Are We There Yet?

ISBN-13: 978-0-9914332-1-6
ISBN-10: 0-9914332-1-1

First printing, May, 2014

Cover design by ThomasMax

Published by:

tm

ThomasMax Publishing
P.O. Box 250054
Atlanta, GA 30325
www.thomasmax.com

Are We There Yet?

Enjoy the journey —
fun, sorrows + adventure,
Yet rewarding + beyond
life the Lord,

by Barbara Lunow

Barbara Lunow

ThomasMax

Your Publisher
For The 21st Century

INTRODUCTION

"For I am the LORD, your God, who takes hold of your right hand and says to you,
Do not fear; I will help you." Isaiah 41:13 NIV

This is a story about how God took ordinary people and used them to do His kingdom work. It's about me and my family when we left the western world of the US and flew across the Pacific to an island of primitive tribes to tell them about Jesus. And oh, what an adventure it was!

We got sick, bug bitten, ate strange things, saw hairy spiders and other creepy crawlies, were surrounded by dark and dirty, and sometimes threatening Papuans, suffered loneliness, missed hearing our own language, faced separation and death, and often had to do things we didn't want to do. But God led us as His children. He made us try new things, and gave us wisdom when we didn't know what to do. He encouraged us when we were discouraged and strengthened us when we were weak. He was always there, the Faithful One. Come with us on the journey, and see for yourself what marvelous things God did, using everyday followers who simply wanted to walk in Jesus path of *'hurting flesh'* which is the way of the cross.

The story is narrowed down to our first term, from June 1968 to June 1972, since thirty-three years and eight terms in one book would prove a daunting task, as well as a boring read. The beginning years that I'm sharing were diverse and full of drama and tragedy as we adjusted to life in another culture and climate.

In that time, and following, God was opening up tribal groups faster than the mission community could enter them. We were few in number because visas were hard to get. There were missionary casualties along the way, due to serious illnesses, accidents and death. The devil worked hard trying to knock us down, to discourage and defeat us before we barely got started. Yet, the time we went to Papua was the golden age for opening doors to the tribes, and as my children say, "We were there when it happened!"

My husband Dan (Wolfgang) and I served together in West Papua, Indonesia from June 1968 until April 2001. After a period of orientation, our first year and half, we worked in a primitive tribe, called the Sougb (So-gb), a group of approximately 13,000 people. Dan's main focus was linguistics and Bible translation, as well as teaching and training church leaders.

Besides language learning, I started out practicing nursing in a village clinic and training medical workers for basic clinics throughout the tribe. In the 1980s, I developed a six year Sunday School curriculum and taught the course and lessons to Sunday School teachers. Another translation project was the Sougb Culture Reader, which included history stories and folktales that were passed down orally by the elders. One of my greatest joys was teaching a weekly Widow's Bible class. These women were ignored and neglected in Sougb society. But they found identity and a name in the promises of scripture.

My main job through the years was transcribing the scriptures, which my husband and his team of national helpers translated. We eventually printed the Sougb New Testament, followed by the shorter Old Testament several years later.

Following our relocation to the US in 2001, Dan continued translating materials in the Sougb language, while I transcribed and formatted them. Besides the New and Old Testaments, the translation projects we set out to do are completed, with printing a four-volume set of New Testament lessons/commentaries and revision and printing of the Sougb Songbook in May 2012. Dan, and our son Jonathan, return regularly to Papua for encouragement of Sougb church leaders and the missionaries who are ministering in other tribes.

Meijiresou (Me-jee-re-so), which means your life to you, as you read our story,
Barbara Lunow, Fort Mill, South Carolina, April 2014

ACKNOWLEDGMENTS

Friends and family asked me many times when I was going to write a book. Thank you, for putting the seed thoughts in my mind and nagging me enough to do it.

My gratitude and thanks go to Mom and Grandma, my daughter Lorraine, Wanita Peterson and Wanda Hatfield for keeping all of my letters and returning them to me. Through the letters, I have been able to restore order and to recall events and feelings with more accuracy and detail.

Roxanne Hanna, of Sunscribe Publishers, helped me with an edit and gave me valuable suggestions. I appreciate her positive feedback and encouragement to pursue publication of my manuscript.

There's nothing like reading your own writing to a sympathetic writers' group. Thank you, to my writer friends for their expertise in grammar and punctuation, their suggestions and questions about the parts that needed clarification. I value our critique sessions which gave me the confidence to go ahead and write. Thanks go to other friends who took the time to read parts and pieces of my manuscript and give me their opinions on the writing.

Most recently ThomasMax Publishing and Lee Clevenger-Editor have dealt kindly with me in all my questions and fears of publishing my manuscript. I am deeply appreciative of their professional advice, given with kindness

For my husband, Dan, and my children:

Lorraine, David, Jonathan, Marie and Matthew.

For our Irian Jaya co-workers in ministry:

Thank you, dear Family,

for your love and the comfort of your

company on the journey.

ABOUT THE AUTHOR

Barbara Lunow was born and raised in Iowa, the 2nd of 6 children. After high school, she became a nurse, followed by a year of Bible College, and a 3-month course at the Summer Institute of Linguistics in Grand Forks, North Dakota.

She and her husband, Dan (Wolfgang) went as missionaries under The Evangelical Alliance Mission (TEAM) to Papua, Indonesia where they ministered to a primitive tribal group of 13,000 people for 35 years plus. Initially, Barbara used her nursing skills in the local village clinic. She taught health workers so they could open clinics in their own villages. Barbara also translated and prepared a six year Sunday School curriculum which she taught to teachers. She started a weekly Bible Class for widows, which opened the eyes of the Sougb church to the desperate needs of the aged. Over the years she typed all of the Sougb Bible text into the computer, and typed and prepared several other teaching books for printing.

Barbara has always liked to write; including the book reports and essays assigned in public school. Her personal writing experience began in earnest with letters and reports sent to family and supporters about their mission ministry. She wrote weekly letters and culture stories to her children when they went to boarding school and on through their adult lives in the US. Her letters to supporters developed into a monthly logbook which was noticed by the editor of their mission magazine. She adapted a number of those letters for articles which were published in the TEAM Horizon magazine. She also elicited stories and folktales from the Sougb elders. These stories were edited and printed for use as a reader in the Sougb language. She translated that booklet into English and is currently adapting the articles and stories into an educational book for children.

Barbara is the mother of five children; two of them were born in a small mission hospital in the central highlands of Papua, Indonesia. She now lives with her husband in Fort Mill, South Carolina.

Prologue: "The Beginning before the Beginning"
The Himalayas, India

"Lorraaaaine! Daaavid! Wheeeere are youuuu?"

Our frantic calls out into the mist and fog were left hanging in the air in front of our faces. We could hear muffled sounds on the mountain path above us and little blurbs of light silently floated up into the clouds, but there was no answering response to our cries. My seven year old daughter, Lorraine, and five year old twin son, David, seemed to have vanished in the haze.

The Bus

Where were we? We were on a mountainside of the Himalayas in northern India, in the dark, trying to find a small cottage. The comforts and familiarities of the US were far behind us, as we made our way to the mission field for the first time. This was a stopover to visit friends, Alton and Ruth Olson, who were medical missionaries in India. It was all arranged. We had specific instructions to take a deluxe tourist bus up the mountains. But we missed that bus because our plane from Germany, where we visited family, was late on arrival into Delhi.

At the bus station the eager-to-please ticket master assured us in his clipped British-Indian dialect, "Do not worry, there are other buses for you. One will be leaving soon. I can take you to it."

It was very hot and five-year-old twin brother, Jonathan, shuffled his feet as he stood close to the shelter of my skirt with Lorraine and David waiting patiently beside him. My husband, Dan, turned to talk it over with us. "I don't know what else we can do. We don't have any other instructions for a plan B. We will have to go on the other bus."

He turned back to the ticket agent, "Can you give us tickets for five seats?"

Of course he could. They were First Class tickets on a fourth-class bus. Our premium seating consisted of one long, wooden bench at the front of the bus, behind the driver's seat, with a supporting board stretched across the back. The other passengers sat on shorter benches, minus the backboard. They were able to hold each other up, simply because they were packed as close as possible to a bench -so much so, that they nearly spilled over into the small aisle between them.

Before we boarded the bus, the laborers, wearing dirty-white, bloomer trousers and blousy, long-sleeve shirts, beckoned to Dan and me. Motioning for us to watch the procedure, they made a great show and ceremony of counting our luggage, all eleven pieces. Several men climbed on top of the bus and grabbed each suitcase from another porter down below, placing the additional piece haphazardly on the pile already stacked there. We nodded and smiled assurances as we watched them complete the job before our family climbed aboard.

The bus sputtered and groaned its way out of the central bus station onto the road, dodging the many push-carts and pull-wagons with their wares piled high. There was no air conditioning on this poor-man's bus; we felt only a powdery, dusty breeze coming in through the open windows. Our nostrils inhaled the pungent smells of sweaty humanity, mixed with fuel fumes and other pollutants from the roadway as we made our way through the throngs of people. They appeared unperturbed by the incessant honking of the horns from all manner of vehicles, and they boldly walked in a line stretched across the width of the road. The crowds moved aside only when a bus or truck came directly up behind them and shattered their eardrums with a blast of the horn. Our bus chugged along, forever dodging people and swerving around the many animals on the road.

David, Jonathan, and Lorraine were agog looking out the window, exclaiming over each new sight. This was their first experience as new missionary kids (MKs) seeing an Eastern culture firsthand, right out the open bus window. Actually, it was Dan's and my first look at the Far East, too.

Along the roadside there were mud-covered, water buffalo in the rice paddies, dusty gray elephants carried huge logs in their trunks, and many *holy cows* were roaming freely. Amidst the drab colors of the animals an occasional peacock walked sedately along, dragging his lustrous, variegated-blue tail behind him. All the creatures appeared oblivious to the crowds and congested traffic teeming around them.

There were people, people everywhere, mingling in the heat and dust of the roadway. The dark-haired women wore saris in varying muted colors. Men looked of the same mold in their long-sleeved, white, flowing tunics and road-weary, baggy trousers. The Sikhs identified themselves by their wrapped turbans. And always there were the dirty, sickly beggars in tatters, crowding around the buses with their hands out, pleading for any coin or piece of food that might be tossed their way.

An Indian woman wearing a brilliantly colored sari with gold-threaded trim was sitting alone on the second-class bench behind us. She leaned forward and in precise British English spoke in my ear, "May I help you, if you require my assistance? My husband is a professor at the University."

"We are the Lunow family. We're going to visit friends up in the mountains. Yes, we would be happy to have you help us. Please." Our volunteer, tour guide was with us for about half of the trip. I was sorry when she left the bus at the stop before the mountains.

The beggars were everywhere. As soon as the bus slowed down on the road, they crowded close, reaching out to us. "Can you tell us if we should give something to the beggars? How are we to know how much to give them?"

The Professor's wife spoke again in my ear, "It is expected that you give something. You do not have to, but it would be good. In the Hindu religion, it is important to give to the poor and gain merits for Nirvana, like your heaven. I can suggest an amount that you might give. It is a little more because you are white people and can give more."

"Oh, we only have a little paper money we exchanged at the bus station," I worried out-loud. "We do not have any coins."

"For that I may be able to help you. Give me your paper *rupees,* and I will give you some of my coins in exchange."

The handful of coins from our friend was long gone by the time we reached our destination. At least we shared what we had with a few beggars who reached their hands out for our help.

The other passengers on the bus were of lower caste than our Hindu friend. India has divisions of the social classes, starting from the wealthiest people on down to the poorest. We could tell the caste just by looking at what they wore. The poor people on our bus had similar dress for the women and men. The women's saris were made of cotton and were very drab. The men looked alike in dirty-white, blousy shirts and baggy trousers.

We foreigners took center stage and attention. I'm sure they had never seen white people riding on the public bus before. Of course, everyone was curious about the children, watching their every move. Lorraine had a baby doll wrapped up in a blanket. It opened and closed its eyes and cried whenever she tipped it backwards. The passengers were fascinated with it.

I felt a tap on my shoulder, "They are asking to please hold the baby."

Lorraine didn't utter a word of protest and handed her doll to our new friend. We soon heard repeated dolly cries amidst murmurs and exclamations, as they passed the doll all the way to the back of the bus on one side and on down to the front on the other side. Then someone graciously handed the doll back to our lady friend.

Handing it over my shoulder, she said, "They are saying to please tell the little girl, thank you, for letting them hold her baby and making it cry."

Beyond that diversion inside the bus, there was so much to look at outside that none of us said much. We were busy taking in all the strange new sights. David was the one who had to know everything about everything going on around him. He was especially curious about a peculiar thing that happened several times during that long day. Every few hours voices from within the bus would begin calling out to the driver. We couldn't understand what they were saying, but shortly after the calls rang out the bus driver pulled over to the side of road near a rice paddy. A number of people then got out and waded into the paddy with their backs to us. Several minutes later, they all turned around and trooped back into the bus.

David could restrain himself no longer and the question came, a bit too loudly, "Daddy, what are they doing?"

"Shush, David, don't stare and embarrass them. These people are going to the bathroom out in the rice fields."

"Oh, is that all," was his only thought on that subject.

By mid afternoon we arrived at another main bus station near the foothills of the mountains. Our interpreter was getting out there, "You may go to the WC, the toilet, in the small building over there, but be careful."

No wonder the people-in-the-know chose to go out in the rice paddy! The public toilets were in a cement block building, divided in two, men and women on either side. A multitude of large flies buzzed around and the odor was suffocating. Dan issued a stern word of warning, "When you go in, don't touch the walls. Do not touch anything else either!"

I didn't have to repeat any words of caution to Lorraine because we hurried in and out of the women's side as fast as we could. There were no sinks or toilets, just footprints imbedded in the cement designating where to squat over a little channel of water running down the middle of the room.

When the beggars saw us outside the bus, they began crowding around. We clustered together and hustled ourselves back to the buses. The sick and maimed followed, and we gave out nearly all the coins that we had left. Some kind soul shooed them away when he saw that our money was nearly gone.

By this time everyone was thirsty, but we were afraid to drink any of the water offered at the station. Dan went to buy several glass bottles of soda from the vendors who were selling their wares. Since the caps were sealed, we felt safe about drinking from the bottles. (This was long before you could buy drinking water in plastic bottles.)

Back at the bus, our driver informed us, "Here we change bus. There is a new bus to go up the mountains. Come with me. I will show you."

Our new-old bus appeared much smaller and even more decrepit than the first one. Again, the porters crowded around and made a great show of taking our suitcases and bags down from the number one bus and piling them onto the roof of the number two bus. Up on top, they ceremoniously pointed and loudly counted, "One, two, three, four, five," and so on, until they reached the magic number of eleven pieces.

The new driver directed us to our front-row benches first. Then the other passengers were allowed to board. With the steepest part of the trip before us, the bus lumbered its way out of the station.

The Monsoons

As we progressed up into the foothills of the mountains, the loaded bus heaved and groaned each zigzag of the way. The road became like a narrow shelf hanging onto the side of the mountain, wrapping around and around, as it climbed its way up into the clouds. The driver elbowed his horn at each new curve. Of course, other buses were also coming down on the same narrow road. Those drivers continually blasted their horns, driving straight at our bus, until at the last second they veered away to the right, or left, and squeezed past.

I tried not to look at the oncoming buses. Instead, I deliberately looked the other way and focused my eyes on the broader views. Lorraine and David weren't facing forward either. They sat staring wide-eyed out the side window. Jonathan looked white-faced with a tinge of green around the lips. Nobody talked. We hung on to the window's edge, the board in front, and to each other.

My mind finally let go of thoughts of sudden death, and I started looking at the grand vistas around us. They were spectacular. One side of the bus looked down sheer cliffs to the sunny plains. While turning my head, I craned my neck to look straight up into the mist-shrouded mountains of the Himalayas on the other side. The air felt heavier and clouds began drifting down, while the bus strained and struggled, climbing higher and higher.

Suddenly the monsoon rains started and the temperature dropped dramatically. Our windows were stuck and wouldn't shut, so the wind blew the torrential rain into the bus. We scooted to the end of our bench towards the middle aisle. Streams of water cascaded down the mountainside and began flooding across the road. The skies blackened, and dark clouds came rolling down.

The kids were getting anxious and I kept telling them, "We're almost there."

"But look at the road. It's like a river with the water flowing down." Jonathan was crying. He was the one who worried the most.

Suddenly, with a gasp and a moan, our bus drove into what looked like a large turn around in the road and ground to a stop.

Our driver indicated that this was it, "Cannot go any more. There is a big pile of rocks on the road up there." He waved his hand in the direction of *somewhere up there.*

We climbed down off the bus into heavy rain and no umbrellas. We were hoping to see our friend waiting for us. But alas, there was no Alton. The porters climbed on top of the bus, counted out our soaked luggage and piled it in a heap on the wet blacktop beside us. The bus driver no longer paid any attention to us because he was busily loading up waiting passengers for the drive back down the mountain. Thankfully, the rain was letting up and was down to a drizzle when the bus left us standing at the side of the road.

"Does any one here speak English? Is there anyone?" Dan asked several times.

Finally a man stepped out of the mist and descending darkness and nodded a greeting. "Do you know the missionary doctor from up the mountain? He was to meet us."

The man looked blank, "Missionary? Doctor? I don't know about him."

He turned to the crowd, asking them in Hindi, and turned back to us, "Oh, yes, he came here before. But you did not come. He left. But do not be afraid; we will take you to him."

The Climb

Our resources were gone; we had no more rupees to pay porters, no more liquid to drink, and no more food to eat as our airplane snacks were long since eaten. I also felt like I had no strength after flying all night and traveling all day in the heat and dust of the plains of India, not to mention our most recent hair-raising drive up to this spot. Then a man speaking in broken English tells us that he will take us to our friends who live up there, near the store of Mr. So-n-So? How could we possibly trust him? But no one else appeared to rescue us. We decided we would go with him.

Our new manager immediately took over. He called for carriers who began hoisting suitcases, one to each shoulder, while forming a line to climb farther up the mountain.

Lorraine and David were excited, "Daddy can we go with them? We sat all day long, now we want to walk with them. Can we? Say yes. Please." And they stationed themselves in the middle of the porters' line.

Jonathan stood close to Dan and me. He was reluctant and more than a little wary about joining in the venture, "No, I don't want to go. I have a bad headache."

Did I mention that I was about seven months pregnant at the time? My feet and ankles were swollen, my legs ached, and I could barely walk after sitting all day. And I was expected to trudge up an uneven mountain path, to who knows where?

Our man-in-charge comforted me, "Do not fear. I will get you a pull-cart."

"Oh, please. But I will ride only if my son can too. He does not feel well," I told him.

By then I was beginning to doubt the advisability of getting into any vehicle, much less something someone had to pull. Our rescuer managed to procure a little wagon. It was open to the elements with a narrow, wooden plank barely wide enough for Jonathan and me to sit on. Between the two poles in front of our seat stepped a thin, poorly-dressed porter who intended to pull our cart, with us in it, on up the mountain.

Lorraine and David had already disappeared into the mist,

following the carriers up an unseen path. We heard their voices chattering and the murmurs of the porters for a brief time, but all sounds quickly became muffled. There was silence as darkness and clouds swallowed them up. Would we ever see them again, I wondered?

Dan set his pace, walking alongside, as the porter pulled us up the steep, uneven pathway. My feet and legs began to ache worse than on the bus. We came to a zig-zag corner and the porter strained to pull us around it.

Jonathan started to cry, "I can't see. Where are the lights? Where are Lorraine and David? They're gone! I know they're lost."

The porter kept pointing and nodding, like he knew where we were going, but that didn't reassure Jonathan, or me, one bit. "No more, let us get out and walk. Please!"

Jonathan was so relieved, worried, or scared (maybe all three), that when he got his feet back on solid ground he promptly threw up. Thus began our calls into the darkness and mist to try to find Lorraine and David. Did our porters really know where they were going? Were they actually taking our children and our luggage up to our friends' house? We didn't know where we were. We couldn't talk to them. We had no more *rupees.* Could we trust them? In the end, they were all we had. We had to trust them and God.

How in the world did we arrive at this unearthly place in time, foolhardy and unreal as it seemed to us right then?

Getting Started

I was born on January 7, 1941, in Fort Dodge, Iowa, the second of six children, three boys and three girls. Mom named me Barbara after herself and my grandma. We lived with my Grandma Tigner in her little four room house. My dad was an alcoholic and money was always scarce. Mom hated it, but she applied for Aid to Dependent Children, welfare, which allowed her to feed us and get our clothes for school. I remember that we each got one new pair of brown leather tie shoes for school, at least one size larger for our feet to grow into them in a school year. We went barefoot all summer, no shoes needed. Those hard times as a child helped me on the mission field because I learned how to make do with what I had.

When I was in sixth grade, we older kids begged Mom to get a divorce because Dad was physically abusing her and Grandma. Of the six of us, I was the one who was most terrified of Dad when he was drinking. Mom finally got a divorce when I was in middle school. I asked to live with my grandma after Mom remarried. My two sisters and three brothers moved with Mom to Chicago when I was in high school.

As early as I can remember Mom took us to a small community church close to home. I couldn't wait to go to Sunday School because I loved the Bible stories. They were all about God, how He made everything and everybody, including me, and He loved us so much that He sent Jesus to die on the cross for our sins. There was an old upright piano in our classroom and we learned all the children's songs, doing the motions with great zest and joy. Later on, we started going to a larger Baptist Church. The pastor from that church came in his station wagon to pick us up every Sunday. I remember having perfect attendance in Sunday School for seven years.

All six of us kids attended Daily Vacation Bible School for two weeks every summer. When I was ten years old, I knew that I had to accept Jesus as my personal savior. I prayed with one of my teachers, and from then on I knew I was God's child. In Vacation Bible School, the challenge was on to memorize Bible verses and win a free trip to summer camp. I won several times and loved going. At camp we had daily Bible lessons, fun crafts, swimming and games, and evening meetings. What I liked best was the missionary meetings, the stories and pictures they showed about bringing Jesus to people in other lands. When I was twelve years old, I knew in my heart that God wanted me to be a missionary, too. One night I threw my stick of commitment on the campfire and promised God that I would go wherever He wanted me to go. I never turned back from that promise.

In high school our youth leader, who was also a nurse, encouraged me to think about becoming a missionary nurse. A man in our church paid for me to go to nursing school in Minneapolis, Minnesota. What a deal that was, costing a total of $700 for the three years! However, as part of our student nurse's training, we worked as nurses' aides for the hospital, without pay.

My husband, Dan, and I met when he was working as an orderly at my training hospital, while going to the University of Minnesota. He emigrated from Hamburg, Germany, in 1954. His given name is Wolfgang, but his American friends nick-named him Dan. (Dan tells his own personal story about growing up in Hitler's Germany in a "New Commander-in-Chief.") When I met him, he told me right away that he was studying to be a missionary. At that time he was in pre-med, but he switched to linguistic studies because he thought he was better suited to be a Bible translator. I always thought God was calling me to be a single nurse, and I was okay with that. But we both felt God was leading us together to serve Him in foreign missionary work. Although penniless students, we married at the end of my nursing studies.

Someone gave Dan a mission magazine from The Evangelical Alliance Mission (TEAM), which told of their need for translators in Dutch New Guinea, now called Papua, Indonesia. From then on, Dan felt called to New Guinea. There went my dream of nursing in a little mission hospital; I knew that a translator would end up going to a primitive tribe out in the jungle somewhere. We were accepted as missionaries with TEAM and planned on a church planting and Bible translation ministry. I never regretted going to the Sougb people, but we sure had a lot to learn along the way.

Our family quickly grew by three, with Lorraine coming first, then David and Jonathan, our twins. Lorraine was barely two years old and the boys not yet a year old when we headed south for Bible classes at Columbia Bible College (now Columbia International University) in South Carolina. Dan took graduate courses, and another student's wife and I alternated babysitting our kids, taking classes on opposite days of each other. I also worked part time on the night shift in the OB ward of the local hospital.

At the end of the school year, we packed up and drove directly to Grand Forks, North Dakota, to attend the Wycliffe Summer Institute of Linguistics. Dan had already finished two summers there, but TEAM required me to take at least one summer session. Dan was chief babysitter while I studied. The course was technical and intense, but I managed to do okay with my grades. What a stretching experience that was, especially after the full year at Bible School.

Families were housed in long narrow dorm rooms, no air conditioning, just a ceiling fan. There was a huge bathroom down the hall. The first couple of weeks were fine, but then pink eye made the rounds. Next, Lorraine ran a high fever, which was the beginning of red measles. I soaked her in the tub in the dorm bathroom to get the fever down. She cried because the light hurt her eyes, and I had to turn off the lights in our room. I took my books and studied in the hall. The boys avoided the measles because they had received the new measles vaccine. Lorraine also developed several earaches during the summer.

What a relief it was when the three months were over, and we were out of that stuffy dorm room.

Formal classes over, we traversed the country with Lorraine, David and Jonathan bunked in the back of our old station wagon; no seat belts were required then. We were out sharing our missionary vision, building financial and prayer support for going to the field. Some of those early supporters prayed for us and our kids all through our lives in Papua and their lives back in America. What a heritage that is!

With our support team together, we applied for a visa to Irian Barat, Indonesia. By the time we were ready to go, Dutch New Guinea had been turned over to Indonesia and renamed Irian Barat, or West Irian. Our first visa application was promptly denied, but the second time it was miraculously granted, in March of 1968. By then there was great urgency to get going to the field, because I was pregnant. Did we dare risk waiting for the new baby and then try to get a passport and separate visa? Our own visa would expire by then. No, we couldn't take the risk.

So it was, we boarded a plane for Indonesia, and I was six months pregnant. I carried an official *Letter of Permission* from my doctor, so that the airlines would allow me to travel. I'm sure no airline today would permit a woman in advanced pregnancy to fly around the world, but we did it then.

Our first stop was Germany to see Oma and Opa Lunow, Dan's parents because he hadn't been home since 1954. Lorraine celebrated her seventh birthday during the two weeks that we were there.

The plan after leaving Germany was to go to India for a week with our good friends, the Olsons, then on to Irian Barat, Indonesia.

Back on the mountainside

Finally, out of the muted stillness, we heard Lorraine's voice calling, "Daaaaddy! Daaaaddy! We're here. Keep coming."

As promised, the porter-guides had led them up to *Mr. So-n-So's* little store on the side of the mountain. Struggling up the pathway through the mist, Jonathan was overjoyed to see his brother and sister sitting among our suitcases with the carriers standing guard close by.

Together again, Dan cupped his hands around his mouth and called out into the darkness, "Alton, Helloooo! We're here. Helloooo! Alton!"

After several calls and what seemed like minutes of silence, an answering shout came from down below us, "Helloooo! Wolfgang, is that you? I'm coming up."

A minute later, our friend Alton walked out of the mist and darkness, "Oh, Wolfgang, so you did make it on another bus. Welcome, brother."

It was a few more steps down another winding pathway, and we arrived at their stone cottage. The carriers deposited our luggage on the doorstep and after Alton paid them, they silently disappeared into the night.

The time with Alton and Ruth helped us transition from a western culture to an eastern one. It rained every day, but they did their best to show us around and give us an idea of what it was like to do mission work. We visited medical clinics, and Alton showed us the little hospital perched on the side of the mountain. I was glad to know Alton was a doctor and Ruth a nurse, just in case I needed their medical services. Although, Alton assured me everything was fine with my pregnancy. Ruth cooked up some tasty rice and curry dishes, which were also new to us. Our kids took their new experiences in stride and played with their friends, Bradley and Nathan Olson.

After a week, Alton chartered a taxi to take us down the mountain and on to Delhi for our flight. I was thankful to have a more comfortable ride, and it was definitely less death-defying than our memorable drive up in the bus. The visit seemed short; except by the time we left, I was feeling ready to finish our trip, only there were a few more miles to travel before Baby-Day was scheduled to arrive.

Chapter One: "Is it hot, or hot hot?"
Jakarta, Indonesia

Flying out of Delhi, we landed in Indonesia on our own private jet on July 22, 1968. At least, it seemed like it was our personal plane because there were only three other passengers on board. After political turmoil, and the overthrow of the old regime, Indonesia's new government closed the door to new visas. This resulted in nearly-empty planes in and out of the capitol, Jakarta, on the central island of Java. Our three kids made the most of it, enjoying their popularity with the stewardesses, regaling them with their entire life stories. They also filled themselves up on the limitless free sodas and peanut snacks that were offered.

In Jakarta, we collected all eleven pieces of luggage, stacked them on two carts, and pushed them through immigration without anyone checking our stuff. We exited the terminal doors into the hazy, humid air of Jakarta. The mission van was waiting at the curb to load us up and bring us into the city. It was only across the sidewalk to the curb, but we were dripping with sweat already. Ah, how wonderful; the van had air-conditioning!

Into the city

Not far from the airport, we drove within sight of the ocean and the harbor. The ships were lined up at dockside reminding us that Jakarta was at sea level. There were active volcanic mountains not far away, running through the middle of the island. When we opened our windows a crack to see the boats better, a strong odor of dead fish permeated the air and up went the windows again.

"Jakarta looks a lot cleaner, not as crowded as India," Lorraine observed. "There are more real cars here, too, but not all kinds of carts."

David added, "Yeah, and I don't see any of those holy cows roaming around, either."

Pedestrians were walking along the side of the road, instead of all over the road. The air felt heavy and gas fumes were so rank that it seemed like we were pumping gas at the gas station. Mingled with the fuel odors, we detected strong whiffs of some spice and another kind of sweet fragrance.

Ever sensitive and curious, David wanted to know, "What's that smell? It smells like someone is cooking."

"It is from garlic. We use much garlic and onions to cook," Our driver piped up from the front seat. Ah, so he understood some English.

There was another heavy, spicy scent and we soon discovered that Indonesian cigarettes are laced with cloves and that distinct aroma permeates the air too. The men were smoking, but we were shocked to see children smoking too.

All along the road into the city, we saw a number of impressive monuments and huge statues with fountains in the middle of circular intersections. Some looked like soldiers in battle; others were of mythical figures that we didn't recognize. Still others were jutting out of the tops of buildings. We began pointing them out and counting them.

Our chauffeur, turned guide, shrugged his shoulders, "Oh, they are statues and buildings from the former President Sukarno." He didn't sound very impressed and that's all he had to say about that.

Traffic became more congested with the usual taxis, cars and buses rushing by each other as we neared downtown Jakarta. We also noticed other smaller, unrecognizable vehicles; some had three wheels. Another variety was the two-wheeled carts, pedaled by what looked like a bicycle from behind. Still others were motorized four-wheelers. All of them carried passengers to various destinations. These mini-vehicles wove in and out of the general traffic, and our driver was on constant alert trying to miss the little guys.

I don't know if there was a speed limit, but traffic seemed to go faster, rather than slower, in the city. Like India, the drivers were more aggressive using their horns, cutting in front of other cars, or riding their bumpers from behind. They also liked to straddle the center line of the road, trying to see around larger vehicles in front of them. In our case, this daredevil tactic made for several close shaves with oncoming cars. We again found ourselves hanging on to each other for support.

Despite the hazards of third world traffic, the driver delivered us safely to the Dutch Christian Church Guest House. What a relief to be that far! Mr. Ken Riggenbach, the mission chairman for The Christian and Missionary Alliance (C&MA) welcomed us and, in the next breath, gave us the bad news that the guest house rooms were full; we would have to go somewhere else.

"I have booked you at a small hotel not far from here. Our driver will take you there until there's an empty room here. It's a local place, and they only speak Indonesian, but I think you will do fine. I'm sorry we can't have you here, but this hotel has received our guests before. They'll take care of you, and we can be in touch by phone."

We handed our passports to Ken so he could begin the process of checking us in with the various Indonesian offices. Then he introduced us to Otto and Carol Koning with their three children and to Don and Carol Spencer. They were waiting for travel permits to go on to Irian Barat, the same direction we were headed. It felt good to meet someone from our own mission, TEAM. The Konings were returning from home leave in the US for a second term. The Spencers were first time arrivals too. I wanted to stay and talk longer, but our driver was waiting to take us to the Indonesian hotel.

Before we left the states, the home office had told us that we might be in Jakarta for a couple of weeks to process all our papers. The government required adults and children to have proper ID cards with pictures and to carry travel permits wherever we went in Indonesia. Besides the immigration department, the military intelligence branch wanted to know where we foreigners were at all times. After the standard registration process was done, we needed additional permits to live in Irian Barat (*West Irian*) because at that time it was considered a restricted province. Once all permits were in hand, travel passes would be issued. They were to be presented at police stations and other government offices wherever we went.

Little did we know that this first-time registration process was only the beginning of the reams of immigration forms and travel documents required of foreigners. And they always wanted our pictures. Dan laughingly told us, "Well, they must be papering the walls with our passport pictures because they keep asking for more every time I go to a different office."

In fact, we never actually had possession of our passports. They were always in some government office being processed. Or the intermission business office held them in a safe to show when asked by the government.

The Hotel

All the paperwork pending, we headed to the local hotel. The humidity and heat were nearly unbearable for me and certainly uncomfortable for the rest of the family. Our room was on the ground floor, without fans, or air conditioning. When we closed the big wooden shutters for privacy and safety at night, the room was even stuffier to sleep in. I felt exposed to the public because anyone walking by outside could see through the slats in the shutters, or they could climb in since none of the windows locked. The din of traffic continued all night with horns honking, engines revving up, and radios turned on full volume. At the crack of dawn, the call to prayers blared from loudspeakers in the mosques. That sound became familiar because the *faithful* pray five times a day in Indonesia.

If the outdoor noises weren't enough, the inside sounds kept us awake too. Mosquitoes flew in masses through the screen-less windows, and we could hear their constant buzzing. The kids were covered in bites because there were no mosquito nets on the beds. We didn't know where, or how, to ask for mosquito spray, either.

The hotel staff was kind and gracious, but none of them spoke English, although they knew words like "eat," "drink," and "WC for bathroom." Both sides smiled a lot, and we motioned with our hands to get our messages across. A worker knocked on our door that first morning and pantomimed like he was eating and escorted us to the breakfast table. That was the only meal offered, always the same; white bread with chunky pineapple jam and cups of thick black coffee or sweet milk tea. We ventured out near the hotel to find food in little restaurants along the sidewalk. Most of them had picture menus, which were best for us. Everything came with white rice, and we pointed at the meat and vegetables on the menu that we wanted put on top. If it turned out too spicy, the kids inhaled the white rice and were satisfied.

On our second day there, we were brave enough to pile into a small pedi-cab, called a *becak*, and go to a larger hotel to eat familiar western food. The hotel people showed us about how much to pay for a ride by pointing to the differently colored Indonesian bills that we might need for the trip.

The pedi-cabs were fun. They lined up at curbside on the street outside the hotel and the passenger seeking a ride went out to bargain for the price of the fare. There was no set rate because it depended on how far you were going and how well you could bargain. The fare had to be settled before you stepped into a vehicle, otherwise the driver could ask whatever he wanted at the end of the ride. When we came out on the sidewalk, the drivers flocked around us pointing to their particular cab, hoping to steer us in that direction. We figured out later that we could have asked for two becaks, but the kids wanted to ride with us, and we were scared that we might get separated in traffic.

Becaks were mounted between two large bicycle type tires, and the driver perched in the back on a bicycle seat. The small open passenger cart sat in front, and your feet fit down in a trough below the seat. Each driver customized his cab by painting it in bright colors. Most of them also had a low, rounded canvas roof overhead which folded back like a convertible top. Otherwise, passengers were totally exposed to the elements and received the full benefits of the noise and gaseous fumes that the city had to offer.

The seat on the pedi-cab was barely wide enough for two adult Asian people. But with the price agreed on, Dan and I managed to squeeze Lorraine in between us, and we put one boy on each of our laps. When we were all settled in, the driver happily pedaled us on our way.

(We loved our short trips in those little pedal-powered carts. Everything was new to our eyes and there was so much to see, hear, and smell. Having a working olfactory sense is so important when describing a place in Asia. Pictures can't show the smells, and that is a great loss for the armchair traveler. In this writing, I can only tell you about odors, fragrances and scents and leave them to your imagination.)

As our driver pedaled along, people-watching was a favorite pastime. The women wore batik sarongs in traditional designs with the earth tone colors. Some of them had on the beautiful lace jackets that are typical for Indonesia. Most of the men wore long sleeve-shirts and roomy trousers that were gathered around the ankles. Those carrying especially heavy burdens had short sleeve shirts and wore shorts. Very few people that we saw were in western dress. They all had on the plain slippers with the strap running through the toes.

Street vendors were everywhere carrying their weighty wares, which were hanging in woven baskets on either end of a long pole balanced over their shoulders. Each peddler used a distinct call to indicate what he or she was selling. Everyone, except us, recognized their cries.

I chattered away, trying to make it an educational experience by pointing out different people, "Let's try to guess what they are carrying in their baskets. Look at that man, he's walking bow-legged, and his back is bent over. Oh, there's a lady with a sarong slung over her shoulder, and it's full of bottles. Maybe she's collecting empty ones."

David joined in the game, "Hey, look at the ones with full bottles.

They're everywhere. I wonder what's in them."

The two of us were at least in the spirit of things, "I don't know, but it must taste good. Lots of people are buying from them."

Pedestrians paused long enough to buy a bottle, or just a drink. The single drink was conjured up when the vendor whipped out a glass and poured a dab of colored *strop* into the bottom of it, and then filled the rest with water from another bottle he carried. The buyer drank it right then and there and handed the glass back to the peddler. We drove by too fast to see what happened to the dirty glass. I did see another seller swish out one of her used glasses with a little water and then wipe it off with a handy towel tucked into her waist. The glass went back into her pack. No more need be said about that.

Cars also stopped right in the middle of the street; an arm waved money out of the window; and the trader balancing the pole trotted out with his special gait to make his sale. Those selling syrup waited for the customer to down the drink, collected the glasses, and went on their way. Meanwhile, traffic slowed down and drove around them.

Beside the main street, where we traveled, there was an open canal. It was partially filled with unknown, foul smelling drainage and rainwater. The water appeared oily and stagnant. We observed people bathing, others doing their laundry, and men with their backs to us urinating in it. Lorraine, David, and Jonathan were unable to tear their eyes away from the ditch, although they ignored the urinating part.

David's face told it all, "Are they washing their clothes, and then they take a bath, in the same water? It smells like a sewer. Yuk, it stinks!"

I was embarrassed and shushed them, "Think about it. They must be really poor people, maybe with no other way to get water. I'm sure they wouldn't wash in it unless they had to."

We made it to the big hotel, had our hamburger and French fries, and then watched, smelled, and heard the city sights all over again as our driver pedaled us back to our local hotel.

The Mission Guest House

After a second night of traffic noise and droves of mosquitoes, the Mission Guest House had a room open. The driver of the now familiar van came to transport us, and after many good-byes of *selamat jalan* and shaking of hands, we departed the little hotel. I surprised myself and felt I would miss it because the workers were so nice, and I knew we were hearing the language and seeing more of the culture staying there.

Since the van came in the morning, we got a better look at the mission guest house this time. It was an elegant, old Colonial place, converted into a mission house when the Dutch left Indonesia. Turning into the driveway, I looked down the street and saw military guards outside another big old house. "Look at that place. Who lives there? They have guards outside of it."

"Ah, a big General lives there," our driver informed us.

Well, with the military right on our street, it must be a safe neighborhood. It was already much quieter than our former hotel.

The Konings and Spencers were still waiting on travel permits, and I was glad for the extra time with them. Now I could talk in English and be understood. The Konings also spoke Indonesian and helped translate when we needed to communicate with the house helpers. Carol went so far as to write out a list of everyday phrases for me. They also explained important cultural manners, lest we transgress a taboo, such as handing something to someone with our left hand.

David and Jonathan were glad to make friends with Otto Junior who was their age. They ended up being in boarding school together and have remained close friends all their lives.

Again we had only one large room with several beds, but it was more comfortable than the one at the hotel. The heat and humidity still bothered me. I felt hot and sticky all the time. At least the room had ceiling fan, which I turned on and never turned off. It was another ground floor room, but the windows had screens and were up high enough to give us privacy. A guest house worker came in every evening during our supper time and sprayed for mosquitoes. He also closed the inner shutters at night, and they were secure.

One luxury for me at the guest house was their laundry service. I set our dirty clothes outside the door early every morning. The clothes miraculously disappeared and returned all washed and freshly folded, or ironed, by late afternoon. We had an especially large pile of laundry that first day because our clothes hadn't been washed since India.

The guest house also served all meals, plus an afternoon snack of cookies and juice. The meals were Indonesian style with lots of rice. The cooks allowed for our Western taste and used less spice than usual in their cooking. They placed extra hot sauce on the table instead, so we could help ourselves. The servers only smiled when we asked them what we were eating, and they weren't offended with our questions.

Lorraine and David gamely tasted all the different foods placed before them. Jonathan preferred eating what was familiar and was cautious about trying anything new. Each meal had enough fruit and vegetables that we could avoid some of the spicier foods and still be satisfied. At that point, I didn't like too much spice either.

The important question about eating at the guest house for the kids was, "What day is today?" They were waiting for one special day per week when the Guest House served an American meal: hamburgers, buns, French fries, lots of American catsup, and ice cream with chocolate syrup topping. That was the day they could fill up on the familiar. It was pure bliss to be served comfort food, especially since everything else they were experiencing was new and different.

Culture Differences

Entering into a totally new culture for the first time, we didn't always know what was expected. We often got ourselves into fixes because of misunderstandings in the language. One family story that was nearly a disaster is worth the telling.

It all started with Dan asking the server at the table a simple question, "*Ini panas?* Is this hot?" He wanted to know if the dish was spicy, or not. We had already discovered that the most innocent looking vegetable dish could be hiding any number of unseen hot pepper seeds.

The server looked surprised. "Oh, no, not hot," he shook his head.

"Oh, good," we said. Dan and I had a bite, only to immediately gasp for air and reach for our water glasses. Wow, who said that dish wasn't spicy?

"Who was he kidding? Did he tell us that as joke?" That's when we found out that English and Indonesian words for *hot* are not equal. There are two separate words for hot in Indonesian. Our waiter thought we were asking about *panas,* the *hot* referring to temperature, as in warm, rather than *pedas* the hot that meant spicy hot.

We learned many things simply by trial and error, mostly on the side of error. Another hot story from our first week in Jakarta always gives us a laugh. It was our first afternoon at the Guest House, and the boys were hot and sweaty. They asked if they could take a bath to cool off. We gave them permission, and they walked down the hall to the bathing room.

A few minutes later one of the workers came timidly to our room and tried to tell us, "The boys are in the water."

"Yes, yes, we know they are," Dan nodded in agreement to the man.

Shaking his head no, the man stammered, "But they are having a bath inside. Come." Dan went with him and there they were. The boys, with their new friend Otto James, were having a wonderful time splashing around inside the square, cement-block tub that was filled with nice, cool water.

Jonathan greeted Dan, "Hey, Dad, this is really cool. We could swim in here all day."

The trouble was that the square, four-feet by four-feet *bok*, cement tank, was for all the guest house occupants to use. You take a dipper, about the size of a two quart sauce pan, dip it in the bok and pour the water over your body, soap up, and dip again to rinse. But you're standing outside of the tub.

Dan became number one party-pooper as he enlightened the boys, "But, you guys, this water is for everyone. All the guests need to use this water too. You can't jump in there and swim around. You'll have to use the dipper and splash it over you outside of the bok." What a disappointment that was! It was the dipper method or none at all.

Our paperwork was barely started when the Konings and Spencers received their travel permits. They would leave before us, and oh, how we envied them. Our turn came over a week later, and I eagerly packed up for yet another stage of the journey.

That initial entry into Indonesia was only our first extended stay in Jakarta. The mission office and Guest House were always there to help us out and even watched over our children on their trips back and forth to high school. We greatly appreciated the Jakarta connection and their many services to us over the years.

And so, the next morning, or was it still the middle of the night, we checked in at 2 AM at the domestic airport, which also happened to be the military airport. This time all eleven suitcases were weighed and charged over-weight fees, which were double what we paid in the US. No wonder it looked like the other passengers were carrying all their worldly goods onto the airplane, rather than checking them in.

At the airport, it was still dark when we boarded, but we could see that we were going on a propeller plane this time. Goodbye to the big jets. No matter, we were headed for our final destination, the island of New Guinea.

Chapter Two: "Are we there yet?"
Biak Island

Besides the drone of the engine resounding inside the smaller plane, the propellers also made a loud whirring noise. The plane rattled and shook the whole trip. I began feeling sick to my stomach from the constant jiggling, and started to worry that I would shake into labor with the turbulence. This was our first experience in a twin engine aircraft and it was a good introduction to riding in smaller planes. At the time, though, I didn't think there was anything good about it. In fact, I was positive that we, I, would never make it to New Guinea.

Our kids were sitting three in two seats, despite the fact that we had paid for three full tickets. We tried to tell the stewardess, but she only nodded her head and smiled and nothing changed. Welcome to the third world. The plane was also packed out with military personnel in full dress uniform. I'm convinced they took one of my kids' seats. Their presence did nothing but increase my anxieties, wondering where they were going and why.

We expected to fly all the way to West Irian but the plane was only going as far as Biak, a smaller island that runs to the east of Irian. It was mid-afternoon when we landed on an old World War II airstrip built by the US forces. It was acclaimed to be the biggest and longest coral airfield in the entire Pacific arena.

Pentecostal missionaries, Mike and Mae Hanas, met us with a warm, *"Selamat dating,* peace in your coming." They took us to their house on the Bible School property for the night. Mike kindly took our travel passes to the police station to be stamped and Dan didn't have to appear in person.

That first overnight was the beginning of a lifetime of friendship with Mike and Mae. Their door was always open to any of the missionaries because Biak was the port of entry to Irian at the time. Our kids also stored up school travel memories in their many sleep-overs at Uncle Mike and Aunt Mae's house. Mike was the one who helped them a number of times with exit permits, tickets and other glitches in their travels to and from high school in the Philippines.

One story that I heard about was when a group of the kids traveling from high school ended up at the Hanas house on the beach when they were gone. Their houseboy met them at the airport in the Land Rover, saying, "I am by myself, but *Bapak* Hanas says you are to come with me, and I will take care of you."

My informant told me, "Mom, it was a blast. Kobus took us in Uncle Mike's old Land Rover to a restaurant to eat. When we went back home, we sat out on the beach into the evening. We stayed up just talking and having a good time. Finally the girls went to sleep in a bedroom and the guys slept all around the living room. It was great, and we all got to the plane in the morning."

But on that first night in Biak, we all slept in a small room with bunk beds in a room at the Bible School. Mike woke us up before dawn on August 2, 1968 to get ready for the airplane. The Mission Aviation Fellowship (MAF) Aero-Commander, piloted by Clell Rogers, flew in from the base in Sentani to pick us up. The Commander was considerably smaller than the prop plane, another down-size from the jets, but it was MAF's largest plane. Pilot Clell told us to weigh everything --bodies, suitcases, and all hand-carry pieces. No, he wasn't going to charge us overweight. But MAF has specific weight limits for each plane in their fleet; and they carefully follow those rules for safety's sake. After our weigh-in, the pilot, Uncle Mike, and Dan proceeded to load the aircraft themselves. Then we five and a half Lunows scrambled aboard, eager and excited to get going.

Pilot Clell took his seat and clicked his seat belt on. He looked back at us, while he fumbled around and grabbed a paperback book from the side of his seat. He began to flip through the pages as he informed us, "This plane is new to me and here's the manual to help me fly it. I have to make sure I know how to do it."

The kids heard him and whispered, "Mom, what did he say? Doesn't he know how to fly this plane?"

Unaware that our pilot was known for his practical jokes, it took a few seconds to decide that he was just trying to scare the new missionary family. MAF pilots are some of the best trained pilots in the entire world. Of course, he knew how to fly that plane.

Off we flew, two hours away from our appointed destination. What a thrill it was to fly low enough over the brilliant blue waters of the Pacific and actually see the whitecaps of the waves below us. To the west, we made out a dark, jagged land mass. As we flew closer to the land the plane banked a little, until we were parallel with the water's edge. Soon we were flying over dense, dark-green jungle, with murky, brownish streams and rivers cutting ribbons through the lowlands on their way out into the ocean. Farther in the distance to the west and stretching to the south, we made out the shadowy outline of the mountain peaks of the interior. Finally, we all craned our necks, getting our first glimpses of the vast interior lands of the many tribes of the island of New Guinea.

"Do you see anything yet?"

"What's that?"

"Where?"

"Are we there yet?"

We were all asking the same questions, and no one was answering. This time the questions weren't just rhetorical, they were for real, as we searched the land below with our eyes.

We had been traveling for seven weeks. The kids were especially tired of suitcase living, with all the packing and unpacking; tired of maintaining and collecting their few worldly treasures in those little briefcase-like bags. Nope, there were no backpacks then. I was tired too, and feeling ready to see a doctor soon. My last checkup was in India with our friend Dr. Alton and we had flown many air miles since then.

The plane swept nearly full circle out over the jungle, giving us a panoramic picture of shades of green. On our descent, we glided over a huge lake, nosing down and lining up for landing at a long cement strip before us, Sentani airport. It was another one of those World War II airstrips built by US forces. The plane taxied over to the MAF hangar on their base.

"Now?"

"Yes!"

"We're here!"

Sentani, MAF Base and Mission School

A worker came out and opened the double side doors, and helped the kids and I down, while the two men got out and started unloading the plane. Lorraine, David and Jonathan eagerly helped stack everything to the side.

By then several MAF families gathered to greet us. Names fail me as to who was there, but I do remember how glad everyone was to see us. We were the first families, Spencers and Lunows, to be granted visas after a five year hiatus. Missionary visas were hard to get because of a change-over from Dutch rule to an Indonesian government in 1963. During the transition period, the United Nations came in to oversee that the indigenous people were treated fairly. Our visas were the first to be issued by the Indonesian government, which was predominantly Muslim. The door to Irian Barat had finally opened, if only a crack.

The welcoming party loaded us up in a Volkswagen van, called a *kombi,* or VW bus, and drove us the seven minutes up *The Hill* to the school compound. The jungle crowded in along both sides of the road effectively blocking out any sort of grand view we might have had to look back and see Lake Sentani. The tropical growth around us was gorgeously lush in all shades and hues of green, with brilliant colors of red, orange and yellow blossoms climbing up the tree trunks and into the topmost branches. I was enjoying this new scenery. My kids weren't noticing any of it.

They were all excited about something else, "Mom, look at the banana trees. They're real bananas growing on them. Can we eat them like that?"

"Well," I confessed, "I've never seen a banana tree growing either, but I'm sure you can cut the stalk down and eat them, just like they are."

The Missionary Kids School (MK School), run by C&MA was up on The Hill, as well as dorms for boarding students, teachers' housing, and several guest houses for parents when they came out to see their kids. The buildings were all located at the foot of Cyclops Mountain, with the tangled jungle growth all around.

It was summer vacation and only a couple teachers were at home. Several of the old guest houses were former q*uonset huts* from General MacArthur's occupation with the US forces during WW II. Other houses, called Kingstrands, were made of heavy gauge, corrugated aluminum that originally came in sheets and were bolted together as they were built. All the houses on the hill were built on cement slabs, although houses in other areas were on huge timbers off the ground to keep them from flooding out in heavy rains.

As we drove up on the gravel roadway beside the house, we detected a faint breeze which made it feel slightly cooler than Jakarta. The smells from the city were definitely missing. This was more like country fresh air, only much hotter.

I reminded everybody, "We have to get used to the heat and humidity because we are just south of the equator. Let's enjoy any breeze we get. The weather here is going to be sticky like this all year long."

Those words were directed at my family, but I also needed to hear them for myself. In my obviously pregnant condition, the heat made me feel clammy all over, tired all the time, crabby most of the time, and short on patience a lot of the time.

It was no surprise when Carol and Don Spencer came out on the veranda of the guest house to greet us. They were always one step ahead of us in the paper trail process, and their documents were nearly finished then, too. They would be going to the South Coast to begin Indonesian language study the next week and we were sharing the house with them before they left. The plan at the time was that we would follow them to the South Coast as soon as our immigration work was finished.

Since they were ahead of us, they already knew about buying food, the drinking water, and other necessities of daily living. It felt good to rely on their expertise, rather than figuring everything out on my own. Don explained how to fill and run the kerosene refrigerator. He also showed us how to start those old kerosene burners, which replaced a stove. They are mounted on a pedestal about seven inches high with a small tank at the base.

Don demonstrated as he talked, "First, fill the tank with kerosene. Then fill this little trough, which is wrapped around the bottom of the pedestal here with alcohol. Next, pump up the pressure with the pump that sticks out the side of the tank, right here. Then light a match to the alcohol, but wait until it's just about burned up into a blue flame. Now, slowly turn the valve to light the burner." The pressurized burner roared into life with a quick, hot flame.

I protested, "I'll never be able to light one of those things! We'll never get to eat, if I have to use these burners." Given time, I learned how to do it, but I always hated those things.

We were also glad to find out that we had neon lights suspended from the ceilings. Of course, the electricity wasn't always dependable, but it was better than kerosene lamps. There were a couple of table top fans around too. I had expected to do without electricity.

Meanwhile, the kids were bored with kitchen stuff and had already run down the hall to find their bedroom. The beds were shrouded in canopies of mosquito netting, which were drawn back for the day. Their imaginations kicked in and the mosquito nets immediately became tents. Oh, what endless possibilities of pretend games they dreamt up. It was no matter that the netting effectively cut off any breeze, or cool air, that might be available when they were closed. The kids claimed their beds and spread out their few belongings.

After lunch with Don and Carol, I unpacked some of our necessities and took a short rest. Then I tried to figure out a food list for our immediate needs. Carol made my job easier because she had already gotten a huge net bag of fresh vegetables for us. MAF flew *veggie runs* once a week, from the interior tribal people, out to the coast for the missionary community. They divided everything out into large string bags, with an average assortment containing green beans, cabbage, a few white and sweet potatoes, squash, bundles of leeks, and the occasional tomato. Fruits, such as bananas, lemons, papaya, and pineapple could be bought from native people selling alongside of the road, or they brought them directly to our door during the week.

Since there were no stores at that time, the missions joined together and MAF stocked a storeroom where we could buy canned goods and staples like rice, powdered milk, sugar and flour, and other household supplies that had been flown in from the Australian side of New Guinea. They also kept a kerosene fueled freezer with a limited amount of frozen meats. Thankfully, Aunt Carol had gotten a few of those items for us. The rest could wait until tomorrow, at which time I thought I would be more able to deal with shopping for the family.

With the essentials, such as food for the day and beds made, life was looking up. Lorraine, David and Jonathan were wildly excited about going outside and checking out the surroundings. The school was a priority and we hustled over there to take a look. It was ranch style, long and low, with classrooms for grades one to eight, which was as far as classes went. The louver windows were open and we cupped our hands around our eyes so we could see through the screens to the inside. The rooms had ceiling fans, blackboards, charts and maps on the walls, with normal study desks lined up in rows, waiting for each student; nothing unusual at all.

Lorraine sounded relieved and surprised, "Well, it looks just like my school in America."

Jonathan had a different idea of what his new surroundings would look like. "I thought everything in New Guinea would be black; like the trees, the grass, the people, everything."

Lorraine areed, "Yeah, I thought it would be really different, but it isn't that bad." I don't know what pictures they had in their minds, but now they could see for themselves that *everything* appeared quite normal after all.

We met a couple of teachers on the grounds. John and Mary Hazelett were busy moving into their house. A number of things needed fixing and Dan promptly volunteered, "Let me help you in any way I can. I know a little about plumbing and some electrical things. We're here for paperwork, otherwise I will have time on my hands. "

"Thank you. That sounds like a good plan to me because I don't know much about doing any kind of repairs," Mr Hazelett smiled.

Dan spent the next two weeks of our waiting period sweating profusely and working on electrical wiring and plumbing at the Hazelett's house. Yes, they moved in by the time school started. The repair work was Dan's side job, his main one being regular trips to town to check in at the government offices hoping to speed our paperwork along.

(Mrs. Hazelett was the first grade teacher. Lorraine started Sentani School in second grade and missed her as teacher, but the other kids had her. Mr.Hazelett taught eighth grade, but his other passion was band. Nearly all the students, third grade or older, joined the band. They practiced every afternoon after school. Mr. Hazelett kept their attention by throwing erasers their way, or so I was told.

Other missionaries, like Aunt Marianne Rosenberger, gave private lessons in the wind instruments. I always enjoyed attending band practice, at least once, when visiting the kids at school. Otherwise, we rarely heard our kids play, unless they played for a Christmas special when home on station.)

Have you detected the references to calling some of our new missionary friends aunts and uncles? The whole mission community, regardless of mission affiliation, was one big family. We all felt that way. It was natural for the MKs to refer to the other missionaries as their aunts and uncles, even though there was no blood relationship.

(When we went on our first furlough, the kids were confused about stateside aunts and uncles, and the ones they already had in Irian. The kids went to their dad, "Well, the aunts and uncles here in the states are your mom's real brothers and sisters that she grew up with. Out is Irian your aunts and uncles are called that because we all work together as a family. The adults look at you kids like you are their own children. We love and care for each other the same way a real family cares about each other. And it's respectful to use the aunt and uncle before their names."

Our kids still refer to some of those *relatives* from former days as their aunts and uncles. However, their teachers were always afforded the courtesy and greater respect of being called Miss, Misses, or Mister.)

On that first day in Sentani, our afternoon inspection of the school grounds was noisy. Two new classrooms were being added to the building. School opening was already delayed one week so they could finish. The carpenters were trained men from the interior Dani tribe. Their supervisors were coastal people, Christian men from the island of Biak.

Jonathan wandered off, following the noise of a big machine. Down the hill, on the other side of the schoolyard, they were digging with a crane. Above the noise, we heard a yell, "Hey, guys, come on down here."

"Wow! Look at that hole in the ground. It's a swimming pool!" Lorraine was elated.

"Maybe it won't be so bad coming here to school if they have a pool," David chimed in. We all agreed that a pool would definitely make boarding school in the future a much greater attraction.

Back at the house in the late afternoon, a rhythmic racket suddenly started up. It was a new sound to us, but well known in the tropics. The frogs and crickets were vying for the best, or worst, music awards of the night. We soon learned when it was four or five in the afternoon because these local singers began their performance every day at the same time. The sounds of the jungle were at their best at dusk and early evening. Cricket calls, cicadas' trills, human voices, and other music and noises echoed from far-away places as the sun went down.

Night time brought adventures of its own. Our house didn't have an indoor bathroom, the toilet room and the shower-room were outside. They were connected by a covered, cement walkway from the back door of the kitchen. We soon learned to do our business while it was yet day. None of us, except maybe Dan, liked going out into the shadows of night, even with a small light of sorts out there. Our imaginations ran wild as we thought of all the creatures that might be hiding out in the dark behind the house. Those fears were later proven to be correct when the boys sent home tales of snake skins in the outdoor shower stalls at their dorm in MK School.

The first night brought another disturbing experience for me. After going to bed, Dan and I heard bumping and clunking noises coming from the kitchen. I sent Dan to check. "Well, so much for little Mickey Mouse mice, we have nocturnal rats running around in the cupboards."

After that cheery word, it was hard to sleep. I envisioned huge rats, running all over the house. How dare my kids sleep soundly and not even know of their presence, until I told them in the morning. I convinced myself that my night of listening was for them, and they didn't even appreciate it.

After a second night of cupboard clatter, we borrowed someone's cat, and she managed to catch one rat. The others remained very illusive and never did get caught. I resolved to stay out of the kitchen at night. So there! The rodents became a part of living in the tropics and I knew I just had to get over it and live with them. But no matter how often we had rats, I never got used to them running around in my house at night. They seemed to grow bigger and the tails got longer every time I heard one, or wrote home about them.

Other than the school construction, the hill was quiet and my three kids were the only ones around. They played outside and inside and never complained about the heat, even though they sweat profusely from morning to night. I'm the one who did the complaining about the heat and humidity. I felt so dragged out all the time. We usually rested in the early afternoon during the worst heat of the day. The best thing was to park in front of a fan and hope that the electricity wouldn't go out. Or you could take a shower, or two, or three, or... Showers were favorites with the kids. I waited until late afternoon for my shower, and then went for a walk because it was slightly cooler then.

On our second afternoon, a call echoed over the hillside, "Come on, the van's here."

Someone drove the van from the MAF base every afternoon to pick up anyone who wanted to go to the old swimming hole. *The Hole*, as named by the missionaries, was located over on another hillside -- up the mountain to a place where a stream poured water into the depths of a large, naturally formed pool. What a fun time the kids had playing in the fresh, cold water. They never missed a day when the van came for them. Dan and I trooped along a couple of times. I usually waded and it felt wonderfully cool on my swollen feet.

Sunday came and we went to the small aluminum-sided chapel near the guest house. Missionaries took turns preaching, and we had a traditional service in English. We especially enjoyed it because that was our first opportunity to meet most of the missionaries who lived on the coast.

That first Sunday was also important because we established a lifelong habit of taking our medicine against malaria. Sunday was a different schedule for the day, which made it easier to remember to take our pills. They were extremely bitter and the kids fussed about the taste. I cajoled and coerced, "Remember all the shots we got in the states before we came? You didn't cry when you had them. Surely you can manage to swallow a few little pills. We gotta do it, so let's just try."

Lorraine had an idea, "How about we see who can swallow them down the fastest." The sibling challenge worked fairly well. The kids finally overcame the bitterness and swallowed their pills every week without complaint for as long as they lived in Irian.

(We learned that being sick with malaria was no fun. But taking the meds was not a sure thing either, if your body became resistant to the meds. I found that out to my own distress and despair later on in my missionary life. I started having malaria break-through, as it is called, and developed low grade fevers and bad headaches, which occurred on the average of every two weeks. It wasn't enough to go to bed, but I felt awful. Leading up to the attacks I was wiped out and my body ached like the flu, so I knew they were coming on. Worse yet, I couldn't think and concentrate with the headaches. But when they passed, I felt so much better that I wondered if I had imagined being sick. The mission doctor worked with me and we tried several other meds before I found one that kept me on track. It took me several years of misery to find the right medication.

Meanwhile Lorraine never did get malaria, and Dan and the other kids only got it a couple of times. Once they took the *cure,* they were fine.)

More travel papers

Back to our arrival . . . We landed in Sentani on a Friday when the government offices were closed. Dan had the weekend free before beginning rounds of the government offices to report and get all the necessary travel documents. Early on Monday morning, he hitched a ride from another missionary going into Sukarnapura, now called Jayapura, the capitol of Irian Barat. Fortunately, Dan was allowed to represent the family, and the rest of us didn't have to go to town with him. An Indonesian visa is only granted for the head of the house, other members are considered mere travel companions. Hooray!

The trip to town took more than an hour because the road was filled with deep pot-holes. When Dan checked in to The Mission Fellowship (TMF) business office, he was relieved that there was an Indonesian man assigned to go with him. The two of them made rounds, going to several different government offices, presenting forms and introductions. They also stopped at Police Headquarters for Dan to get finger prints for his driver's license. By early afternoon, he came home, hot, thirsty and exhausted.

"Well, I have to take more passport pictures to town because every office wants several of each person. It's a beautiful drive, going around Lake Sentani then curving up around the mountains. When you finally reach the top, you have a panoramic view of the bay going out to the ocean. The town spreads out all around the hillsides of the harbor."

"I'd like to go with you sometime and see the view. We might all have to go with you anyhow because we're already out of the two dozen pictures each that I brought with us. The offices in Jakarta took them."

The whole family did go to town that week to get pictures taken. The mission office agreed to pick them up and deliver them to the government offices. We finally got smart though. After taking the second batch of pictures, we told TMF to ask for the negatives and keep them with our passports, just in case more were requested later. And of course, they were.

It was two weeks, and several more trips to town, before all documents were registered, signed and stamped. Traveling back and forth, Dan got better acquainted with people from the mission community. On one trip, he ran into a former classmate, Phil Masters. They had attended the Summer Institute of Linguistics in North Dakota together. Phil told Dan about a planned survey trip to check out a new tribe that he and another missionary wanted to enter. He was in town for government permits to go into a restricted area, where several hostile tribes were located.

The wait in Sentani helped me adjust, somewhat, to the tropical climate. I felt over-heated and clammy all the time. Being so great-with-child I was also tired and lacked energy, which didn't help my outlook on the weather, either. But I finally gave it up figuring that was how it was, just live with it!

A Christian Tribesman
One good thing was that I didn't have to do all the chores by

myself. Our guest house came supplied with a house-helper, which was another new experience for me.

Emerit was a Dani tribesman who prepared vegetables, washed dishes, swept the floors, and washed clothes for us. We couldn't talk together, so he appointed himself as my Indonesian language teacher. He would hold up a piece of fruit, or whatever, and repeat the word in Indonesian, waiting for me to repeat it back to him. *"Ini pisang, pisang,"* as he held up a banana.

I imitated, *"Pisang, pisang,"* back to him. Who knows how much of it was with a Dani accent. If there was any difference, I didn't know it.

Working in the kitchen was another story. Emerit silently watched me trying to do things I didn't know how to do. One day I was struggling with those hard little lemons that grew on the trees in the yard. Making real lemonade was my goal, but I couldn't get any juice out of them. Emerit quietly came over and took one and pushing down, rolled it under his palm on the table, effectively squashing it into pulp on the inside. When he cut it open, wah-lah, the juice was there for the squeezing into the pitcher. I don't know how many times he rescued me from my state of great frustration and started those stupid kerosene burners. Emerit checked the rice for bugs and sifted my flour for weevils before I even realized they were a problem. He knew all the little tricks to making my life easier in the kitchen.

Emerit's family consisted of two wives and four children, and they all lived in a little house out beside the guest house. Mrs. Hazelett clued me in, "Emerit is a wonderful Christian man. He became a Christian after he married his two wives. The Dani church doesn't allow him to serve as a leader with two wives. If he divorced one and sent her back to her family, she would be rejected and most likely turn to prostitution in order to survive. So he decided to keep his wives and their children together. He is highly respected, and even though he can't be an official church leader, the other pastors still come to him for advice in many spiritual matters. He is also skilled in mid-wifery and out here the Danis call on him to help in difficult deliveries. He is so trustworthy that the mission offered him the job of caretaker for the church and their guest house. He gets paid for that, and with working as house-help in the guest house, he can support his family and send his kids to school."

How thankful I am for meeting up with such a godly national man our first day on the mission field. Emerit and his family showed us nothing but kindness and love. What an introduction to the tribal people. It was an encouragement to me to see how God was at work in the hearts of the tribes bringing them into His kingdom.

As our documentation neared completion, Plan A was for us to fly to the south coast town of Agats and begin Indonesian language study with the Spencers. Nearer my due date in September we were to go to the hospital in the highlands for delivery. However, the Baptist mission doctor, Thelma Becroft, nixed that idea. Just before our arrival she was in Agats on a medical trip and immediately called on the two-way radio to the TEAM field chairman telling him, "Agats is absolutely no place for a new missionary to go so late in her pregnancy. I know it's early, but when the Lunows' paperwork is done they are to go directly to the hospital at Pit River." And that was that!

Pit River is the Australian mission station in the central highlands. I don't know about our field chairman, but I was relieved to be told of Dr. Thelma's ultimatum. By this time, my due date was six weeks away. The mountains would be cooler and I was going to see a doctor, sooner rather than later. What pleasant thoughts!

Immigration took their time, third world time, until all our documents were finally processed and in hand. We put in our flight requests to MAF and once again gathered our luggage together; yes, including all eleven of those big pieces. Plus we had various and sundry smaller carry-ons, and any number of additional cartons of foodstuffs needed for our trip to the hospital station at Pit River. We were ready. Oh, were we ready to welcome the new baby into our lives. And I, well I was also getting crabbier by the minute, too.

Chapter Three: "Is it for supper, or for tea?"
First glimpses of the Central Highlands

August 15, 1968 was another early morning for us. In darkness and with masses of mosquitoes buzzing around our heads, we loaded up the van and went down the hill to check in at MAF. Our total weight for this trip was 900 pounds, which I jotted down in my daily journal. That sum just about maxed out the amount the airplane would accept within their safety limits. The weight included our bodies, luggage, and food stuffs, minus the pilot's weight. Pilot pounds, or kilos, were already calculated with the airplane. In later years, our combined weight for luggage and bodies always exceeded the load limit, and it took two flights to fly us anywhere.

This time it was a single engine Cessna airplane, which MAF used for the shorter grass airstrips in the interior. The kids eventually knew all the MAF planes just by the sound of their engines flying overhead. My hearing never equaled theirs when it came to the finer distinctions between a hum, a drone, or a roar of a specific airplane motor.

The pilot seated us, heavier weights in front, and lighter in back so the tail would lift up in takeoff and not drag on landing. Dan was next to the pilot in the front, I sat with Lorraine and Jonathan in the middle, our shoulder straps securely fastened into our seat belts across our laps. My belt was loosened out of necessity. David was perched behind us with suitcases stacked up beside him. He was especially pleased because that seat had a small escape door in the side of the plane, and he could slip out of it when the plane landed. The Cessna also had a pod, which looked like a pregnant belly, with a hinged door attached to the bottom of the plane. MAF modified the planes adding the pods in order to carry more supplies. The space was packed with as much of our stuff as they could possibly shove into it. That flight we bulked-out with all our stuff, before reaching cargo weight limit.

By take-off time, the horizon was beginning to brighten. We silently gaped out the windows as the plane briefly skimmed over the tops of banana trees and other jungle growth. Flying low over Lake Sentani, we slowly climbed higher over the lush landscape on the other side. The clouds were showing tinges of pink and the sky soon changed to a golden glow, then into burnished orange-pink and yellow hues. The white pathways of the rising sun streamed out between cloud layers.

It was truly glorious to see the morning skies unfold from our seats in the heavens. No, I promise I won't go into great detail and description of every cloud that we saw. But those first experiences of what it's like flying into the dawn of a new day in Irian are part of our memories, part of our feelings for that land where God led us as a family. How breathtaking and wonderful it was to see the breaking dawn. The small plane maintained at an altitude where we could plainly see the land below us.

The jungle spread out like one continuous, plush carpet in shades of verdant green with splashes of white and red-orange colors scattered in the top-most branches of the trees. The sun shimmered on the waters of the meandering streams and rivers that flowed deep below the canopy of the forests. We flew above and alongside of great, white egrets that were gliding in slow motion over the emerald tree tops. The plane's engine roared in our ears, but I still sensed the utter silence and great vastness of the wilderness that lay below.

Watching it all, I was acutely aware of going into the great unknown --a place in time, far away, vastly different from anything I'd ever experienced before. I talked to God, "Lord, you promised to take care of us in this land. It's scary not knowing what it will be like. I know you can keep us, but help me to have faith and believe in my heart that you will. Help me to feel your presence with us."

Lorraine set the scene we were looking at in a poem she wrote, when she was ten years old.

"As God Watches Over"
As God watches over the deep jungle green
As God watches over the creatures unseen
As God watches over the birds in the sky
Just that much does God watch over You and I.   Amen"

We rarely talked, but we silently poked each other and pointed when we saw something interesting down below. It was a game of who would be first to see signs of life, like a village, a garden clearing, a smoke trail from a fire, or even a hut down in the depths of the trees. The sightings were rare, with only miles and miles of green and rivers below us.

By full daylight, the mountains were looming closer. The air felt cooler. I urged the kids to put on their sweaters, but it wasn't easy to do because their sleeves got tangled up in their shoulder straps. The plane climbed higher, pointing its nose up into the sky. Near the foothills of the mountains we finally spied more huts scattered here and there, but there were no villages on that side of the ranges.

Flying between giant cotton balls of clouds, we were suddenly up and over a long ridge of mountains. Below us stretched a great valley, encircled all around with higher peaks misted in clouds. It was the Grand Baliem Valley, a place I'd only read about in mission books. The slopes of the mountains and the valley floor were covered in what looked like cultivated rows of gardens. Smoke plumes wafted up from the gardens and round huts of small villages snuggled together on the valley floor. The broad waters of the Baliem River snaked its way from one end of the valley to the other.

What a thrill it was as we caught our first glimpses of the interior lands of the tribes of Irian Barat. It didn't matter that this was not the area that we would be in because other mission groups were already there. It was still exciting, realizing that this was a place long unknown to the outside world. And now missionaries lived there, telling the tribes about a God who created their world, a God who made and loved them.

Australian Baptist Hospital Station, Pit River

Our excitement mounted as we flew over the main valley and saw a couple of airstrips up other valleys which branched off of the Baliem. We headed into one of them and the pilot pointed, mouthing to Dan that we were nearly there. We circled down and the plane lined up and flew straight in to a small grass strip on a mountain ridge. We landed on the level and then sped, almost perpendicular, up to the top at the landing area.

Waiting off to the side of the airstrip, we saw a missionary couple surrounded by naked, dark skinned people, the Danis. Many of them stood with their arms crossed over their chests, hands clutching their shoulders, trying to keep warm in the cool mountain air. At last, we had our first close up look of inland tribal people.

The missionary couple came out to the plane and greeted us in their Aussie accent, "Welcome to Pit River. I'm David Brown and this is my wife Helen. We'll show you down to your cabin. Helen is a midwife and she'll be helping you when the baby is born."

That was the cue for the Dani people to crowd around the plane. Not to see Dan and me, but the center of their attention was our three kids.The curiosity was mutual as both sides stared at each other. White children were always the center of attention with the tribal people. Once our kids cleared the path, Dan and I found it easier to establish relationships and friendships.This first time, the Danis had no problem surrounding our kids and reaching out to rub their white arms and touch their lighter hair.

Before going interior, Dan tried to prepare the kids, "Remember, the tribal people might not have any clothes on. That is the way they live, and they are not embarrassed about it. So don't you be either. And don't stare at them!"

As far as looks go, the Danis fit right in to that word of warning. The women wore short grass skirts, slung low on the hips, with the bottom of the skirt just above the knees, but they were bare from the waist up. The men wore only a penis sheath, which is made out of a long, narrow gourd and tied with a vine-string around the waist. All the children were totally naked. Danis were stocky and muscular, with dark-brown, nearly black skin, and tight curly hair. The hair was in various lengths of matted or twisted styles. Somehow, with their dark skin and the gray ash covering their bodies, they actually looked like they were clothed.

Many of the women had large, woven-fiber bags with the strap across the front of their foreheads, and the bag spread over their shoulders hanging down their backs. They carried loads of fresh garden vegetables, sweet potatoes, or firewood. Several smaller net bags appeared to have only leaves and grasses in them, until we heard a baby fuss.

Lorraine nudged me and pointed, "Mom, I think they have a baby in there."

I asked Helen Brown about it, "Oh, yes, that baby is snuggled up in a bed of fresh leaves which stay warm and moist. It's like a humidity chamber. When baby soils the leaves, mum dumps the old leaves and gathers a pile of new ones to line the bag. It's actually very clean and fresh." The babies must have loved being hauled around in the bags because we rarely heard them cry.

Meanwhile, the pilot was unloading our luggage and setting it to the side because he had other places to fly that day. Those famous eleven pieces were accounted for, only the pilot didn't count them out-loud like the bus coolies in India. The Danis started picking up and shouldering suitcases, along with a multitude of food boxes, the kids' carry-on cases, and the open tray of thirty eggs. The caravan, with carriers in the lead, made its way down the path along the side of the airstrip to the cabin below. Everyone was talking and chattering in at least two distinct languages. A couple of naked little boys grabbed David and Jonathan by the arms and they all went bounding down the steep path ahead of us. Since I was less than graceful at that time, I hung onto Dan's hand as I waddled my way down the steep trail. Of course, we two were at the tail end of the line.

The cabin was on a rise near the two room mission hospital, which was below the bottom of the airstrip. It looked very rustic, set off the ground on timbers, with smoke floating up from a blackened stove pipe. The walls were of rough-hewn sawn lumber, painted a brownish black color, smelling strongly of creosote. Painting creosote on wooden buildings kept the termites out. The cabin roof was thatched with bundles of the long *kunai* grasses. The Danis used the same grass for the roofs on their huts.

It was dark inside the cabin, coming in from the bright sunlight. There were only a couple of small louver windows. The living room-kitchen was one long open room. The back door was located beside the cast-iron cooking stove. The kitchen cabinet held a small stainless steel sink with a hand pump on one end for well water. The long cupboard shelves below the sink were open for placing dishes and storing food. The floor had a roll to it because it was of thick bark, uncurled and flattened out. The house was sparsely furnished, with a daybed on one side and handmade wooden table and chairs in the middle of the floor. One bedroom had a double bed, the other had bunk beds. Each room had open shelves for our clothes. The only bright spot in the bedrooms was the patchwork quilts on the beds. I was delighted to find a small bathroom inside the house, even if it was a bucket-flush toilet and a canvas bucket with shower head attached for bathing. We loved that little cabin, especially at night when the generator was humming and the one neon light was on. The evenings were cool and it felt cozy and comfy to be inside.

A young Dani man was assigned to keep the fire going in our stove, and he did that most faithfully. Every morning he carried firewood in and started the fire. He also helped in the house, washing dishes and sweeping. The broom was made of long reeds tied together and he simply swished the crumbs through the cracks in the floor. Since there was no wash machine, he hand washed the laundry every day and hung it outside on a vine-line. We all watched the weather so he could take it down before the afternoon rains. I no longer bothered about ironing clothes; we just folded them and put them in the cupboards.

Showing, and not telling, came in handy again because we couldn't speak to each other. I showed him how to make the beds, especially the top bunk, by standing on a chair and doing it myself the first time. We got along fine. If the lemonade was finished, I set the pitcher out for him to see. He knew what the small piles of potatoes and green beans out on the cabinet meant. The kids had no problem communicating, motioning for him to follow them outside when they had something to show him or tell the waiting throngs. Whatever he thought they were saying, he spoke in Dani and it was all settled.

Now is the time to *fess-up* about those eleven pieces of luggage that we hauled across the world with us. Before leaving for the field we shipped a supply, or outfit, of household goods and clothing that I estimated we would need for a term of four to five years. At that time there were no stores in Irian Barat and our shipment would take at least six months before it arrived in Sentani. After that, MAF flew everything interior to our station.

How can you actually know what your family, especially growing kids, will need six months to four years down the line? At least for the immediate future, all was well because of those eleven suitcases. One huge duffel bag was stuffed full of boy or girl baby clothes, including several dozen cloth diapers. One half of another black, hardboard foot-locker contained baby bottles, blankets, plastic pants, training pants and a handheld baby food grinder. I felt especially fortunate to have several packages of the new disposable diapers -something that had just come out on the market. I planned to save them for travel only. Unpacking the baby clothes and putting things on the shelves in our little cabin made me feel like, yes, this was real. We were going to get a baby soon. We were there.

Besides the baby clothes, each of us had our own suitcase of clothing and personal items. Extra space in the two trunks contained clothes for the next few months until our goods arrived. I hoped and prayed that we had enough of everything until then. Otherwise we'd all be running around in native dress. Not really, I could always sew new clothes for the kids.

I was way off on my estimations with Dan, though. His only pair of tennis shoes was already rotting from the wet weather and all the walking he was doing. I sent a note out to the MAF mission bookkeeper, Gene Newman, "Would you be able to get a pair of tennis shoes for Dan from Papua, New Guinea when the MAF plane goes over for food supplies? I am sending a tracing of his foot because I don't know how they measure his size in Australia."

A note came back, *"Size 12 wide shoes!!! Who wears one that big, was the question from the store in Wewak? The pilot looked all over for some shoes for you, but the largest was a size 10. There is another flight next week and I will send a letter to the store in Lae. Or we can try to get a pair sent up from Australia. Let me know if you want me to special order for you."* Gene Newman

Getting Dan a new pair of shoes became a big joke with the mission community because the whole island somehow heard, via two-way radio, about the order for a big pair of shoes. Orders, medical needs, and important traffic were relayed on the radios. As a result, nothing was private, and we learned a lot about each other, whether we wanted to know it or not.

First things first, though. The morning after our arrival at Pit River, I went over to the mission hospital for a check up. The hospital looked like a larger version of our cabin, only with an aluminum roof. It had two rooms, one for general assessments and dispensing medicines; the other was for surgery and obstetrics. There were no in-patient rooms, which meant I would go directly over to our cabin after the birth. The hospital was rustically humble, but adequate. A doctor and two Australian nurses staffed it. Dr. Thelma Becroft was on vacation. I hoped that my baby would wait for her return, but I wasn't worried because the midwives were more than capable to help me deliver.

The other nurse-midwife, Jean Crowe, checked me over and reassured me, "Everything is fine."

To my question, she was reassuring, "No, I don't hear two heartbeats. I would say this is a single birth. And you are not ready for delivery yet."

Jean also ordered a pint of fresh cow's milk for me from a nearby village where the missionaries had given the Danis a couple of milk cows. They were to bring the milk to our house every few days. I was also told to exercise by taking walks every day. That was not easy because all foot paths were either uphill or downhill. I managed to get out every morning before the afternoon rains came. Dan, or the kids, usually walked with me.

Adventures in Dani-land

The children lost no time in playing outside in the sunshine every morning and making new friends. Dani boys hung on our doorstep from dawn to dusk, waiting for someone, anyone, to come out the door. The fact that none of my kids spoke a word of Dani didn't deter anyone. David chatted away as if everything was fully understood. Lorraine played with the boys because very few little girls came around. None of the kids ever mentioned the fact that all their new friends were naked. It just wasn't a problem to them.

Lorraine's hair was long and wavy, and silky in texture. "How do the Danis keep their hair so curly? I wish mine was like theirs."

David was more interested in the carved wooden combs that they had sticking up out of their heads. He kept trying to wear one, but was disappointed that his hair was straight and too slippery for the combs to stay in. A couple of young boys brought mouth harps made out of bamboo and vine-string, and showed the kids how to play. No problem, all three put them in front of their teeth, hollowed their cheeks out, pulled the string at the end and twanged away, making music.

Jonathan never said much, but the kids on the doorstep always looked for him because he was the ball guy. His volleyball was a huge hit. They also used it as a soccer ball, dodge ball, or whatever kind of ball they wanted to make it at the moment. Even the Dani men came to play with it, and sometimes they didn't want to give it back. But the kids were good sports about sharing and letting the men play with it. That generosity apparently did not go unnoticed. Early one morning a little boy who always hung around the house brought Jonathan a small bow and arrow that he had made. Jonathan couldn't believe that he was actually giving it to him, for free, for keeps.

He brought it in to show us, "Boy, they sure must love us. I love them too, and I like to play with them." Back outside, the other boys gathered around clamoring to show both Jonathan and David how to draw the vine and shoot the arrows.

Mornings were best for outside play because of the afternoon rains. The kids developed peeling noses and red faces because we were above 6,000 feet, and the higher the altitude the stronger the ultraviolet rays. I dug into the suitcases and found my zinc oxide and slathered noses and cheeks with it, producing ghostly white faces. Otherwise, the kids' skin was so tanned that sometimes their knees looked dirty and we scrubbed them extra hard at bath time.

The constant presence of people in the yard, and at the door, eventually wore on me. After awhile it began to wear on the kids too. Jonathan, especially, liked his space, "Couldn't we play alone once in awhile? I like to play with them, but do they have to be around all the time?"

It was worse when they brought any of their toys outside; their little cars, or Lorraine took her doll. Even the dads and the moms came running when they saw toys. No one ever tried to take anything. Murmuring quietly, they circled round and watched. I told the kids, "Just be patient and kind, and let them look. They've never seen toys like yours before." So we put up with the constant company outside our door.

The next thing I noticed was the kids had insect bites around their waists and legs and they were scratching all the time. There were no mosquitoes in the highlands. Looking closer, I could actually see tiny brown critters jumping around in their shorts and inside their shirts. I had never seen fleas before, but that's what they were and there wasn't much I could do about it. As long as the kids played in the grass and with the other children, they had fleas. Those fleas were survivors! They could even hold their breath going through the laundry and come out alive. I can verify that fact with my own eyes.

Since we were on an extended stay at Pit River, the kids and Dan went on a couple of trips. One day we were all invited to a Dani pig feast to honor a government official who had come to inspect something or other. I stayed at home, declining to walk over the steep uneven path. This was their first time experience of going to a native village and having *pig-in-a-pit,* which the interior highlanders are famous for. The kids had to wait until boarding school before they had another pig feast.

The first one is always the most memorable. When the pig party was over, the kids came home with delectable tales about the feast and the food, "Mom, you really missed it. You should have come. They dug the food up out of the ground. It was all mixed up with meat and vegetables, packed on steaming rocks and buried under dirt. And then we ate the food on big leaves with our fingers. It was really good!" Yup, they were most certainly trying to make me feel bad about staying at home.

The procedure for a pig roast is worth talking about. The men dig out a big hole in the chosen spot early in the morning. They line the hole with rocks and then build a fire inside and cook the rocks to get them hot. Next, the women bring banana leaves to cover the rocks. That's followed by a layer of leeks and onions, cut cabbage, sweet potatoes and other vegetables. The next layer is the butchered pork, with another thick layer of cabbage and vegetables on top. Everything is covered over with the huge banana leaves, and the hot rocks below steam and cook the food. The aroma wafting out of a roasting pit is enough to water your taste buds and try your patience for the feast to be ready. After an all day roast, they finally peel back the layers and serve the vegetables all mixed up in one big pile and the tender pieces of pork set to the side. Each serving is dished up on a banana leaf, and you dig in with your hands, unless you brought your own plate and spoon. Eating with your hands makes it taste better, at least we think so.

On another day, Dan and the kids went on a three hour walk down the valley. The Dani guides, accompanied by many other village kids, took them to see a steel cable bridge that the government built for the people to cross over a steep ravine with a raging river below. On their way back home they experienced another thrill, when they took a different path and crossed over a Dani suspension bridge. It was a swaying, vine bridge, with the river easily visible through the slats in the so-called flooring; a real Indiana Jones kind of bridge. On that trip, the kids attracted more people as they walked along and the crowd followed them home. They all returned with red faces and blistered noses, despite my generous application of zinc oxide before they went on their hike.

A Tribal Funeral

One day the Danis began building a huge bonfire right on the hillside near our house. Shortly after, a little procession of people came crying up the path, carrying a large wrapped bundle. They put their burden on the woodpile and set it ablaze.

The children ran outside, "Hey, let's go see the bonfire."

Running back to us, they reported, "Wow, it's a big fire!"

It took Dan and me a little while to figure out the connection between the news of a mother and newborn dying in the hospital and the bonfire outside our house. Dan hurried outside to talk to the kids, "I'm sorry, this isn't a regular bonfire. It's for a lady who died at the hospital this morning. The people here don't have a lot of land, so they can't bury people when they die. They cry and mourn them and then burn the body; like they are doing here."

His explanation was simple and the kids didn't seem to have any trouble with that. We allowed them to remain outside watching the fire, but Dan called them inside before the body was visible and everything burned to ashes.

The kids handled that spectacle better than me. I was horrified to think that my children were out there watching bodies burn up on a pile of wood! We hadn't known until that event that the Danis cremate their dead. I like to think that our acceptance and explanation of this custom helped the kids to understand it better. Little did we know then, but our children would have to face death a number of times in their missionary kid experience. But as far as I know, they never attended a cremation service again.

Settling into a routine

Because we were staying in Pit River for so long, Dan made arrangements for a teacher at the government school to help us with conversational Indonesian. He was all excited to get started; one hour in the morning and one hour in the afternoon. The tutoring ended up being more for Dan, than it was for me. He took tests for the first two units while at Pit River. I studied vocabulary lists, and that's about as far as I got. I had other things on my mind, mainly the new baby.

Daily chores also took me a long time: working with the woodstove, cooking from scratch, and heating water in tea kettles for showers. I also felt that that I should keep a closer eye on my children when they were outside playing. Plus, I was home-schooling Lorraine for her first semester of second grade. No wonder I wasn't enthusiastic about studying a new language right then.

Along with the daily jobs, I started baking my own bread, twice a week. Flour came in forty pound sacks and our house-helper immediately sifted out the weevils when it came in. Depending on what stage of development the bugs were in, we looked for little whitish, wormy crawlers in sort of web-like clusters, or at an earlier stage, they were small black bugs crawling around. The sifters were of very fine mesh, not like the courser screen from the US sifters. They were round, with a rim, and you shook them by hand. If the flour was damp, there was no way you could sift flour through the screen. Our Dani worker took the whole bag outside to sift it and let the breeze blow the dust away.

Grandma T had given me her old-timey bread recipe and I practiced baking bread while we were still in the US. Her general rule-of-thumb called for one teaspoon of salt, one tablespoon of sugar, and one tablespoon of melted shortening per cup of liquid, with flour added, making one loaf. The recipe went like this:

    1/3 Cup warm water, plus
    1 Tablespoon of dry yeast, plus
    1 teaspoon of sugar, mix, set aside to bubble
    3 Cups of water or milk
    3 Tablespoons melted shortening
    2 Tablespoons of sugar
    3 Teaspoons of salt

Add yeast mixture to the liquid, gradually add about 4 cups of flour or more, until the dough is no longer sticky. Cover with dish towel and let it rise and punch down two times. It takes a couple of hours depending on the weather. Shape into loaves and put into greased pans, let rise, bake in medium heat (350 F.) oven for 40-50 minutes. Thump the bottom of the bread for hollow sound, which indicates it's done.

I passed on Grandma's recipe to Lorraine and she's used it in her adult life with her family, and at their school to demonstrate bread-making. We also used the bread dough to make cinnamon rolls with each batch of bread.

So, here goes my first try using the wood-burning stove to bake bread at Pit River. The stove didn't have an oven thermometer and I had to get a feel for how hot I thought the oven should be. When the fire was lit, it was a matter of not stoking up the firebox with too much wood and maintaining a consistent heat. That first try wasn't the best, my bread was sort of heavy and flat, but it sure smelled good. We ate it anyway, as was my food rule for whatever I cooked. (After years of practice, my homemade bread and sweet rolls are still a Lunow family favorite.)

The Cessna airplane brought in supplies and mail from Sentani every week. We received only a few letters from the states while we were at Pit. This is snail mail we're talking about because in those days it took five to six weeks for letters to come, sometimes even longer. We didn't hear from my mom or Grandma T for several months, even though I wrote to them every two weeks.

(How slow communication was then, and how depressed I got

when we didn't get mail. It was wonderful to eventually get coastal phone service, followed by satellite phones, then to email, high speed internet, and now even Skype. High tech and quick communications for us came years later and we saw only the beginning of it in our time.)

The airplanes from the interior bases flew in to Pit River several times a week with various medical emergencies. Every time we heard the plane come in low and land, my kids ran up to the top of the airstrip just to watch. Stretcher patients were most exciting because some of them actually had arrows sticking out of their bodies from the tribal wars. There was an encephalitis epidemic in a nearby village and a number of critically ill babies were also brought in to the hospital. A woman having trouble with delivery was flown in too.

One noon we heard the plane, but on landing the engine suddenly stopped. The Danis started yelling and calling. The kids and Dan ran out the door and up to the strip to see what had happened. The plane had gotten caught in a downdraft at the bottom of the airstrip and nosed into the soft grass. Thankfully, no one was hurt.

But whoops, we all got scrambled eggs from that accident because there were several egg trays on board. To top it off, the patient coming in was a pregnant lady with high blood pressure! She did okay while there and her blood pressure eventually went down after she delivered. Another plane came in a couple of days later with a pilot and mechanic. They repaired the downed plane enough to fly it over to the MAF station.

Dani wasn't the only language that we struggled to understand at Pit River. Aussie-English also proved perplexing at times. They had a number of sayings and phrases that we'd never heard before. One funny mix-up was when we got an invitation to supper for pancakes. Our American supper is a full meal, so we didn't feed the kids before we went. Well, the promised pancakes ended up being only two to three inches across, one or two each, and were served with jam instead of syrup. Drinks were water or hot tea. Yup, the kids were starved by the time we got home.

The next invite was for tea, late afternoon again. We learned our lesson from the first invite, and Dan politely asked, "What do you mean by tea?"

"Oh, sorry mate, tea is a full meal for an Aussie."

Now we've got it straight, until next time.

Besides a meal now and then, we missionaries met together on Sunday afternoons to listen to recorded sermons and sing familiar hymns in English. The sermons on tape on Sunday evenings also became our family tradition. We enjoyed the times of fellowship with these new missionary friends at Pit River. They not only welcomed us, but answered our many questions and helped supply extras we needed but missed bringing with us. Their hospitality and willingness to inform and teach us was greatly appreciated and hugely encouraging to us as new missionaries.

It's a Girl!

I was gaining weight daily and felt like I was ready to deliver any minute. Friends in the states expressed their concerns about my having a baby on the mission field. I wasn't scared or worried about it, especially after two deliveries already, once with twins. The two mid-wives were also positive, and they inspired my confidence in them. I believed God would be with me, whether in a two room mission hospital, or in a sterile OB department in the states.

Dr. Thelma made it back from her vacation a full week before I went into labor. Whew! It was a little before midnight on a brilliant starlit night, when Dan and I walked over to the hospital. An hour later, at 1 AM on September 9, 1968, Marie was born. She was our fourth child and second girl. Everything was normal, no anesthesia, and only one shot for pain.

"Thank you, Lord," was all I could say. And I promise I'm not going into any more great and gory details than that. The best part for me was having Dan there. He wasn't even allowed near the delivery room in the states. This time he shared in the whole process and miracle of Marie taking her first breath and then bellowing her lungs out.

The midwife, Helen Brown, bundled up our baby and handed her to me. Just then we heard the door to the outer medical room creak open. Dr. Thelma looked out and saw Jonathan standing there barefoot and in his pjs.

His eyes were wide as he looked in the delivery room and tried to explain to us at the same time, "I woke up and called for you, but you didn't answer. Then I saw the light in the hospital window and so I came over."

He suddenly glimpsed his new sister all wrapped up beside me and came over for a better look, "Did we get a girl baby?"

When assured that it was a girl, his next question was, "Did our baby come bare-naked, or did she already have those clothes on?"

Of course, he was thrilled and proud to be the first to see her. "Can I go over and tell Lorraine and David that we got a baby sister? We prayed for a girl."

"No, honey, let's wait until daylight before you go tell them."

The next few hours we stayed at the hospital so the midwife could check on me and baby. Dan and Jonathan rested on a cot near my bed. By dawn I was feeling ready to go over to our cabin. First, our proud Dad went outside to show off his new daughter to the Danis who were standing around waiting for medical care. Glancing over to the cabin, Dan saw two little figures clad in pajamas sitting on the steps.

He waved and called, "Hey, come on over and see what we got." They were already on the run, excited to see their new baby.

Jonathan couldn't resist his bragging rights, "I was the first one to see her, you know."

"Well, you should have called us when you left," David retorted.

Lorraine summed it up, "Now we have two and two, our family is even."

It was time for me to move back to the cabin. Dan and Nurse Helen helped me onto the stretcher. What, no ambulance? Nope, the EMT brigade was comprised of a half dozen Danis clad in their gourds, with wooden comb picks stuck in their hair. They lined up on either side of the canvas litter. It was quite a sight and quite a ride for me and baby Marie.

At the house, Helen settled us into bed and checked both of us one more time. Then she gave me a bed bath and it felt wonderful. Marie also received her first bath and she howled the whole time. How she hated the exposure to the air and being cold.

"Can I pick out the baby's clothes for today?" Lorraine was first to ask. From then on, it became a contest among the three kids to choose Marie's clothes after her bath. Each of the kids had their favorite outfit to dress their live doll in. I acted as the referee, making sure that they took turns choosing. That duffel bag of baby clothes was well worth the haul across the world.

We put Marie on the bed because there was no crib in the cabin. It was a little scary having her beside me all the time. I was afraid I would roll over on her. That first night both Dan and I were overly conscious of her every little breath and snort. But we made it through the night without anybody getting squashed.

I was still weak and felt sick, running a low grade fever, the first couple of days. Dr. Thelma came over and checked me and discovered that I had retained a piece of placenta in my uterus. Fortunately I didn't need surgery because I expelled it on my own the next day. After that I felt better and started to regain strength.

Dad does double duty

Day to day living was in Dan's hands that first week. I'm sure he didn't know that being nursemaid to me would be part of the deal. But Dan cheerfully helped me to the bathroom, to bathe, and to take care of myself in the general aftermath of having a baby. May I point out that kind of thing was something no real German man would ever do in the *olde country.*

Dan did it all without flinching and with humor, telling me, "Well, having a baby on the mission field is a family affair. You have to do what you have to do. Didn't I learn how to change diapers when we had our twins? Now I can do this."

One thing he didn't do was wash the cloth diapers by hand with only a bucket to rinse in. Our Dani helper did that, and Dan was most grateful for his services.

Although we all knew Dan was not a cook, he managed to follow my instructions so that everyone had enough to eat. One day he cooked up some mean scrambled eggs, according to the kids, "Mom, Dad's eggs taste better than yours." I tried them and they were right.

The third day after delivery TEAM missionaries, Uncle Doug and Aunt Julie Miller, came to see us. We hadn't seen any of our mission co-workers for awhile and we needed their encouragement. Julie gave me a bouquet of gardenias and a chocolate candy bar, and made me feel coddled. She also cooked for us that day. Hooray! The two older Miller kids and Marie were in the same age bracket, They became good friends and went from K through high school together.

On a daily basis, my kids helped out by choosing their own clothes and getting dressed every morning. They did chores, like setting the table and cleaning up. All three were more than eager to run and fetch whatever I needed for Marie. They were so thrilled with her that they came into the bedroom just to look at her and make sure she was alright. That's when they asked their many questions.

David was puzzled and wondered, "Whatever color the mother is, that's the color of the baby, isn't it? What language will our baby speak?"

Thinking of our status, Jonathan's question was, "Is our baby a baby missionary too?"

Lorraine's questions were more immediate and motherly, "Mom, the baby is crying, can I pick her up and hold her now?"

With a doting Dad, and three older siblings to respond to her every sigh or whimper, Marie got carried around an awful lot. But I remained the most important person in her life because I was nursing her.

We sent out birth announcement cables from the TMF office on the coast to my mother and Grandma T and a couple of our churches. The content was relayed to the office via the station's two-way radio. It took over a month to hear back from anyone. My mom told us that her cable arrived the day after we sent it. I'm glad they got the news sooner, than later, even though we didn't know they received it right away.

I was realizing more and more how hard it was to have such a long gap in communication with family and friends across the world. In fact, the day that Marie was born, we received a bag of letters from the US. It was mail sent five weeks earlier, old news by the time we read it, but all new to us. Still, I am thankful for letters and how encouraging they were no matter when they were received.

As soon as I felt better, I started home schooling Lorraine again. She could have gone to boarding school, but she was so excited about a new baby that she didn't want to go away to school just yet. All of our children would eventually go to boarding school because we lived in extremely isolated situations, and some places were not safe for children to stay at home with their parents. Dan and I felt that one semester of home schooling would help us adjust and acclimate as a family. Besides, I was being a little selfish and wanted to keep Lorraine home as long as I could. I appreciated that she was always my cheerful helper, willing to do whatever was needed. She never complained and had great ideas for entertaining herself and her brothers.

We carried the second grade school books with us from America. Lessons were usually in the mornings when Dan was also studying Indonesian. Lorraine helped me by being easy to teach. She did well accepting my feeble efforts, along with my emotional ups and downs. Her one big problem was concentrating when the boys were making a racket playing. Naturally she wanted to be outside playing too. Of course, there were interruptions with baby Marie. I also took over cooking duties again. Some days I was short on patience or demonstrated none at all, with all that was going on in our little cabin.

Dr. Thelma wanted to make sure that I was strong enough to go to the South Coast and she ordered that we stay a month longer at Pit River. Life settled into a routine of sorts with studies for Dan and Lorraine.

David and Jonathan grew more restless and complained to me, "We always have somebody around us when we're outside. And when we come in, we get told to be quiet because Dad or Lorraine is studying, or the baby is sleeping."

I think those were fair remarks for how they were feeling. Dan and I tried to be more sensitive to their needs and spend more time with them. Thankfully they were good sports, and were long-suffering and very patient, especially when outside with the Dani kids in their faces all the time. They tried to be quieter in the house, but never quite mastered that virtue.

Great sorrow and loss

All of the routine schedule and restlessness was interrupted on another memorable day, September 26, 1968, when the news came across the two-way radio that two missionaries, along with their four native carriers, had missed radio contact with their wives the day before. The party was on a ten day trek to survey an uncharted region that had never been entered before. It was Phil Masters, Dan's friend, and Stan Dale from the Regions Beyond Missionary Union (RBMU). They wanted to make contact with the people of that area in the hopes that they would be invited into their territory so they could introduce them to the gospel.

When the men didn't make the scheduled evening call, their wives turned on the radio at dawn the next morning, hoping for contact. They waited until early afternoon, when they heard someone from the Lutheran mission station calling to report that two Dani carriers had just arrived there exhausted and barely able to talk. The carriers said their party was attacked, but they ran for their lives. MAF responded immediately and they flew to pick up another RBMU missionary who spoke Dani to go meet the two carriers and find out more details. Sadly, it was too late in the day for any search and rescue because of afternoon cloud build-up and rains.

By then, the whole mission community had heard the tragic news and was listening on the radio. Since we didn't have a radio, midwife Jean Crowe came over from her house beside the hospital to tell us what was happening. "They say the men were in hostile cannibal territory. The way the carriers are telling it, there is little hope the rest of them are still alive. We can only wait until they search tomorrow, and pray, and hope that MAF can find them in the morning."

At dawn the next morning MAF canceled all other radio traffic to clear the channel for the search. Mission station radios listened to the verbatim, eye-witness accounts of what was happening on the ground and in the air over the next few days.

The first search plane flew two missionaries and the two carriers over the deep gorge, called the Seng Valley, where the attack took place. It was so heavily forested and dense that they couldn't see any signs of life. Several other planes searched over the same territory without seeing anything. The pilots decided the best option was to wait for the MAF helicopter to come from Papua New Guinea. It was disappointing when it arrived in the afternoon and the clouds had already covered the mountains. The mission family sorrowed and prayed through another night.

The next morning, as soon as the skies cleared, a plane led the way, circling over the Seng Valley. The helicopter followed at lower altitude, maneuvering its' way down to a river bed, then hovered while the passengers dropped two feet into the cold waters. It took three shuttles to haul two missionaries, one of the carriers, one policeman, and two soldiers to the sight. Meanwhile the MAF plane continued to circle, hoping to scare off any unseen tribesmen on the ground who might try to attack them.

The landing party carried a trail radio to give a live report of what they saw and what they were doing. With the Dani carrier leading, they walked up the riverbed a short distance and discovered two bloody areas among the overhanging branches. Signs of an attack were everywhere. Hundreds of arrows were sticking into the ground and the surrounding bushes. They found pieces of blood stained clothing. The missionaries' trail radio was smashed and broken to pieces, along with a battered camera. A New Testament lay on the ground with an arrow stuck through it. The two missionaries must have died there.

As the news from below was relayed to the listening island, the pilot flying overhead warned the ground party that he was seeing a huge crowd of people in a cluster of huts on the mountainside downstream. He could also make out people lining up on both sides along the ridges above the men in the river bed. They were waving bows, arrows and long spears, and jumping up and down, apparently hollering at the men as they moved along the riverbed.

The helicopter quickly returned and shuttled the search party to a clearing about a mile down from the attack sight, but it was closer to the village where the people were gathering. In that very clearing, the grass was all trampled down and they found Phil Master's glasses, slashed boots, and more bloody clothing, but no remains. They determined this was the actual scene of the probable cannibal feast.

Even though we thought about the possibility of a bad outcome, we still hoped for life, until that final word confirming the deaths of the missionaries and one of their carriers. It was horrifying, especially when we realized how the men were killed.

There was no way Dan and I could shield or hide any of the terrible news from our kids. They were hearing everything at the same time we heard it. We decided to go ahead and explain as simply as we could, and then answer their questions as they came. The kids had already seen patients brought to the hospital with arrow and spear wounds from tribal wars. We also talked with them about the darkness of people's hearts and the kinds of things they do when they don't know about the love of Jesus.

Now the situation was far graver and missionaries were actually killed. The kids were thinking this all over. Jonathan came to us, "If we love the people that are in Agats when we go to them, will they hurt us?"

It was a valid question and we had no guarantee. I talked about trusting God, speaking to myself, as well as to the kids, "You know that Dad and I believe that God goes with us wherever He asks us to go. Whatever we face in our lives, in this place, we know that God is here too. He doesn't promise that hard things won't happen, but we are trusting in our hearts that God will take care of us, like He promised He would do in the Bible."

The children seemed satisfied with what we did tell them.

Me, well I had similar thoughts to Jonathan's, only I didn't verbalize them. Dan and I talked with our kids, but I found it hard to talk with Dan about how I was feeling. There was a great heaviness in my chest. The pain I felt for the wives and children in their losses was unspeakable to me, I couldn't talk about it with someone else yet.

As I thought about it, I realized this was happening in the real world, it wasn't just a story in a mission book. The stark reality was that three men were killed trying to bring the gospel to a tribe. God's call to work in this land was not without great cost. I asked myself again if I could trust God, with surety, to guard and keep me there. And even more importantly, could I trust Him for my children?

I carried on a one-sided conversation with God, "Lord, is this where you want me to be? Why did the kids have to hear such a terrible story of death and cannibalism? They're so young. Is this what it means to take up my cross and follow you? Not just for me, but for my kids too?"

Ah, but then the Spirit reminded me, "Hey, your kids are also God's kids." That thought helped me to let go of the worry and accept that God would keep His promises and be with all of us.

I felt weak and mortal right then, but I finally was able to honestly tell God, "Okay, Lord, I'm still willing to stay and do whatever you ask me to do. Please, God, remember that I can't do it without your help and strength. I have to feel your presence with me, and with us, as a family."

I still wondered in my heart what God might be doing, what were His greater plans for the tribes in Irian. As a family, we'd only been on this island for two months and so much had happened already. What lay ahead for us? I knew in my head that God could handle my tomorrows, but it was taking a while for faith to filter down into my heart.

The next week, it was time for us to go to the South Coast. Another missionary couple from the C&MA mission needed our little cabin while they waited for their baby. It was Paul and Jeannie Burkhardt, and we added them to our list of good friends. Our boys also became lifetime buds with the three Burkhardt boys. How blessed we were to have such genuine friendships within the mission community. We all felt like we were real family, truly the family of God.

Meanwhile, I was dragging my feet about leaving Pit River because I knew we would be going to the jungle with the heat and high humidity. But the Spencers were waiting for Dan and me to come down and study Indonesian with them in Agats. Lorraine, David, and Jonathan were looking for more adventures in another place too. It was time for me to get myself ready, physically, emotionally and spiritually. Once again, we packed suitcases. I ordered cartons of canned food from Sentani, enough to last for several months. They would be flown down later when there was a connection. Take-off time had arrived for the South Coast and its great swampland.

**New arrivals to Irian Barat, Indonesia, September, 1968.
Barbara with baby Marie, Lorraine, Jonathan, David
- Pit River**

Chapter Four:
"Can you see the end of the world from there?"

Wheels to floats, the South Coast

Marie was one day shy of being a month old when we climbed into the MAF wheel plane for our flight down to the South Coast on October 8, 1968. The mountains were rugged and densely covered in trees, but we saw many clearings along the steep slopes and in the ravines that were planted in sweet potato gardens. We climbed higher to get over the ranges.

"Watch the baby for any signs of blue lips. The cabin isn't pressurized and we have to be careful with babies on board," the pilot warned me. But no worries, Marie was a natural at flying, she snuggled in and slept the whole way.

The contrast from mountains to swamp and jungle was staggering. We flew through a pass which they call the South Gap, and suddenly the jungle was there below us. It's a solid carpet of lush, dark green, ribboned with dirty brown rivers. Once in awhile we glimpsed a few huts along a river bank. Tiny jungle clearings appeared here and there. The cool vapors of the mountains drained away and we felt the hot, muggy air of the jungle come seeping into the plane. My spirits plummeted as we glided down to sea level.

The flight over the shaggy-green carpet below us was nearly an hour. The jungle was so dense that I didn't see the 600 foot runway until we were treetop level, nearly at the touchdown end of the muddy airstrip. Thankfully, the pilot knew where he was and he landed the plane without a rumble. Yawsakor was the changing station for the float plane. Agats, our final destination, was on the river.

Senior missionaries with TEAM, Chuck and Bernita Preston, met us at the strip with a warm greeting in more ways than one, "Welcome to the South Coast. Come on down to our house for lunch while they move your things to the float plane." We didn't know it then, but the Prestons became our greatest encouragers in the days ahead.

Don Beiter, the pilot for the float plane, told us to eat a quick lunch because he wanted to be on his way to Agats before the tide went out. The kids gulped their food down and begged, "Can we go down to the river now to see the float plane? Please dad, please."

"Okay, but stand on the dock and don't get in the way."

We hurried with our meal too, but with less urgency. After finishing sandwiches and a drink, Dan carried Marie on his shoulders, and we headed down to the big river.

The path to the dock was alongside the river bank and we saw some Asmat men out in their long canoes. They are a proud and fearsome people, known as cannibal warriors to the outside world. We saw them standing tall, and perfectly balanced, in their long dugout canoes, skimming over the water with the river's current. They rowed, holding carved, long-handled paddles to stroke the water in rhythmic accord. It was a magnificent sight, watching them for the first time, as they silently glided down the river in a procession of ax and adz hewn canoes. As grand a sight as that was, it was sobering to realize that only a handful of them had ever heard anything about God or His son, Jesus. They lived to attack enemy villages, always seeking revenge.

The kids were waiting at the dock, "Are we ready yet? What's taking so long? We wanna take off on the water. Will it be bumpy or smooth? Who gets to sit in the back seat this time?"

Aunt Bernita took baby Marie while I gingerly stepped onto the pontoon, which was sloshing up and down in the black, murky water. We stepped on the wing strut and up into the plane. I was wearing a dress and climbing in and out of an airplane in a modest fashion was not easy. At that time women didn't wear long pants because it was culturally unacceptable to the Indonesian and Christian communities. The pilot indicated our seats, and waited while we belted in. After I got myself seated, Bernita handed Marie to me without mishap. Papa Lima's propeller started to rotate and we backed away from the dock, turned, and skimmed over the water in a smooth lift off, airborne again. We flew low over the treetops and had a clear vision of the jungle below. Looking down on sparkling waters of the river, I realized the float plane could land almost anywhere on the water. What was there to worry about?

The kids were more thrilled about flying in the float plane than I was. My imagination ran away with me, worrying that someone would drop Baby Marie into the muddy river when we were out on the dock getting on or off the plane. Of course, that never happened.

Agats was less than an hour away in flight time. We touched down on a broad river, which flowed into the sea around the bend from our landing place. The tide was already going out and an open strip of shallow water and mud were beginning to surround the dock.

The boys were looking out the windows, "Hey, look at those guys just lying there all stretched out. They're covered with mud. Yuk! Now they're all jumping back in the water."

"Well, at least they get washed off that way," Lorraine concluded.

The mother in me is thinking, "But Lord, the river is filthy, and what about the crocodiles and snakes swimming in it?"

Looking around, the world was in muted shades of gray, black and brown along the river. Then I noticed bright splotches of a reddish color scurrying along sideways on the black river bank. "Thank you, God, only you could put that splash of color in the mud." It was little, red crabs coming out of mud burrows for a fresh breath of air during the low tide.

"Hey, look at the big pinchers on them," David pointed. "Those kids in the mud don't look like they're afraid of them."

When the plane was as close to the dock as possible, Dan climbed down onto the pontoon, then turned to give the rest of us a hand. More helping hands reached down from the dock and managed to lift us, one by one, from the swaying pontoon. Aunt Carol and Uncle Don stood there grinning at us. Carol eagerly reached out and took Marie from my arms. We huddled together under her umbrella, trying to keep the baby out of the blazing sun.

Bill and Verena Hekman, the senior missionaries, stepped forward to shake hands. "*Velkomen.* So, you are here now in Agats," Bill greeted us in his Dutch accent. He was to be our Indonesian language teacher for the next five months.

Agats Town

Meanwhile, the pilot was juggling our luggage, handing it up to the dock. When we were all together: passengers, luggage and food cartons, the carriers picked up everything and marched on ahead with our kids in the lead. I grabbed Dan's hand in order to keep my balance on the uneven planks, even though it was culturally taboo to cling to him in public. The kids were waiting at our tin house with the baggage when we got there.

The boardwalk was made of pit-sawn logs nailed down to timber piles, which were in turn sunk deep into the mud. During high tide the water came up under the boards. It was about three city blocks up to our houses from the river. There were no railings on either side of the walkway and below, parallel, were drainage ditches for tide water and raw sewage from town. We were careful to stay in the middle of the boards.

In reality it was the only safe place to walk. Agats was at sea level and recorded 172 inches of rain a year. The ground remained soggy and squishy all the time. "Don't try to walk on the ground or you will end up sinking all the way to China," became our constant warning for the kids. Naturally, they had no trouble balancing, walking, or running on the timbers.

Are we there yet? Oh, yes, we had arrived at *the-end-of-the-world, or Mudville,* as missionary friends described Agats. My first reaction was to wonder how in the world anyone could live there. Standing on the dock, the heat was already oppressive. I was sweaty and sticky just walking up to our house. The landscape was water, water everywhere, and the colors were gray, dark and black, depressing.

"If a person can't walk on the ground, where will the kids play when they're outside?" I was questioning God again, in my heart, "How is this ever going to work for my family? For me?" God surely was patient with me and my questions in those days.

Agats was a government post with Asmat villages located out on the rivers close by. The town itself was populated by the military, government personnel, and the two missions with their teachers. The military group was conspicuously visible as they walked around town in their uniforms, rifles slung over their shoulders. TEAM mission had a middle school and dormitory for the Asmat and other tribal boys. The Catholic Mission had the same type of school, plus a small hospital. There were a couple of Chinese owned trade stores with a minimum amount of stock, mostly basic supplies, like: rice, salt, sugar, cooking oil and fuel for lamps and boat motors. The back of those stores was where they lived.Townspeople dressed in western clothes and spoke Indonesian. They didn't mingle with the tribes people because they considered them primitive heathens.

Asmat people came to town every day to trade fish, wild meat, fruits and greens for staples like salt and cooking oil, or paper money. Their Indonesian was rudimentary, enough to bargain and trade. Coming to town, the men proudly walked along the boardwalks wearing ragged tee shirts, or simply their own skins, with maybe a shell covering over their private parts. Their women were scantily clothed in dirty sarongs, or tee shirts and skimpy cloth skirts. Some of their apparel needed a bit of imagination to figure out what it was, other than a rag covering up a body part. Once in awhile a woman appeared bare breasted, wearing a traditional grass mini-skirt, the original hipster, about mid thigh in length. Whatever they wore, or didn't wear, the men and women walked straight and tall in comparison to other shorter, stockier tribes, like the Danis.

Our House

Like Sentani, the house in Agats was made of corrugated aluminum with screens on the big square windows and hinged aluminum shutters to close down, if needed. All the buildings in Agats were mounted on wooden piles. Hopefully our house was elevated enough above the water so that the high tides might not lap through the cracks in the floor boards. There was a small porch all across the front which joined the boardwalk. An aluminum door opened directly into the middle room, which was the living-guest room. The kitchen was at one end and two bedrooms on the other end. Sanded, wooden planks covered the floor, but cracks between them opened to the ground below.

The kitchen had three of those wonderful, tongue-in-cheek, pump-up kerosene burners to cook on. There were a couple of small metal ovens that fit over the burners for baking. By then I knew how to light them. They worked okay, but it was hard to determine the temperature or adjust the heat, and the burning kerosene wick often smoked up the food. The little, square stainless steel sink had running water from a tank of rain water collected off the roof. There was also a small kerosene-run refrigerator.

A huge room, made of ironwood, was added onto the back of the house. It had glass louver windows with screens, and was termite proof. That room was truly life saving because it remained cooler during the day and it had fewer mosquitoes at night. The aluminum part of our house absorbed the heat and mosquitoes flew in through the many cracks in the walls. There was a small bathroom with a toilet and a shower stall built in a back corner, with running water from the rain tank behind the house. A pantry closet was in the opposite corner, with shelves all around to store case lots of food. This room was connected by a wooden breezeway to the main house. I used the space between the two buildings for doing the laundry, and the kids often bathed in the big wash tubs stored there.

In the bedrooms mosquito nets again shrouded the beds. Our bed had a full net covering, which was strung from a wire frame surrounding the bed and dropped down to the floor. I put Marie's crib on my side of the bed. It had screening around on all sides and a screened lid on top. I added a mosquito net over the whole thing, just to be sure. The nets were frustrating to open and close when tending to the baby. If Marie was restless at night, most of the time I gave up and put her in bed with me. I didn't sleep well with the extra body in bed because it was so stuffy inside when the nets were closed. Aside from all my complaints, I knew that we were shielded from the mosquitoes at night and that made all the hassle worth it.

Other problems were magnified in the dark. Our first night in Agats I noticed the sheets felt damp. I thought maybe they hadn't fully dried. I soon found out that none of the linen, bath towels, or clothing ever dried completely, even when they were hung out in the sun. The damp bed sheets at night were one of the hardest things for me to deal with, especially since I already felt sweaty and sticky all day long. It was depressing and I never overcame that feeling; I just tried to get used to it.

Fortunately, my family boosted my moral when I was down. The kids were excited to get up every day, and according to them, there was always something awesome to do or experience outdoors. "But Mom, why can't we hunt crabs and frogs in the ditches? All we need are a couple of cans with lids on. The school kids will help us and watch out for us."

They were right because the ditches were alive with a variety of frogs and the red crabs from the river bank. I suspected they might be filled with all manner of other living creatures too. Who knew what sort of water was mixed in there with the tide waters. Of course, somebody had to fall into a ditch at least once and it was David, wearing his Sunday clothes, no less. He was not only embarrassed, but he hated getting all muddy. They were the only good clothes he owned.

The Asmat village boys were curious when they saw our kids, and always came running if they saw them outside playing. Unlike the highland kids, they didn't crowd around, but allowed our kids their space. Language was no barrier. All of the children made friends, without saying much to each other at first. But it wasn't long before the boys started to speak Indonesian. Most of the time they played outside on the boardwalk, or they sloshed around with sticks in the canals. The native boys loved it when David and Jonathan brought their little Matchbox cars out on the porch walkway in front of our house. They had never seen toy cars, or real ones, for that matter.

Lorraine bluntly and truthfully described their new friends to me, "The kids here are a lot dirtier than the Danis from Pit River, aren't they? They stink too. Maybe they don't bathe. Are those raggedy shorts their only pair?" Those were the simple facts, but none of it deterred the kids from playing together.

One morning an Asmat boy proudly presented David and Jonathan with a stuffed baby crocodile. I'm sure it was the only treasure that little boy had. Lorraine steered away from the gift. "I don't like that thing. I don't even want to touch it." Her reaction surprised me, until I found out the boys had already tried to scare her with it before they showed it to me.

The school boys were also eager to play, and they came straight from class still wearing uniforms of white shirts and dark shorts. Unlike the village playmates, their skin was shiny and clean, no mud. Lorraine, David and Jonathan learned most of their Indonesian vocabulary from them. David fearlessly plunged ahead, talking as if both parties had perfect understanding of each other, even when he used his own made-up words and hand motions. How I envied my kids in their language abilities.

Again, Lorraine was disappointed with Agats, "I thought there would be girls to play with here. The Hekman girls are so far back in the jungle that I can't go to their house by myself. Besides, they have each other. The boys always have other boys outside. Girls don't go to school and I don't see any village girls coming to town, either."

True, the students were all boys. Like the Dani girls, all the girls in Agats stayed at home and worked, or watched younger siblings.

Even though she was lonely for a girl friend, Lorraine was a good sport and hung with her brothers outside. Inside, she was my idea girl, always planning and making things for special occasions and for non-occasions too. Supplies were limited to what we brought in our suitcases, but that didn't matter to her. She enlisted my help and at times cajoled her brothers to join us.

For Halloween, she designed costumes from old clothes, a ghost, and two witches. The boys and I cut out black colored cats, smiley face pumpkins, and witch hats to hang around the house. We baked cutout cookies shaped like pumpkins and then sat eating them while singing and telling stories, trying to scare each other.

At Thanksgiving, Lorraine wrote a play, which they performed twice; once for Dan and me, the second time for Spencers and Hekmans. David and Lorraine were the pilgrims, Jonathan was the Indian. The Nativity play at Christmas included the Hekman girls. We made paper chains to hang around the house and baked cut-out cookies then too.

I learned a lot about attitude from Lorraine. She was always my cheerful one and could put a positive light on most anything. She accepted conditions as they were, and never failed to encourage me in the process. Whenever her little sister needed something, she was there, dependable and helpful, and distracting her when she was fussy. Marie loved it when Lorraine was watching her. The boys entertained Marie too, except they weren't as steady with the babysitting. Marie didn't care, she dearly loved all three of her siblings, however much time they spent with her.

Life outside in the sunshine remained the most alluring activity for the older kids. They soon had rich brown tans and their hair bleached out. Jonathan's turned nearly white, which fascinated the tribal kids. One especially hot, sticky day they came begging, "Please Daddy, please, can you take us down to the river so we can swim and cool off. It's safe. The Asmat kids swim there all the time."

Of course, I'm the one who didn't like their idea, and I wondered aloud that Dan was even thinking about taking them to the river. I sighted the facts, "The river and sea are teeming with crocodiles, snakes, octopus-eez, sharks, and who knows what all. Kids have actually disappeared swimming in that river! How can you even think about swimming down there?"

"But Mom, it's so hot," they countered. "Besides, Dad will be right there with us. We'll ask the people if they've seen any crocodiles down there lately. It'll be okay. Honest. Please, can we?"

Naturally, their desperate pleas won out. Dan took them down to the dock where we had disembarked from the float plane. They jumped into the river and swam with the other kids. The joyful word came back to me, "Hey, Mom that was really cool. It was okay. We didn't see any crocodiles either."

I don't know, or remember, or maybe I blocked it out, whether Dan ever took them down to the sea again. He probably did.

The mud and water around us never bothered any of my family, except me. The day came when I had to give up my nagging about it. I finally accepted that every time the kids ventured outside, staying dry and clean was not even a remote possibility. So I set up two huge galvanized washtubs filled with water on the breezeway. Then I ordered the kids, "Okay, this is what you do. When you come inside, take off your clothes. Dump them in the tub of soapy water outback. Then you can jump into the other tub of water and take a bath. Put on clean clothes when you're done."

The kids added one variation to that and often used the clean water tub as a wading pool when it was especially hot, even if they hadn't been outside.

The tropics required awareness and adjustments in other ways too. Being at sea level and on the equator, it was hot, humid and rainy most of the time. The smallest scratch or insect bite could develop into an infection overnight. Once sores got infected they took longer to heal, often requiring antibiotic ointment, or even a penicillin shot. The flies were eager to land and spread more germs if the wounds weren't covered with gauze or a band aid.

The kids were always getting scratched, cut, or bruised at play. My standard words of warning were, "Wash that scrape off, don't scratch that bite, it could get infected."

There were various other tropical bugs and sicknesses traveling around, and it seemed like someone in our family caught everything going. The people who knocked at our door habitually had runny noses and coughs to share with us. Fortunately, when the flu hit we all weren't sick at once, but a couple of us got it twice. It was a bad flu with nausea and vomiting, and of course, diarrhea. The danger was always dehydration.

When Marie was only a couple months old, she got the flu and fussed the whole time. She ran a fever and was thirsty, and wanted to nurse all the time. At least it seemed like that to me because I was the one nursing her. I had to be sure to drink extra water for myself because I knew breast milk was still the safest for her.

During the hottest part of the day, which was noon to about 4 PM, we all took an afternoon rest. It was impossible to maintain a regular pace in that climate without resting and drinking plenty of fluids. A short nap gave us more energy for the remainder of the day. I should say that I'm the one who ended up napping, along with Marie, and sometimes Dan.

Our first week there, I woke to Lorraine whispering in my ear, "Mom, can we get up now? We don't have to sleep do we? I can read to the boys."

"Okay. But be quiet for a while, and then you can get up."

Another problem with the climate surfaced after a couple of weeks. Our luggage and leather sandals changed from brown to a powdering of yellow-green mold. The backroom storage area began to smell moldy and musty. Rust spots peeped through on my cooking utensils. Flashlight batteries swelled and some even exploded inside the carton. A few rusted inside the flashlights. I shared the problem with the Hekmans and they offered to sell us a couple of their metal, fifty-five gallon drums that they used to ship supplies from the US.

"Make sure everything is dry and clean when you put it in the drum. Then clamp the lids down with the metal rim and you should be okay."

Because of all the rain, there were puddles everywhere, in any little depression. The dampness produced hoards of mosquitoes. Jonathan was the winner for the most bites. Bugs of any kind could find him and have themselves a meal at his expense. With the mosquitoes though, I was also conscientious about taking our malaria meds every Sunday. By that time Lorraine, David and Jonathan gulped their pills down without any fuss.

Swallowing medicine, of any kind, was another story with Marie. She was still nursing and it was a jolt to drink that nasty, bitter, awful medicine, even though I doctored it up with cool-aide. Every week it was the same fight getting her to down it. I threatened, cajoled, tasted it myself to show her, and when all else failed, held her nose so she was forced to gulp it down. She never did take the liquid baby stuff without protest. When she graduated to toddler size, she finally took crushed pills in jelly. We all clapped and hollered the day she managed to swallow the regular pills down.

Besides our mosquito nets and malaria pills, another precaution we used was to spray in our bedrooms. I sprayed the nets, as well. We also discovered mosquito coils, which we lit and put under our beds. We put them in a large lid, or on a metal plate, to catch the ashes as they smoldered without flames. One coil lasted most of the night, giving out a malodorous scent which wafted up and out from under the beds. We hated the smell, but had to be serious about prevention.

(In later years, there was a period of time that I repeatedly had light attacks of malaria, despite taking meds for prophylaxis. The break-through came every three weeks, and I felt worn out all the time, plus I had nagging, continuous headaches. I kept going, but it was hard to concentrate with a low grade fever and sore, tired eyes. After several trials, our mission doctor helped me find a preventive regime, a daily pill, which helped to keep it under control. The rest of the family was blessed. Dan only had malaria a couple of times, along with the boys and Marie. Lorraine doesn't remember ever getting malaria in all her years in the tropics.)

Other than the mosquito population, there was one big benefit of so much rain, it kept our drinking water tanks full. We collected rain water off the roof into huge aluminum tanks. The water then came into the house by gravity feed through plastic piping. Dr. Ken told us we didn't need to boil the water because the aluminum roof was heated from the sun and the water was clean. If it didn't rain for a number of days, we were in trouble. I used a lot of water to wash clothes and for the daily baths, and soakings for the kids. We ended up with low water a couple of times. Spencers didn't have kids at that time and so we carried buckets of water from their house to ours. The night rains beat down on the tin roof of our house and at first we thought it was horribly noisy. After a while, we grew to love the sound of rain on our roof, especially when we were cozy and comfy inside. Of course, rain on the tin roof at church when the preacher was preaching was a different story.

Household Remedies

I was gradually learning little tricks to make our lives easier in the tropics. The more seasoned missionaries were great to share their vast knowledge of survival. Aunt Verena Hekman had a number of suggestions, as well as Aunt Bernita Preston. We already had the tubs of water on the breezeway. Besides throwing muddy clothes in the tubs, all of our dirty clothes went in them to soak at the end of the day. The water prevented armies of ants from getting into the clothes and eating little holes here and there wherever any food or drink had spilled. The ants were well organized and aggressive, but didn't like to swim. We changed the water every third day or else it got sour and smelled. I usually had our clothes washed every three days anyway.

Aunt Verena's number one remedy was Vaseline. "It's very good for baby's bottom and sores, but you can slather it on the legs of your kitchen table too. The ants won't crawl through it to get up on your table and into your sugar bowl."

That was good news to me because I had already discovered that any bit of food left out on the table or dropped on the floor would be blackened with ants in minutes. Vaseline also worked well on the legs of Marie's crib, as a barrier to keep the ants from crawling into bed with her. Putting the legs of the table inside tins of water on the floor also kept the ants out, but I liked the Vaseline method best. Boric acid and sugar was a good mixture to kill ants. Roach tablets thrown into the back of cupboards helped keep them out. At least I didn't see so many of them. Spray cans with insecticide were expensive and hard to find, but I bought several cans whenever we saw them in a store. I tried to keep things clean in order to prevent any infestation of bugs, but it was a constant battle. Spiders and flying ants were also visitors, especially at night. How I hated all those critters!

Actually, I hated the rats running around overhead at night even more than the bugs. I heard them in my cupboards and saw their droppings on my shelves. The kids and Dan slept blissfully through it all. Sometimes I elbowed Dan to wake him up, just to prove that the rats were there and I wasn't imagining things. We tried again with a borrowed cat; Spencer's. She actually captured a rat right away, but then ran around playing with it for half the night. We set traps, but somehow the rats avoided them, as they descended from the rafters and roamed around freely in the dark of night.

Another perceived insult, to me, was the day one of those little geckos fell from the rafters when I was sitting at the table. Splatt! It fell onto my neck. It felt cold and clammy. *I* felt cold and clammy. Both of us were stunned. Then the little guy made a flying leap off me, and in the process, he lost part of his tail. Geckos were supposed to be our friends because they go after mosquitoes and other flying biting bugs. Right then I wasn't sure that gecko was my friend.

Food orders and otherwise

After a lot of guessing, I managed to send my first order of basic food and household supplies to MAF. The tins came twenty-four to forty-eight per carton. We were surprised to see Blue Band margarine and Kraft cheese in tins that could be stored on the shelf until they were opened. Kraft canned cheese was a favorite with my kids, so much so that their one request when going to college was for me to send them canned cheese. The flour, sugar, and powdered milk came in forty pound bags. We also ordered trays of eggs, thirty count to a tray. We kept them out on a shelf and turned each one over every couple of days so the yoke wouldn't stick to the shell.

We also ordered small packages of frozen meats from the MAF freezer in the central highlands. They were supplied from a freezer in Sentani on the airplane base. The meat originated in Australia, via Papua New Guinea, and was expensive, with not much choice. Of course, everyone wanted hamburger. We rarely got it because Agats was at the end of the food chain and other stations got theirs before us. If hamburger was gone, we gave MAF permission to send whatever they had in the freezer.

One time when we got two little steaks in place of the anticipated hamburger, Lorraine sighed in acceptance and uttered her philosophy about the situation, "That's the way it is on the mission field. You sometimes get what you don't order, and you never get what you want."

There wasn't much choice for soaps and household supplies. Before we could buy powdered laundry soap, there were bars of laundry soap, called Sunlight soap. I did the same thing I remembered my grandma doing when I was a little girl. I got out the vegetable grater and hand-grated the soap into flakes to go in the wash tub. I also bought a three inch by three inch screened shaker to put a piece of soap in and swish around for suds in the dishpan. It took years for liquid dish soap to appear on the market. Lux was the only bath soap available. There was one brand of cleanser, Vim. Colgate was our toothpaste brand. We bought cartons of wooden stick matches with the inscription "Made as Sweden" written on each little box, which, of course, meant they were not from Sweden at all. Flashlight batteries came by the carton, and were of such poor quality that they died by the carton, just as quickly as we got them. Then there were the huge boxes of toilet tissue, of which we had no choice either. It came as it came.

MAF continued their twice a month highland vegetable runs to the South Coast stations. We were careful and tried to make the fresh vegetables last for the two weeks. I put the perishable veggies in the refrigerator. Fresh fruit was almost nonexistent. Occasionally, other south coast stations sent us bananas, a papaya, or a couple of pineapples. The town of Agats was being taken over by the sea and nothing grew in the salt water, except coconut palms. The kids loved to eat the fresh coconut, even drank its cleansing juices with gusto. Their school friends climbed the palms and whacked them down with machetes. They husked the outside, split the hard inside, and chipped out the coconut chunks and the kids were ready to eat. Sometimes they chopped a hole in top first and drank the coconut water before opening up the shell.

I tried to be creative in my cooking. We had a nutritious diet and enough to eat, but there wasn't much variety. It seemed to take me forever to cook because everything was made from scratch. It was hard to see my family gobble it down, after I spent so much time getting it ready.

Besides the canned goods order and vegetables flown in, the Asmat people brought us fresh vegetables and meats from the jungle. Sometimes it was a rare and exotic offering. Other times it was fresh fish, greens, or long jungle beans. I was willing to try the more questionable food, but wasn't always sure of how to cook it. The day cassowary bird came to the door, I was really bummed because I had never seen a cassowary before, let alone cooked one.

"What am I supposed to do with it? I don't know how to cook it. What if nobody will eat it?"

I was grumbling away when Lorraine sweetly asked me, "But it was nice of that man to share it with us, wasn't it?"

Well, that put me in my place and I decided to buy it and try it. After all, it was poultry, wasn't it? Cassowary is a bird next in size to the ostrich. I heard later that missionaries had a special recipe for cooking it, "Put the cassowary and a rock in a pressure cooker, and when the rock is done, so is the cassowary." I had sense enough to put it in the pressure cooker to tenderize it, minus the rock, of course. The meat was a little tough and dry, but it tasted okay, kind of like the dark meat of chicken. Following my standard rule, we ate it anyway.

On another morning, someone brought a crocodile tail and flopped it down on the porch. That was one thing I was NOT prepared to cook, despite Lorraine's thankfulness for fresh meat. I passed on the offer of fresh croc pot-roast. I am thankful that my kids didn't insist that we buy it. They were good sports about trying foods, even if they decided they didn't like it. And they were more than willing to sample delicacies that the schoolboys offered, such as: fresh grubs, fried grubs, beetles, bugs, unknown birds and small wild animals, and other un-reported goodies.

David on the boardwalk at Agats

Jonathan, David and friends in dugout canoe - Agats

Chapter Five: "What is the mission field?"

Pirimid, TEAM Annual Conference

In the middle of adjusting to this new life, we received a ten day reprieve from the heat and flew off to the mountains again to attend our mission's Annual Conference. It was held in one end of the Baliem Valley at Pirimid, on a Christian and Missionary Alliance station. They had built a couple rows of cabins, and a large combined dining room and conference building on the property near the airstrip. The missions used these grounds for conferences and seminars because it was central in location and also cool there.

"Mom, why are the suitcases out in the sun? Are we going somewhere again? I thought we were staying in Agats for a long time."

"We're going to the annual mission conference. Be glad about it. You MK kids don't always get to go, but this year you do. They will have teachers from other missions for Daily Vacation Bible School, and they will do other special things with you too. It'll be like a vacation, AND it's in the mountains." The kids were excited about another trip, but they didn't care about cooler weather. Dan and I were the ones who were excited about a respite from the heat and humidity.

It wasn't a simple thing to leave the station. I made lists of duties for closing up because I couldn't remember it all. Besides packing clothes for a cooler climate, we also had to close up our house. That meant emptying and turning off the refrigerator, washing all dirty clothes, and shutting all the huge window shutters before we flew away. Any food left out or in the fridge would spoil. Clothes left in dirty water would sour and stagnate. Closing up was important and we followed the procedure every time we left our home for more than a couple of days. Coming back, we reversed the process, and brought all our fresh food, eggs and meat with us because there wouldn't be any at home. Just living in Papua required much forethought.

Still, we were glad to go to Conference because Dan and I finally met the rest of our TEAM coworkers. Our mission areas were in what are called the Bird's Head and the South Coast areas, with other mission groups serving between in the central highlands and coastal lowlands. Conference was a time of refreshing and fellowship, spiritual renewal, and business meetings. Cooks and children's workers came from the mission community. We, in turn, helped the other missions out when they had their annual meetings. It was a great arrangement.

That first year at Conference was so welcome. I could freely speak English again. I didn't have to concentrate and listen to every single word to make sure I was getting it. There was one session with government people speaking in Indonesian, which I didn't understand. But Dan told me I didn't miss much on that one. The officials always rambled on, saying nothing, even if it took them a long time to say it.

It was also a relief having a babysitter for Marie during meetings. The local Dani women volunteered to help out and they earned a little money that way, too. Marie was a few months old then and she loved the teenage girl who carried her around outside all day long. It was wonderful; she wasn't clinging to me all day long.

Another joy for me was that I didn't have to worry about cooking from scratch for the next meal; I could go to the dining room with everyone else. We had guest cooks from other missions helping out.

The speaker for that year was Dr. Delber Kuehl who was a Director of TEAM. Dan and I already counted him as a friend because he and his wife Delores went to our home church in Minneapolis. Delbert was the one who encouraged us to apply to TEAM. He had morning devotions and Bible teaching every night. I was looking forward to the time after Conference when Dr. Kuehl was coming around to visit all of the TEAM stations, including Agats.

Lorraine was excited; she finally met up with other girls her age. David and Jonathan also made instant friends with the other boys who were there. It was the beginning of lasting friendships with other MKs who became like sisters and brothers to my children. Every morning the kids had Vacation Bible School. They also planned some of the fun night skits. In the afternoons, they played or went on adventures with their VBS teachers. One year they hiked down valley. Dani guides took them into a huge cavern, which they called the Bat Cave. They also trekked and crossed over the Baliem River gorge on the hanging vine bridges.

There was always one afternoon set aside for a very merry *un-birthday* party, complete with presents, cake and homemade ice cream. The missionary in charge of the party asked for presents from supporting churches, which were sent to the field during the year. The party was a conference tradition which all of the kids and parents enjoyed. Being alone on interior stations, the BD celebrations were with family and some of the little kids had never been to a real party before.

Since we were new to the field, Dan and I had a separate orientation meeting with our Field Chairman, Hank Bock. He sent us information when we arrived in Sentani, but it was nice to meet him in person and ask our own questions. The Bocks were serving in Anggi with the Sougb people, formerly called the Manikion tribe. It was the station in the Bird's Head where we were originally assigned. The area was restricted for new missionaries, even though the Bocks were allowed to stay. When the field reassigned us to the south coast, our visa was granted. Hank told us that the field would like to place us in Nohon with the Spencers, when we finished Indonesian language study. Uncle Don and Aunt Carol were to do village evangelism and supervise the Nohon Bible School, taught in Indonesian. Dan was assigned to linguistics and translation for the Auyu language, which was the tribe at Nohon. My job was mom and medical work. Since we didn't know anything about the needs of the south coast, we trusted the field to make the right decision concerning our placement. The conference voted to assign us to Nohon.

Somewhere in the middle of Conference an intestinal flu made the rounds. Those who were afflicted were sick for a day or two. In our family, Marie was sick first, then me. The "conference bug" became a habit of mine. I can't think of one conference when I wasn't sick for a couple of days. I usually ended up missing meetings those days. I didn't have the resistance when we lived together in a mixed group like that. Dan and the big kids managed to avoid contact with the bugs that were bothering other people.

We also heard about more fighting and unrest in the area of the Seng Valley. This was where the two missionaries and their carrier had been killed the previous September. Jim Sunda, who was on station at Pirimid, relayed the news that the Seng Valley people were making threats to a Dani missionary couple in a nearby area, and they were on the march with spears, bows and arrows. Two RBMU missionaries flew via helicopter to see if they could negotiate a peace. Several military men and a policeman from the interior government post at Wamena went in with them. The Seng Valley people eventually agreed to a peace settlement. They allowed the native evangelist and Bible teachers from the Dani tribe to enter their territory.

At the same time this was happening, it was reported that the leader of the Rebel Movement in the Bird's Head was ready to surrender. The stations involved in the rebellion were Minyambou, Testega, and Anggi. The main leader sent word that he would turn himself in during the week of our Conference. His surrender eventually ended the guerilla warfare and brought peace to the area.

Agats, return to language studies

After Conference, we flew back to Agats-on-the-Water. Oh, my! Knowing what it was like to live there only made it harder to go back. As the plane lowered in altitude, the air became heavier, and my spirits sank deeper. I dreaded it. I felt trapped. I didn't want to go back. *"It's too hot, too humid,"* I argued with myself. But in the end, I knew in my heart that God's appointment was for me to be there. This was where our family was to live for now. I could do it with God's help, Dan's help, and my kids' cheerful attitude.

There we were again, back on the muddy river bank and up onto the dock. The kids eagerly ran ahead, leaving me to plod my way up the long boardwalk. The house was musty, the fridge wouldn't start right away, and our sheets were damp, again. Was anybody else depressed or sad about this?

Not on your life, Lorraine, David and Jonathan were actually excited, pleading with Dan, "Oh, Dad, do we have to unpack now? Can't we go outside and play first? We promise we'll put our stuff away later." Their excitement about returning to Agats was a teaching moment for me. The kids made no mention about it being hot in Agats, amazing. We were back to study and the daily routine.

Daily Schedule

How did our days go? For one thing, they started early. We had to be up by 5:30AM. That was when the two schoolboys came to do our laundry before they went to school. They hung the clothes out on a rope tied between two large poles behind our house, and I took everything down in the afternoon. I didn't like that job because the backyard looked lush and green, but it was wet and squishy underneath. It was hazardous to walk out there, without sinking down into the mud below the surface. The schoolboys seemed to know how to do it without disappearing into the *quick-mud*. They also washed dishes and swept the floors in the two hours they worked before going to school in the mornings.

I was always thankful for anyone who could help me, part time, or full time. I knew I could not keep up with housework and daily living, and survive, without house help. We never considered our workers as our servants, but they were our helpers in the ministry. The two hours from the schoolboys each morning wasn't enough time and we eventually asked for a Dani couple from the highlands to come and work full time for us. The Danis were recommended by other missionaries as enthusiastic, reliable, and trustworthy workers in their homes. When Seruwi and Pu'me came, they took over the house work, which relieved me to care for Marie, home-school Lorraine, cook and do a little medical work. Their little boy, Lazarus, soon became a kid-brother to my kids and we treated the parents like family. After all, they left everything that was familiar to them in the highlands to come and help us.

At 6:45 AM every day we made two-way radio contact with the MAF base and other TEAM mission stations. As required by law, we spoke in Indonesian for all radio contacts. I didn't like it because my Indonesian vocabulary was limited, which made it harder to report weather conditions for the airplane. The government later backed off of the order and allowed us to use English again, for safety's sake. The main reason for the two-way radios was for missionary air traffic. We were allowed to relay important messages, to order supplies, and call a doctor at any time for emergency medical help, but the radio was never used as a telephone for chatting. The main channel was for weather and following the plane and a secondary channel was for other plane related business. The channels for mission and medical contacts were different and used only at assigned times during the day. The government collected annual license fees on all radios.

Whether in English or Indonesian, we used the international alphabet word list to spell out words for radio traffic and for call letters of the airplanes -such as Alpha for A, Bravo for B, and Charlie for C, etc. The missionary kids knew all the MAF airplanes by their alphabet names, like; PL was Papa Lima, and CA was Charlie Alpha. (When on furlough in the US, my kids often used the letter-words as code words over the telephone.)

I liked to leave the two-way radio on during the day and listen to the other stations give their requests and news. It wasn't about hearing all the gossip, but I felt more connected when I heard other voices out there. The radio traffic also made for a long prayer list when we heard about the needs of others in the mission community. I already mentioned that any urgent news always ended up on the radio. We heard it, regardless of how private a matter it might be. Our daily schedules revolved around the radio contact times.

We asked the Asmat people to bring their produce to our front porch before radio schedule began. It took us a good hour to buy everything because Conference gave us the extra assignment of purchasing food for the fifty or so boys in the dorm at the mission school. They brought produce like sago, fish, clams, crabs, greens and occasionally, jungle fruit. The time consuming part for both of us was paying for it. The sellers expected us to know an approximate price to pay for a coconut, or whatever, and to bargain from there. Fish and meat we weighed on hand-held scales, but still needed to know the bargaining price. Dan and I never did get the hang of it, but we tried. We paid for the food with nylon fishing line, fish hooks, paper money, or maybe a pair of drawstring shorts, if it was a large amount. The school boys came to our house every morning, collected the food, and took it to the dorm to cook over their own fires.

The plan was to start home-schooling for Lorraine by 8:30 AM. With daily interruptions, we had to be flexible. I wanted to get lessons done by noon, before it got too hot. Lorraine was doing first semester of the second grade curriculum. I also began Kindergarten lessons for the boys. To my surprise, Jonathan was the one who was all gung-ho about school; well, at first. David soon overtook his younger brother, of ten minutes, in his zeal to learn. Or maybe it was David's sibling rivalry kicking in to outdo him. Once he caught up, David remained excited about learning and school.

Dan also studied Indonesian three times a week with Uncle Don and Aunt Carol. Bill Hekman was fluent in Indonesian and taught the classes, but I couldn't go. I managed to study written lessons one hour a day by myself. Later on, we got an Indonesian lady teacher to come twice a week for conversation with me. I finished six of the language units and took two of the unit tests while we were in Agats. Any test I managed to take was a sign of progress and encouragement to me.

Language study was an on-going struggle, starting with Indonesian and then studying a tribal language. The kids were the ones who learned the languages by osmosis, or so it seemed. Lorraine, David and Jonathan spoke Indonesian fluently just by talking with their Indonesian speaking friends. Marie eventually learned to speak the tribal language, just like a native, as per the testimony of the people. The kids learned by listening and imitating, no textbooks needed. My children often explained to me what was being said, or what was going on during the day. I often heard, "Mom, he is asking you... Mom, she wants to sell you... Mom, they need..."

Plane day was another time when home-schooling for Lorraine was on hold until the plane had come and gone. The schedule was usually once every two weeks and was a major event in our lives. When the noise of the engine was overhead, nearly all of Agats trooped down to the dock to watch it unload. All of our goods were carried from the airplane, through the crowd, and on up to the house. On-lookers had no trouble figuring out what we received. The fresh vegetables that came from the highlands were an especially coveted item for the Indonesian teachers, since they had no way of getting anything fresh. I usually put in a larger produce order in anticipation of the requests to buy them from us. The mail sac was more important to me than any of our supply orders. Woe to the pilot who forgot the mail bag. Lorraine waited for lessons awhile longer until I sorted, and had a quick look at the letters from home.

Speaking of people at the door, besides the Asmat traders, Indonesian soldiers, teachers and government officials often called in the late afternoons. Dan welcomed them because it gave him a chance to practice his language skills. The cultural way was to talk a little first, then get to the point of the visit. They usually wanted something more than simply conversation. Since the guests thought Dan wasn't actually doing anything all day long, they chatted longer than usual, before revealing their requests. I offered room temperature sweet tea and cookies because that was the polite thing to do. With the formalities and courtesies over, it was another story dealing with the requests.

The Indonesian visitors asked us for things that weren't available to them. This was most everything because they didn't have access to stores, nor did they have a two-way radio, like we did. If Dan told them he couldn't get the article they wanted in the capitol of Sukarnapura, they asked him to order it from America. Favorite items were radios and watches, but some were legitimate needs, like clothing, or medicine. It took wisdom and diplomacy to deal with the requests in such a way that it would not offend our visitors. We wanted them to understand we weren't there for private enterprise, but felt we still needed to be sympathetic to their needs. Agats only had a couple of trade stores selling basic food and fuel supplies. It was a fine line to know when to help them out and sell them our personal goods, or to say sorry, we can't do that.

Daily chores, home-schooling, studying, and taking care of Marie took up my time. Everything that was so simple in the US took much longer to do in the tropics. There was no fast food or fresh frozen to pop into the oven. We rarely had leftovers because my kids were good eaters. Other than breakfast, which was granola or cooked oatmeal, toast, and maybe bananas, I planned a menu for two meals every day. Thankfully, we had rice from those front room stores. I decided what to cook according to the fresh vegetables that I had on hand. Meat was limited to a small piece for each person, or better yet, I ground it up and stretched it with gravy on rice. Eggs, cheese and bread filled us up for the evening meal. I baked homemade bread in those tiny tin ovens on top of the kerosene pressure burners several times a week.

I still felt stressed and tired out, despite the school boys coming every day. Nursing baby Marie sapped my energy. She rarely slept through the night, I think because she was thirsty. She always refused a bottle, but she started drinking water and powdered milk from a cup when she was about nine months old. That was a turning point that relieved me, although I still nursed her during the day for a couple more months. When she finally started eating solid foods, and her tummy was full, she slept through the night.

About that time, I started practicing medicine out the front door. My nurse instincts couldn't ignore it when the ones bringing us food and vegetables also brought sick babies with pneumonia, or malaria, or some other visible illness. At first they only begged with their eyes, but later they got braver and asked for medicine for their babies. The sores they showed me were always grossly infected, smelly, and had flies all over them. I bandaged those up, praying in Jesus name, while at the same time trying to hold my breath and keep from gagging. Occasionally, a teacher came to ask for a specific medicine for an illness. I gave it to them, if I had it because there was no one else to help. It was well known that the little hospital in Agats didn't have medicine or supplies. My small medical practice always took more time than I expected. Strangely, the kids didn't seem to mind waiting for me to get to their lessons.

Indonesian church services were on Sunday mornings in a little church back by the Hekman's house. I never understood much, but Dan did very well. One of his language assignments was to prepare a sermon in Indonesian. Even though he read most of it when he presented it, I remember that his first time effort was great. Dan and Uncle Don also went with Uncle Bill by outboard motor boat to Asmat villages for services.

Before going to church, I taught the kids a Sunday school lesson. One time Lorraine was inspired and worked out a flannel-graph story from the Bible lesson we had that morning. I asked her to present it a second time to the families, when we met that Sunday afternoon. The three mission families met in one house, or the other, and listened to a preaching-tape in English. We sang a few hymns and also prayed together at that time. I really enjoyed those meetings together, for the fellowship and because I understood everything.

By October of that year, I started sewing on nametapes and checking out clothes for Lorraine to go to boarding school in January. The process forced me to think and gear myself up for her leaving. Dan and I decided to send Lorraine to Sentani School for second semester. She was torn between being home with her baby sister, and being lonely for girls her own age. I knew in my head that it was the best plan. But the thought of that future parting was digging a big hole in my heart. I didn't know if I was ready for her to leave. Life in Agats was looking darker than ever. All seemed gloom and doom. Or was I the gloomy one?

Visitors

Then, by the goodness of God, a couple of visitors came our way. One was Dr. Delbert Kuehl, our recent Conference speaker. He came to Agats early one morning and stayed until mid afternoon. Lorraine got out paper and crayons and made a long *"Welcome"* banner which she carried down to the dock and the kids held out for him to see when the float plane landed. Delbert wanted personal time with each couple and started by going back to the Hekmans first. I felt like the visit was all too short, especially when he came to visit us last. But no matter, it greatly encouraged me to have someone come see us.

Delbert was at our house when we heard the plane was on its way. He walked with Dan and the kids, and headed down the boardwalk to the dock to meet it. I stayed home with Marie and I could hardly stand seeing him leave. I wished with all my heart that I might be going with him. I felt left behind, as if it was my last chance of ever going back to civilization.

When Dan came back up from the dock, he brought me a short note from Delbert written on a piece of torn notebook paper. *"Dear Barbara, I know how hard it is for you to live in this place. But I also know that God is greater and He will give you the strength and help that you need each day. I will be praying for you and your dear family as I go back to the states. God bless you, Delbert"* God knew that I needed a message to lighten my spirits right then and He used a trusted friend to send it to me. (I kept that note for all my missionary years, and took it out to read every so often. It was like a love letter from God, always lifting me up when I was feeling down.)

Soon after Delbert's visit, Aunt Bernita Preston, from Yawsakor, came for a visit. Dan had a filling in a tooth fall out. The only dentist was on the other side of the island, in Papua New Guinea (PNG). We called MAF about their once a week flight to the other side of the border. The plan was to go to the dentist, and be back within the week. But as we had already learned, plans were made only to be delayed or altogether dumped, with the many unpredictable circumstances that came up at the last minute. I didn't feel like I could stay alone, not knowing for sure when Dan might get back.

When Aunt Bernita heard the discussion about dentists and flights on the radio, she called to say she would come and stay with us while Dan was gone. I gladly accepted her offer and she came with her youngest daughter Tosha, plus her house-help couple. Dan flew back out to go to the dentist. Lorraine was thrilled to have Tosha come for the week and play with her. (Tosha was the same age as David and Jonathan, and the three of them eventually went through school together.)

Aunt Bernita's house-help were not on vacation. They made quick work of all the extra things in my house that hadn't been done in awhile. For instance, leather shoes acquired mold if they weren't wiped down, and metal utensils got rusty if not cleaned properly. Of course, not knowing myself, I didn't teach my house help to clean them, either. Aunt Bernita asked her workers to show my helpers what to do.

This was the first time that Dan had gone somewhere overnight without us. The kids understood that he needed to see the dentist, but they preferred to be going with him. Jonathan had an especially hard time with it. After Dan left on the plane I went out and found him crying behind the rain barrel on the back breezeway.

I hugged him, "Are you missing Daddy already? He'll be back in a few days."

Again that night, when we were having our prayers he asked me, "How long will Dad be gone?"

"I don't know for sure, but the plan is for about a week."

"Well, what if he doesn't come back? Or maybe something will happen to him," Jonathan's anxiously asked me.

Reassurances were needed, and I sat on the edge of the bed. "God doesn't want us to be afraid every time one of us goes somewhere alone. He loves us, and wants us to trust Him that He will be with each one of us, like he promised. I know we can pray and ask God to take care of our dad, and bring him back safely, too." We all prayed together and God heard our prayers, bringing Dan home in just over a week.

It was a double-dip encouragement to me having Bernita stay with us while Dan was gone. She was so matter of fact about life in the jungle, the rain and the mud, the heat and humidity, the mildew and musty odor, and the rats and bugs. Being a seasoned missionary, she walked right in and made things happen. Full meals were miraculously cooked on those burner-stoves. She intuitively offered words of reassurance for how I was doing, and often suggested why not try it this way to make it easier. I never felt like she was pushy or know-it-all, just friendly and helpful. My long hair was hot and heavy on my neck and Bernita's practical solution was to cut it for me. Not a bad job for an amateur hair stylist. She raised her six children on the river banks of Yawsakor and her experienced eye knew exactly what was needed to take care of mine. Besides helping with Marie at night, she took her for one whole day and let me feel lazy.

When I saw Bernita's attitude about life, I thought to myself, "Hey, with God's help, I can live here and do what He wants me to do. Look at Bernita and her family, they're doing it, and with humor and grace. It's possible; I can do it, too."

Uncle Chuck and Aunt Bernita Preston proved to be the Barnabas missionaries on our field, the ones to call when you needed a helping hand. They always had a word of encouragement or helpful suggestion for any situation. I believe I wouldn't have made it through that first term without Bernita's positive support and encouragement.

One special thing happened while she was with us, and it greatly impressed Lorraine, David and Jonathan. It also answered a question that was puzzling David, "Mommy, where is the mission field?

Are we there yet?"

"Oh, yes we're here. But mission field can be any place in the world that you are a Christian and ready to tell others about Jesus, even in America. But when a church, like ours in Minneapolis, especially prays for us and sends us to live here in Irian, so that we can teach the people here about God, that is called the mission field too."

Then Aunt Bernita showed us what mission field really meant. Since they lived in Asmat territory at Yawsakor, she spoke the language. Every morning when the villagers came in to sell their produce, Bernita helped me buy it for the schoolboys. One day an old Asmat lady came to the door. Aunt Bernita talked with her and found out that her only son had died and she was still mourning his loss, wondering who would care for her in her old age. They talked together and Aunt Bernita told her about the love of Jesus. That old Asmat grandma prayed and asked Jesus into her *stomach,* right there on our doorstep. We couldn't talk to her, but Aunt Bernita came at just the right time.

David was so thrilled he could hardly wait to tell Dan when he came back home, "Dad, guess what? Aunt Bernita prayed with an old lady who came to our door, and she asked Jesus into her stomach!" Yup, Agats was the mission field. We were there.

On November sixth the boys celebrated their sixth birthday. Older sister Lorraine came to the rescue again with all kinds of ideas for paper decorations, chains and cut out shapes to hang around. She made cards and wrote out invitations inviting Uncle Don and Aunt Carol for a party. I baked a chocolate cake and made sweetened condensed milk ice cream and we blew up balloons. Packages were on the way from America, but weren't there yet. I put aside birthday cards that came in the mail earlier. One of our churches hid little cars and small goodies inside a pair of shoes that were sent to Dan. I saved those things as presents. It doesn't sound like much when we look back now, but the fun of it was to see what we could do ourselves to make it special. The kids and I became more creative over the years as we made presents and cards for each other.

One special rule that I had for birthdays and other gift-giving days was that no one was allowed to tear the wrapping paper from a package and throw it away. We always recycled the paper. Saving the paper became so much of a habit that I'm still tempted to keep the used wrapping paper here in America. The presents are long forgotten, but my kids still talk about saving wrapping paper.

High Tide

Just when I thought I was adjusting and maybe could make it in Mudville, the high tide crept in one night. Hekmans warned us that from November to January the tides come up two to three feet above normal for three to four nights every week. I didn't keep exact records of the tide's coming, I just know they came. We woke up one morning and all visible ground in our fair city was flooded. Not only that, but the water was just below our floor boards. I could see the murky water through the cracks in the floor. The kids were excited and immediately ran out to sail palm leaf boats off the side of our porch, which was now level with the tidewater. They hailed one of the Asmat boys who loaned them a small dugout canoe, and paddled around in the canals, while the water was still up. By mid-morning the same tide went out and the waters receded until the next time, twelve hours later, when it would slowly and quietly sneak up again.

The scary parts of the high tide for me were the creatures swimming by and the thoughts of how dirty and full of germs and sewage it must be. We didn't know what was happening at first, but the night before the tide a multitude of cockroaches, centipedes, millipedes, and other "pedes" came crawling in through the cracks in the floor and walls looking for shelter and safety. It was like they knew it was coming. During that first night, I woke up and saw several large rats scurrying up the two-by-fours to our rafters.

I was petrified and whispered to Dan, "Wake up and look." I didn't sleep much after that.

In the daylight, we actually saw snakes, huge jungle rats, and other slithering things swimming by in the water. I looked in vain for crocodiles, only half wishing I might see one. Thankfully I never did. Again, it was a great adventure for the kids.

My reaction was more hysterical, "You're all gonna get 'hydrophobia' or some other dire disease resulting in an early and painful death. No, you can't swim, who knows what's in that water." But everyone survived. We're still here today; and another one of my doomsday predictions failed to materialize.

First Christmas-Agats

Christmas was fast approaching and why the military chose that time to collect firearms from the people I'll never know. But they did, going from village to village, and then from house to house in Agats. The Dutch government had previously allowed guns for shooting game, like birds, small furry animals and crocs. But the Indonesian government didn't allow civilians to bear arms. With the guns taken and the military making a list of names and households of those who had them, everybody ended up being on edge. That put a damper on our happy holiday festivities.

December brought some relief from the heat and humidity with the windy season, which cooled things down, although that term is relative. We still didn't feel much like celebrating because we were used to white Christmases with snow and cold. The little house-stores had no decorations displayed either. The lack of any decorations brought it home to us that we were definitely in a foreign country.

"Mom, if we want decorations, we can make them ourselves. I'll get paper and stuff together, and you can help me." Lorraine had it under control.

She was in her element, planning and making colored paper shapes and chains for our tree. What tree? Well, I sent Dan and the kids out to get branches from a type of fir tree with long wispy needles. We tied them together, stuck them in a bucket of wet sand, and the tree was ready. Hopefully our homemade tree would be big enough for all the decors that we were making, and it was.

Early in December we received word that our shipment of personal goods from America had arrived and was in the MAF warehouse in Sentani. We decided to wait on flying it down to the south coast until we moved to Nohon after Indonesian language study. Since we were still living out of our suitcases, I thought we wouldn't have anything new to give the kids as presents. But a couple of churches sent us packages from America, which actually arrived in time for Christmas. Admittedly, they were small gifts but that didn't matter. The point was having presents to open.

Our first Christmas in the tropics arrived. The Indonesian community issued a number of invitations for meals and meetings for Christmas and New Years. Dan was the family and mission representative. On Christmas Eve he attended the midnight mass at the Catholic Mission, along with other dignitaries, such as military and government men. The written invitation for the Mass was the first one we ever received and it was important that he go and also represent the mission. According to culture, a written invitation was the same as a command to appear and could not be ignored. Indonesian teachers also invited Dan and he really enjoyed eating their Indonesian specialties. The teachers were the ones who came to our house and helped Dan in conversational Indonesian. In between those invitations, Bill took Dan with him to several Asmat villages for their Christmas services.

We planned our family time on Christmas Eve because the church services were held on Christmas Day. That became our family tradition in the years to follow. After a sandwich supper, everyone gathered around Dan while he read the Christmas Story out of Luke, chapter two, in the Bible.

The kids gave him a stern word of warning about his prayer, "Daddy, please don't pray all around the world. Make it shorter, so we can open our presents." Gifts were simple, including books, a dolly for Marie, craft kits for Lorraine and little cars for the boys. They were all things received in packages from the US, sent by my Mom and our churches. And yes, the kids carefully took the paper off their gifts so I could re-cycle it.

Christmas morning there was a three hour service in our local Indonesian church. We attended that one together because three Lunow kids and two of the Hekman girls were in the Christmas pageant. Fortunately they didn't have to say anything, just stand there while someone read the story in Indonesian. Jonathan and David were shepherds with towels wrapped around their heads. Lorraine was the angel of the Lord, wearing a white sheet and wings. The Hekman girls and a couple Indonesian kids completed the manger scene. The kids were definitely ready for dinner after that.

Lorraine and I baked several batches of cutout Christmas cookies beforehand. Cinnamon and sugar went a long ways for specialty breads. We shared our goodies with the other families and there was enough that I kept some of it for Indonesian friends who came by for conversation.

The three families combined food for Christmas day. I ordered a small, frozen turkey from MAF, and it came on time. We added white potatoes, gravy and bread crumb dressing to it. Hekmans asked missionary friends in the highlands to send them several bundles of bacteria free lettuce from their own garden for a fresh salad. MAF also brought our bag of fresh vegetables before Christmas. One of the women baked a cherry pie for desert, using a can of pie filling from

America. We ate together and the food was as delicious as any holiday meal in the US. We even had leftovers to divide up and take home.

With our homemade decors and tree, eating familiar Christmas goodies, plus the Christmas program, it felt like Christmas even if it was hot, humid, and no snow. At least we had a breeze.

Chapter Six: "Are they in heaven now?"

Year's End at Agats

Two days before New Year's we had our first company since the visits of Dr. Keuhl and Aunt Bernita. The Gene Newman family was on vacation and they wanted to see Agats, since they had heard so many stories about the place. We knew the family from Sentani because Lois was the station hostess and she took care of us when we first arrived. Gene was the bookkeeper for MAF and the one who ordered Dan's tennis shoes for him. He immediately teased Dan about being Mr. Big Foot.

They arrived on the float plane, and landed on a choppy river. All three Agats families welcomed them at the dock. We had a great time chatting and trooping along the boardwalk, showing them around our fair city. The older Newman kids, Paul, Steven and Joyce ran ahead with all of our kids, while baby Jonathan hung on to his mom.

Gene snapped pictures everywhere, ours included, all the while joking, "Now I can prove to everyone that I was actually here, at the end of the world. They'll never believe it otherwise."

The float plane returned around noon to pick them up and take them on to another mission station for a quick visit before flying back to Yawsakor for the night. The wind was blowing and white caps were forming on the river. Lois Newman was getting anxious about flying in windy weather, but they quickly boarded and took off. They were to fly to the central highlands for a couple more days, before returning home to Sentani.

The day the Newmans visited us a message came over the two-way radio that Vida Troutman, a veteran missionary with C&MA, had died suddenly. We didn't know Vida, but the rest of the mission community knew her as a friend and faithful worker in her ministry. By mid afternoon nearly all the mission planes were headed to Enarotali station, picking up those going to her memorial service at airstrips along the way. A celebration funeral service was scheduled for the next morning.

New Year's Eve, December 31, 1968, in the midst of sadness over Vida's death, the mission community was rocked with another tragedy, like nothing before. I told my mom and grandma all about it in a letter:

"New Years Eve about 8 PM we were having a windy-rainy tropical storm. There was a banging at the door and the Catholic pilot

stepped dripping wet into our home. He asked if we had heard that a plane was lost since morning, and a family was in it. We hadn't heard because our radio wasn't turned on. The pilot had just heard the news himself, and told us he would be ready in the morning to help search, if he was needed. When a plane goes down, it doesn't matter what mission you are in, all the pilots are available to search. He left shortly after giving us the news.

We found out that the MAF plane took off from Yawsakor in the morning with the Newman family to fly to the mountains through that south gap that I told you about. At 11 AM the pilot called on his radio and said that clouds were forming and they would try to go around. That was the last word heard from them. All the other planes were at the Memorial Service for the missionary lady who died. By the time the pilots got the message, afternoon clouds were built up, and they had to wait until the next morning to begin the search.

When we heard the plane was missing with the Newmans on board, we were crushed. We prayed with the kids and talked about the 'what ifs' of a plane crash, especially since the Newmans had just visited us. The kids were remembering that they played together, and now they might be crashed somewhere. It was unthinkable, unbelievable.

Early morning on New Year's Day, we turned on our radio to follow the search and rescue efforts. All the MAF planes were out and flying in the area where they thought the crash might be located. Some natives reported hearing a plane in their area, and by mid-morning they found the wreckage. It was in a steep mountain ravine, impossible to get to with fixed-wing planes. The pilots flying high over the area said the wreckage was scattered down the mountainside and it looked burned out. They couldn't see any signs of life. There were several villages on the nearby ridges. They called for a helicopter from Papua New Guinea.

The next morning the helicopter arrived and, with MAF planes circling overhead, they landed on a clearing near the wreckage. There was line of natives on top of a nearby hillside and they suddenly shoved a white boy down the hill. Paul Newman came running down to the helicopter into the arms of the pilot. He was unhurt, the sole survivor of the crash. His folks, two little brothers and one sister, and the pilot were killed. These people had taken Paul in, caring for him for two days. And get this, they are the same group of people who killed the two missionaries last September! I'll write about it, when I know more.

It's such a terrible loss, a family, and pilot with wife and child. And then the two men last September. We wonder what God is doing, what his plans are. Grandma, you said you thought we were in a God-forsaken land. But I believe God is letting people know about this country. When the world hears about these two incidents, we hope they will pray more and their hearts will be stirred to come as missionaries to this place too."

Death became very real to us during those days. As we listened to the radio reports, our three kids still couldn't believe it. Hadn't Paul and his family just been to our house? Jonathan remembered when they left to fly back to Yawsakor, "Their mommy was right. She didn't want to go on the plane when it was so windy and the waves were high."

"We really need to pray for Paul now because he will be very sad that his mommy and daddy, and brothers and sister, are gone."

"Are Paul's family and the pilot all in heaven now?" David wanted to know.

Dan and I tried to answer the kids' questions as they surfaced, coming any time of the day or often at bedtime. The assurance that we believed they were with God in heaven helped the kids to work through some of their thoughts and emotions. Their questions still came.

"Why did God let them crash?"
" Why is Paul the only one who lived?"
"What will happen to him now?"
"What about the people where the plane crashed?"

We didn't know the answers either, but we tried to help them realize that God knew what He was doing. We could trust God for anything that happened to us. I believe our kids were learning that.

While trying to encourage the kids, I had my own emotions and questions to work through. I wrote in my journal about the crash, mostly trying to reassure myself of what we were doing there in that land. *"My heart is so low. How could this happen to a whole family, the children? I feel like the devil is pressing down hard. Is this a prelude to the year 1969? Surely God is the victor through the blood of His son, Jesus. I must remind myself to look to God for each day, daily living and doing what I feel He wants me to do. I can't let myself dwell on the 'if onlys' of yesterday, and the 'what ifs' of today and tomorrow. Take it all to the cross in prayer and leave it there."*

A few days later, I added the rest of the story to the grandmas:

"Here is more news about the crash with the Newman family and their pilot, Meno Voth.

They got into clouds, flew into the wrong valley, and couldn't turn around. The Newman boy, Paul, was able to get out of the plane before it burned because there was a hole in the back. He unbuckled his seat belt and crawled out and ran across a vine bridge to the village, where the people took him in. He tried to tell them, waving his hands in sign language, saying that his mother and father, brothers and sister, and the pilot were still in the plane. A couple days later, an interpreter told the military that the natives knew, but they couldn't get near the fire in the plane. They took Paul in, gave him food, and put him by their fires at night to keep warm.

The crash was in the Seng Valley, the exact place where the two missionaries were killed last September. Paul didn't know they were in that valley, he thought they were over the ranges. As a result of their kindness to Paul, the military flew into the Seng Valley a few days later and brought back the one tribesman they had taken as hostage when the two missionaries were killed. Now the people of that valley say they want to hear the God talk."

Looking back, and our kids know this too, God called us to minister in Irian at a time when He was opening doors to new tribes every year. People that had been in darkness for centuries were getting glimpses of the light of the Gospel. Areas of great resistance, strongholds of darkness and evil were breaking down. It was an exciting time of group movements and individual life changes. God was preparing hearts to hear, as each New Testament was translated into a tribal language. His Church in Irian Barat was born and growing, but it was not without struggles, sorrow and loss. Yet, we felt it was a privilege to be there and be a part of it all.

Lorraine goes to boarding school

The next event I faced was when our oldest child, Lorraine, left home to go to MK (missionary kids) boarding school for the first time. (As the oldest, Lorraine was the one who always went on ahead of her siblings to new horizons, new adventures. First it was elementary school in Sentani, then to high school at Faith Academy in Manila, and on to college in the US. How I thank God for her positive attitude and adventurous spirit. No, it wasn't easy for her, for me, for her siblings, or her dad. But from that initial separation, and on into the years ahead, she set her sights and went ahead and did it, trusting that God would be with her.)

"*Saya bisa chuga,* I can do that too." Our helper, Pu'me, was watching me sew on name-tapes to Lorraine's clothes one day. How wonderful, from then on the job was hers. She sewed, while I got other things ready to go. The cloth labels were from the US, and I still have some of them stashed away in my sewing box. Memories. Besides tags on the clothes, Lorraine's name was supposed to be written on everything she brought to school with her. It was a job to catch everything.

Since our shipment containing new clothes was in Sentani, we were still living out of suitcases from our arrival the previous summer. I put away a few good clothes for each child and let them play in their grubbies at Agats. In December, Lorraine tried on the stored clothes to see if anything fit, since she added a few inches from last year. The school code required girls to wear dresses with the hemline longer than the child's finger tips when stretched down. Everyone wore sleeveless, straight line dresses, called a "shift." I had dress patterns, but that first semester she had enough new ones packed away to send her off to school in style. Lorraine loved her trying-on sessions. I wish I could say it was as much fun when the boys got ready for school the following year. Their interests were definitely elsewhere.

Our wardrobe conversations served as reminders of the loving care of supporters at home in America, "Mommy, who made these dresses for me? I like the colors, that they're not all the same."

"They're from the ladies at Park Avenue Church. They left the hems down so we could measure you first."

"Well then, who made my underwear for me?"

"Oh, those are from the ladies in Burr Oak, Nebraska. They made all the school tee shirts for the boys too. Those are coming in our shipment drums."

Buying clothing for four years ahead was a huge expense, and I was grateful for the church ladies' sewing groups in those days. The Nebraska women really did sew panties for us three girls for many years. They used quality elastic that never gave out in the tropics. That underwear lasted forever. The Park Avenue and Viking, Minnesota ladies also made quilts. (Dan and I received a large quilt for our bed and still have it today. Each one of the kids eventually got their own quilt, and carried them to the US in a suitcase for college. Lorraine and Marie still have theirs.)

Agats was a barefoot or flip-flop sort of place, and we discovered that Lorraine only had one pair of new sandals left for school. They still fit, although her toes hung out the front. We traced her foot on a piece of paper and enlisted Aunt Bernita to buy her a pair of shoes when she went on vacation over to Papua New Guinea. The kids were allowed to wear canvas tennis shoes, sandals or leather tie shoes for school. That first term I didn't have many tennis shoes stored in the drums either. Leather tie shoes wore out quickly because of the rain and dampness. Flip-flops were for play. The only style they had then was the rubber ones that slipped between your toes, in primary colors, or basic black.

Lorraine's last week at home with family came all too quickly for me. She loved the process of getting her things all organized and packed for school. That week she sorted her treasures and decided what to bring with her, and what to leave at home. There wasn't that much to go through because we only had the suitcases and a few new things from small packages we received for Christmas.

She was excited, looking ahead, "I wonder who will be in my dorm room? How many will be in my class? Who is my teacher? " Her questions served to remind me about her home-schooling. I worried and felt unsure of my teaching skills, having no idea if I taught her all she needed to know, or if she was caught up with her class.

I wanted to make the last week special, but Agats was not a fun town. There were no restaurants, no movies to see, and absolutely no places to go. I noticed that David and Jonathan were more solicitous and teased her less. That was certainly special. She got a new hair-do when I cut her hair shorter so that she would be able to take care of it herself.

Lorraine was feeling the imminent departure too. "Can I take care of Marie this week, before I go?"

One afternoon I arranged for the boys to go down to Hekman's house and play with their girls. That left Lorraine, Dan, Marie and me, for those few hours. It was a special time for us.

On her last day at home, Dan and I took our afternoon rest with her. We lounged on the bed and talked about school, what to expect, being separated from us by distance, but not in heart. Dan reminded her, "Remember, we are praying for you, and lots of people in America are too. We know that God will take care of you away from us because He is with you, and with us, all at the same time."

She shared her worries, "What if I get homesick? Or what if I get sick for real?"

"Oh, everybody gets homesick at some time or other." I tried to reassure her, "It's okay if you cry. If you're too sad, go tell your dorm mom about it. She will help you. And if you're sick for real, the school nurse will take care of you. And she can call us on the radio too."

"But mom, will you write and tell me what you're doing, what the boys are doing?"

"I promise that I will write to you every week." (It was a promise I was able to keep all through our missionary lifetime, the weekly letter to my kids.)

Sentani School

The long-awaited Monday morning arrived, too bright and too early, as far as I was concerned. I was glad that we had decided I would go all the way to school with her for the first time, for my own peace of mind, as well as hers. The three Lunow Girls flew on the float plane from Agats to Lake Sentani, which was a two hour trip over the ranges and down to the north coast. We picked up another MK along the way, Beth Roesler from Ayam. It was a good trip, with blue skies and no air bumps. I felt less secure on the pontoon plane this time when I realized we were flying over the jungle and no water below us to land if we needed to. It was a smooth flight, but a rocking chair landing because it was windy on Lake Sentani. We bobbed our way to shore and disembarked without falling off the pontoon. It was quite a fete for me while holding Marie, but I hung on to her.

The dorm house was up a small hill, away from the school and the main dorm building. Three other second grade girls were to be Lorraine's roommates, but they hadn't arrived yet. Lorraine had first dibs on a bottom bunk and started unpacking her things.

That year the rule was still in place that MKs had to live in the dorm during the week, but they could go with parents on weekends. The rule changed the next year, allowing the kids to stay with their parents any time they were out from their stations. None of that helped Lorraine her first night there. I had to leave her alone in her dorm room, which was really hard for both of us. We prayed together, and Marie and I gave hugs and kisses, and went down the hill to our room.

We were staying at the school for a full week, and Pat Fillmore, the school nurse, invited us to stay with her in one end of the big dorm. She was a TEAM missionary and her original station was at Anggi with the Bocks. When the missionaries evacuated during the rebellion, the field asked Aunt Pat to be the school nurse.

School started at 7:30 AM, while it was still relatively cool. Lorraine's teacher, Miss Elsie Toews, allowed me to visit her class a couple of times. The teachers were missionaries, like us, only they gave their time and talents to take care of the MKs, freeing us to work with the tribes people. The dorm parents served coffee every morning at recess break. I sat at the picnic table in front of the dining room and waited for Lorraine to come. She usually buzzed up to play with Marie, introduced a new friend, and ran off again. I guess that meant she was adjusting and making friends.

Besides recess and meals at the dorm, I only saw Lorraine in short spurts during the week. She came down to our room after school to see Marie and me for awhile, and we had a short time after supper. Then I went up to her dorm to say goodnight. I was glad to see that she finally had girl friends, but sad to know that she didn't need me around all the time.

Marie loved watching all the kids and being outside. She laughed, and squealed, and blew bubbles at anyone who happened to walk by. She was sweaty and sticky most of the time and had heat rash under her chin and in the folds of her arms and legs, but none of it seemed to bother her. The girls in Lorraine's room loved her and passed her around between them. By then she was a little chub and just the right size to hold and tickle.

Every afternoon after school, I took Marie and visited the school clinic. Aunt Pat used that week to give me show-n-tell lessons on medical things that she thought I needed to know. Besides taking care of the MKs, she held morning clinics for the national workers at the school. Anything I learned about tropical medicine from Aunt Pat would be to my advantage later.

One story the MKs always tell about Aunt Pat was her penchant for soaking sores. If ever they complained about a boo-boo, she asked, "Have you soaked it yet?"

I was at clinic one afternoon and saw a row of kids on a bench, each with a large yellow, five pound margarine tin of salted water at their feet, and a wet wash cloth plastered on a foot, or a leg, or an arm.

Those soaks helped prevent the spread of infection and brought many a boil to a head. (To this day, we all remain firm believers in the benefits of a good soak. It's all because of Aunt Pat, the school nurse.)

Each night when I took Lorraine back to the dorm and tucked her in, we both got weepy. As the time neared for my leaving, we found it harder and harder to say goodnight. We had a regular stalling ritual in which I prayed with her several times every night. Then I made the rounds kissing each of her room-mates good night. Marie helped prolong the parting because she took her turn in all the goodnight kisses too.

My heart was aware of the time and how quickly it was passing. I wanted to slow it down and make it last longer. How do you feel in your inner being when all you want is to have your child at home with you? Somehow the promise of coming to see her in another six weeks didn't help the dull ache I felt in my chest. My head told me this was right. I could see how busy and happy she was with her new friends and the school activities, but my heart hadn't caught up with my head yet.

When the week was up and we were packed to leave, my voice got stuck behind a huge gulp in my throat. The tears came, but thankfully not too many. Lorraine was brave too, getting big tears in her eyes but hugging Marie and me together. Then she let us go. I felt God's grace and strength and did what I had to do. Lorraine did too.

Now there are other options to school, mainly with computer courses and online teaching. Other families live on the coast near school and their kids are day students, while the parents make short trips interior. At the time, I know boarding school was the right thing for us. Dan and I did it because we thought it best for our children and we wanted to be in obedience to God's call on our lives, as well. But oh, that first goodbye was soooo hard, and all the succeeding goodbyes, for that matter. With time and years, it never got any easier. Saying goodbye is still hard for all of us Lunows. But we did it with God's help.

Letters from school

Marie and I left Lorraine at school and flew back home to Agats. Did I just say back home? That must have been a slip of the tongue. David and Jonathan were waiting for our return and already missing Lorraine, especially when they had run out of ideas for play.

David fired questions at me, "What dorm is Lorraine in? How early does she have to get up to go to school? Does she like it? Does she get to go swimming every day?"

"I really wish Lorraine was still here with us." Jonathan was the one who felt most secure when everyone was in their place and accounted for.

We were all feeling the empty space in the family circle and eagerly waited for her letters to come. The dorm rule was that the MKs had to write every Sunday afternoon. I did the same in my letters to her. Due to the plane schedules, it didn't mean an actual weekly letter arrived. Sometimes two or three letters came at once. When I knew the plane wasn't coming for awhile, I often wrote several letters ahead. I sent them to the dorm parents to spread out and give to Lorraine over a couple of weeks. I also sent goodies in tins, like: cookies, peanuts, or hard candies. The kids still remember those small oatmeal and Milo tins of yummy things from home.

Lorraine's first letter, which she wrote herself, read like this, *"I love my school. I have many new friends to play with. I am doing fine in my school work. XO XO Lorraine"*

Aunt Pat and the house parents also sent notes, saying that Lorraine was doing fine and adjusting well. Did I detect that they were trying to reassure me that Lorraine wasn't pining away for us? Her days were filled to the brim with school, friends, and activities. To my relief, she told me she was caught up on her schoolwork too.

(Those letters, no matter how delayed, became an essential part of our lives when our kids went to boarding school, and on to other schools. Letters, stacks and stacks of them, are holding the specifics of our memories now. I'm so thankful I kept them and that we can be reminded of where we were, and where we came from, and what we did with the help of the Lord.)

I started working on kindergarten again with the boys. They were definitely less challenged and motivated with their sister gone. The main emphasis was to learn to read. David did well. Jonathan was right behind his brother, but he was always so embarrassed to read out-loud with David sitting by him.

"Mom, make David move. He's listening to me and I don't want him to."

Both of them liked their numbers better than reading. And they were miles ahead of me in speaking Indonesian. A couple of times, when they were really bored, they gathered up their courage and ventured down the boardwalk by themselves to visit the Hekman girls, back in the jungle.

On one of those afternoons, Jonathan came home proudly carrying a fresh coconut. "Look mom. I got it myself. I borrowed a machete from one of the school boys and climbed the palm tree and whacked it down. It's okay, mom, I can do it."

My immediate response was of horror, visualizing my little boy up a palm tree with a machete in his hand. But I was proud of him too.

Culture Clash

Something else happened that spring. I'm not sure if Dan and I did the right thing, but if it still bothers me, I believe we were wrong. Dan was over visiting an Indonesian family. He saw a pile of little toy trucks on their porch, which he knew belonged to David and Jonathan. When Dan came home, he asked the boys about them, "Oh, they gave us candy for our cars."

The kids had talked our boys out of their cars and hauled off nearly all of them. Cultural or not, this was not right. Dan confronted them on it, and asked that the toys be returned. By that time, they had moved everything inside. When they brought out the first return, it was the old battered and beaten trucks.

Dan waited, "*Ada lagi?* Is there more?"

And so it went a few cars at a time, until it became so painful that Dan told them to keep the rest. The boys ended up with less than a dozen cars.

We all learned from that experience. Other Indonesian people in Agats heard the story, via the jungle vine, and told Dan that the family shouldn't have kept the toys. We still felt bad because we knew that confrontation caused them to lose "face," and face is so important in the culture. Maybe we should have just let it go, since they considered us to be rich and able to buy more cars for our boys. We never forced an issue like that again.

Apparently the incident didn't hurt our status with the rest of the Indonesian community because when they found out Dan was nearly finished with language study and we would be moving on to Nohon, they wrote a letter to our field council asking that Dan be allowed to stay in Agats. They explained that he understood them and the way they do things. That was an unexpected compliment and encouraged us that we hadn't destroyed our good relationships with anyone in Agats town.

Finishing up in Agats

Dan was about ready to take his final exam in Indonesian. I was only a fourth of the way through the course, and would continue my lessons in Nohon. Meanwhile, the visitors increased at our door because Dan had started playing chess with several of the military men stationed there. The teachers from both schools came, just to talk, and usually wanted to buy any extra vegetables we might have. They asked if we would take their family pictures with our camera. I didn't sit and chat, but I served the guests lukewarm sweet tea and cookies, and let Dan talk and practice his Indonesian.

We still had Pu'me and Seruwi with us. They were all, and more, than I ever expected them to be in the house, cleaning, baking bread and cookies, and watching Marie. Seruwi was also handy with tools and could fix almost anything. They set up their own routine and just went at it. I appreciated all they did for me and was glad they were going to Nohon with us.

Marie was growing and seemed to be a healthy baby, even though she didn't get regular check–ups from the doctor. Physical exams were done at field conference and Marie would get hers then, in another six months. If I had a question, I could call a doctor on the two-way radio, explain the symptoms and get his advice. Having older kids helped, and I sympathized with the first time mothers who didn't have past experience to help them. I gave Marie her immunization shots. The doctor sent the meds in a thermos with the pilot. I kept the vaccine in our fridge until it was time for a shot. Playing head nurse for my family was never an assignment that I enjoyed.

My mom and grandma were missing out on seeing their latest grandchild grow up in the jungle, so I faithfully recorded Marie's episodes in my letters, *"Baby Marie is growing so fast. She is six months old and has two front teeth, upper middle, a real Bucky Beaver character. She likes to use the new teeth, too; sometimes on me because I'm still nursing her. Just this week she finally took an interest in real food. Before now, she didn't even care for fruit. I can still see myself shoveling applesauce into the boys at her age. But each one is different. None of mine have ever been what you would call quiet. Marie is a squealer and bellows when she is in pain, or thinks she is in pain. Pu'me, our helper, really spoils her, carrying her around all the time.*

They don't believe in letting a kid cry. I don't mind it too much because it's hot and Marie gets so restless."

I thought I should have more time to study Indonesian, but it didn't work out that way. One time consuming job for me was the many visitors who knocked at our door. Word got around town that I was a nurse, and local people came for all and sundry things. The sores the village people had were beyond gross for smell and infection. I often asked Dan to help me wash and bandage them up. The Asmat were so thankful to have a clean bandage, made of stripped bed sheet rolls because the flies ate them alive. The open wounds took forever to heal if they weren't covered up. Many of the adults and children had coughs and chest symptoms, and I gave out the cough syrup as long as it lasted. They loved the red syrup. I know more people arrived at the door for the sweet *strop* than anything else. When it was gone, it was back to the bitter pills, but they kept coming.

Visiting an Asmat church

A fun thing that I did, before we left Agats, was go on a speed boat trip with Uncle Bill Hekman out to an Asmat village. Verena offered to watch Marie. I wrote about it to the grandmas, *"This morning I went out on the river to an Asmat village for church. The wide, black, ugly water rose on either side of the boat, and the dense, dark green jungle growth hangs out over the water. It made me feel claustrophobic going so close to the river bank, but it was a smooth ride.*

The village was totally muddy from the high tide last night. A small church, built of poles and bark, was up off the ground on piles, with bamboo slats for the floor and huge spaces in between. The flooring is also convenient for little kids to go potty, no worries about going outside. The roof was of palm leaves. Everyone sits on the floor. With all the coughing, sniffling, and clearing of throats, it made me think somebody in there was surely dying of 'graveyard consumption,' as my Uncle Dale would say.

Of course, a white lady coming to visit caused quite a sensation. Everyone wanted to shake my hand. Women and children crowded around and pinched my arms and cheeks, to see if my skin was real, or if it would rub off. I brushed their arms right back, and told them we were the same.

There were sixty to seventy people. All the kids in the village go to the Catholic school. The teacher keeps telling them if they go to his school, they have to go to the Catholic Church too. That is not true, but the people believe it. Bill tries to help them understand they have the right to choose their own church.

It was a fun experience to see an Asmat village, but made me feel depressed too. Everything is black and muddy. There was no grass or other greens, except looking up the trunks of the coconut trees to the branches of green palms waving. The houses are brown bark with brown grass roofs. I don't know how they ever survive. I know their lifespan is short, and no wonder."

With Dan and Spencers finishing Indonesian language study, our time in Agats was coming to an end, and I could hardly wait. It meant a move out of the swamps to higher ground. Hooray! No more high tides because Nohon was on an inland river. The village was located on a small sand hill, away from the river.

Most of the packing had to wait until the actual moving day because I was using everything. The plan was for Dan to take our belongings up river to Nohon on the mission boat. The rest of us were to travel by float plane. Before the final move, we were going to see Lorraine at school, and then take a two week vacation in the mountains.

Vacation break at Sentani, Mulia

It was time to pack for a trip to Sentani, a hot place, and the mountains, where sweaters were needed. The stored luggage needed wiping down from mold, and then aired in the sun, before I could pack anything. The kids liked getting the suitcases out into the sun because it meant we were going somewhere on another adventure.

Lorraine had only been gone six weeks, but it felt like six months to the rest of the family. I combined letters to the grandmas, telling them about visiting Lorraine at school, and us going to the mountains, *"The boys are really excited about seeing Lorraine. Jonathan told us, 'I'll be glad to go on vacation to the mountains, but I'll be more glad to see Lorraine.' He's the one who is forever teasing his sister.*

'Well, I'll be glad to see her too, but I won't let her kiss me.' That was David.

When we finally saw her, Jonathan hid behind a curtain, David hung back, and Marie squealed. The overall shyness was brief because the four were back to normal in short order, and the boys have been especially good to Lorraine this week. Besides the boys, Lorraine is doubly pleased to see her baby sister.

She has grown up so much in the six weeks. She even acts older, not my little girl any more. We had her with us for the weekend, and she is with us every afternoon from 3-7 PM. We are in a guest house next to the school, and it is really nice to be so close. We go over to school for snacks at recess time and see her. One night we had Lorraine and her four roommates for supper. They all seem so happy, just a bunch of giggly girls like anywhere else on the globe. My only complaint is that the days are going by too fast.

One day we made the trip into town, Sukarnapura, and took the boys to the beach. Lorraine was in school, so she didn't go. After seeing the black jungle water in Agats, the blue of the ocean was beautiful. The boys dived right into the waves. We went to Invasion Beach, the beach where the Allies landed in World War II. There are rusted out tanks and other military stuff along the shore, with the jungle green growing over them. It makes you feel like you're looking into the past, seeing the rusted hulks. Anyway, the boys had a wonderful time in the ocean. I only waded in the water with Marie and she loved it.

Back at school, the boys wanted to spend every other afternoon in the pool at school. They are getting to be good swimmers, along with Lorraine. We've had Marie in with us and she is not afraid at all. In fact, I think we will have to watch her as she gets older.

We had such a good week with Lorraine, but it went too fast. I didn't know it, but most of the other parents come to see their kids for two weeks. We will have to do that next time.

The night before we left, we had our supper together and Lorraine asked us if she could pray. 'Dear Jesus, thank you that Mom and Dad could come with the boys and baby Marie to see me at school. Please help them so they won't be lonely when they leave. Please help me as I stay in school to learn. Amen.' The prayer was unprompted, and I found my supper hard to eat after that.

Lorraine came down to kiss us all goodbye very early in the morning. I saw big tears in her eyes, but she hurried away so we wouldn't see her cry. The parting this time was harder for me than in January. But her Sunday letter has already come here to Mulia, and she sounds like her usual happy self."

(The two weeks in the mountains was our first and only real vacation together as a family, in all our time in Papua. In following years we went to visit our kids in school each semester, and counted that as vacation. After the kids were gone to high school and college, we had working breaks, going to this or that translation consultation or printing layout session. That one vacation at Mulia remains a highlight in my mind.)

Mulia was another station of the large Dani tribe. There was a small mission hospital and Bible School there, and a couple government buildings. The Danis crowded around and were puzzled as to why one of the boys had brown hair, David, and the other one had blonde hair, Jonathan.

They asked their missionary, Leon Dillinger, 'Where is the *Tuan's* other wife, the one with the white hair?'

Dan nearly got into big trouble for his joking response to that question. Not missing a beat, Dan laughed loudly, "Oh, just tell them that my other wife is in America."

They actually believed him because they were polygamists before the gospel. Whoops, really not such a good story to tell, Dan.

The boys loved Mulia and ran outside every day playing from morning to night, except when it rained and they were forced to come inside. The air felt cool, fresh, and exhilarating and the guys took long trail walks together. I stayed closer to home and carried Marie up and down on the path. It felt good to cook in cool air, on the wood burning stove, and we ate tons of fresh vegetables. At bedtime we snuggled into our dry sheets and warm blankets because the cabin had no insulation, and the night air was cooler after the sun went down. The only flaw in our perfect vacation was that we missed our dear daughter Lorraine.

Chapter Seven: "You ate what?"

Nohon, living among the Auyu people

I thought we would move to Nohon as soon as we got back from our vacation in the mountains. But getting out of Agats took longer than expected, due to the speed limits of the tropics, which registered *slow* and *slower*. Besides that, Dan didn't know how to run the river boat and he was the one to bring our belongings up river. Larry Rascher came down from the Sumapero station to give Dan a crash course in keeping everything shipshape and the motor running. He also instructed him in river travel, avoiding floating islands of jungle growth, and steering in the deep, not the shallows.

Fortunately, the two native watchmen for the boat were to go with Dan on the three day journey. These men knew the tides, and their effect on the rivers. And our house-helper, Seruwi, was also going along. The men started by hauling the packed boxes of our belongings down to the boat. Then they rolled the fifty-five-gallon barrels loaded with our stuff down to the dock. But wait, I'm getting ahead of the story.

The other part of the plan was that the boys, Marie, and I go ahead of Dan on the float plane. On May 1, 1969 we walked the boardwalk for the last time. I think nearly all of Agats trooped down to the river to watch us leave. Now that the moment had arrived, I was actually feeling a little sad in saying goodbye. I had begun to really like the people there, even if I didn't have an ounce of fondness for the surroundings. Uncle Don and Aunt Carol were staying in Agats for now, but they eventually came to Nohon to partner with us.

This time the ride on the plane was bumpy. None of us were in the mood to look out the windows at the vastness and beauty of the jungle below. We were too focused on our stomachs. I didn't throw up, but I felt nauseated all the way. Jonathan was not only sick, but he vomited several times into plastic bags that the pilot carried. Our house-girl, Pu'me, looked green and she also up-chucked once. David remained unusually quiet. Only Marie looked peaceful as she slept in my arms the entire flight of one hour and fifteen minutes. The rest of us could hardly wait to see the river where we were to land, even if we had to disembark into a floating motor boat. At least the landing on the water was smooth.

Marie woke up hollering during the transfer from the pontoon of the float plane to the river boat. It was feeding time. I clutched her to my bosom as I climbed into the middle of the swaying boat. Then I breast fed her as modestly as I could, while everyone looked on. She was only interested in having lunch and didn't seem at all embarrassed. So I figured I should just get over it too. Jim Hyatt, the Nohon missionary who had come out to meet us in the boat, graciously focused his attention on the river bank. Not so with the Auyu school boys, who were all eyes. Thankfully, they said nothing. Still, I survived another first for me with my gallant missionary spirit in tact. And Marie got her tummy full and quit crying. After that little interlude, it was a ten minute boat ride to shore and good ole *terra firma.*

When we got out at the riverbank, the two Hyatt boys immediately grabbed David and Jonathan and ran off with them to explore. The first place they ran to was the swimming pond near the edge of the jungle. The water was a reddish-brown color, and was clear of jungle debris. The pool presented a refreshing contrast from the knee deep mud on the river bank off the dock in Agats.

Of course, the boys ran back pleading, "Mommy, can we go swimming now? We can swim in our shorts. Please mom."

Permission was granted and they took off again. I think they would have lived down by the jungle pool permanently if I had let them. During the summer they became strong, confident swimmers. I must insert bragging rights here because they were the only first graders allowed to swim in the deep end of the pool when they went to school in the fall.

I noticed that the air smelled fresher, more like being in a tropical garden, than by the sea. Grass grew through the sandy ground as we walked up the airstrip from the river landing. It was a wonderful change to no longer sink into the depths of mire and mud, but have sand between my toes. I knew the kids were going to love playing ball and running free up and down that airstrip.

Nohon village looked clean and neat, and tropically beautiful with palm trees swaying in the breezes alongside the airstrip. On the right, the village houses ran parallel to the airstrip. The walls were made of bark with palm-frond thatch roofs, and they were elevated two to three feet off the ground on timbers. The native style church was located in the middle of the village. It had split bamboo half walls and was open the rest of the way up to the thatch roofing. It was built on the ground and had tree-pole pews and a bamboo pulpit in front.

The mission house, located at the top of the airstrip on the village side, felt more welcoming and homelike than our Agats house. It was made of heavy gauge corrugated aluminum and was also built up on timbers about three feet off the ground, like most of the jungle houses in Papua. There were huge open square windows covered in screening, and the metal awnings propped up outside could be dropped down from the top when it rained. The inside of the house was bright and cheerful allowing the sunshine in. The breeze blowing through the windows felt good because Nohon was hot and humid, too. I was happy to see that the floor boards fit together and there were no cavernous cracks between them. They were smooth and finished, and easy to walk on when barefoot, no slivers.

When we arrived in Nohon, the Hyatt family was packing for furlough. We moved in with them for nearly two weeks, before they left for the states. With the Lunows' six and the Hyatts' four, the house was cramped and crowded, and sometimes chaotic. During the day it was even more crowded because Hyatts had a native couple who helped them. And Seruwi and Pu'me were with us. That made four extra people, helping or hindering, depending on how you looked at it. I noticed that Margaret Hyatt's help taught my two workers, and they divided up chores. All four were Danis, and I'm sure they were glad to talk to each other.

Aunt Margaret was a good cook, true southern cuisine, yum. I was glad not to do it for the two families. The only drawback to the delicious meals was that the Hyatts were on a different timetable, they ate much later than we did. We still managed to remain friends, living and working together, despite our differences and close quarters.

Vaseline became a remedy of the past at Nohon. The first time I opened the sugar bin I was thrilled to see white granules, instead of a blanket of black bodies of ants. Good news, there was no need to strain our drinks for ants anymore. I could actually leave some food out on the tabletop for awhile. Vaseline was no longer needed on table and bed legs. Of course, the roaches were still out and about at night, as well as the spiders. My recipe of boric acid mixed with liquid raw sugar worked fairly well in killing the roaches. Spiders were bearable, as long as they weren't too big and hairy because their webs caught flies and other insects.

One advantage with the house elevated off the ground was that it was high enough to keep window-peepers from peering in all day long. As it was, during the day there was usually at least one person standing on the front steps looking in the side windows. We could also see and hear everything going on because a path led from our front door straight down into the village. In return, the main path to the gardens came up and curved around the side of our house leading back to the jungle.

Nohon was our first place without a generator for electricity. We relied on kerosene lamps and the old faithful Coleman lanterns. The trick was to get them lit before it got dark, which was around 6:30 PM. Sometimes we were all so busy that we let the daylight turn to dusk before we filled the lamps. Then we scurried and hurried to get them going, before the rapidly descending darkness hit us all. How quickly the sun went down on the equator, boom, just like that. There were no other lights of any kind shining anywhere else in Nohon. When it was dark, the only outside light was from the moon and stars.

Dan was still on his way with our belongings when Jim told me that some of our outfit drums had arrived on an earlier river boat. That sounded good, but I hadn't planned on unpacking anything until Hyatts cleared their things away.

Then he gave me the bad news, "I'm really sorry to tell you, but there was an accident with your drums. We were moving them from the river boat to my motorboat and a dugout canoe. Four of them were top-heavy and they rolled the dugout over into the river. We managed to fish them out, even the extra heavy one. We couldn't open them to check for water damage because they're locked. Do you have the keys, so I can check them now?"

I searched for the keys in one of our boxes and hurriedly gave them to him. He unlocked the padlock and took off the metal rims, and found that each drum was dry; not one drop had gotten inside. How thankful I was for the thick plastic liners that I put in them. Our stuff would have been soaked with river water and totally ruined, otherwise. Thank you, Lord.

The Auyu language group lived in several villages scattered along the rivers in the government district of Kepy. Nohon was one of the largest settlements. Auyu people were generally short, small framed, with tightly curled black hair. Their brown skin was a lighter shade than the Asmat, and they were less muscular than the Danis. We thought they looked cleaner than the Asmat, maybe due to the fact that they bathed regularly. Every morning they walked past our house to go to a bathing spot in the jungle. Besides perforated earlobes, many of the men and women had holes poked in their noses through the septum, and some through the flesh on top of the nose. Looking at them from the side, their profile was something to behold, especially when they had a pig tusk, a bone, a pencil, large safety pins, or feathers stuck through one or two holes. Others had loose skin flapping, or hanging down, from their noses or ears, where the original piercings had stretched and broken apart.

I also noticed their poor teeth, decayed and discolored, and front teeth missing. "Most of it is poor nutrition," Uncle Jim explained. "Their diet is mainly starch from the *sago* palm, the white milky pith from the inside of the tree. It takes a long time to dry it into those heavy rolls wrapped in banana leaves. They cook it down into a gooey paste to eat. The sago only fills their stomachs, but it has no vitamins to speak of. When they cook it, they throw in a few jungle greens. They catch fish and shoot birds, but they don't have a steady diet of protein. Besides that, they might eat jungle fruits, or pineapple, and coconuts once in awhile."

The young girls and women wore short grass skirts cut just above the knee, and the dry, flat, grasses rustled when they walked. A few wore old tee shirts, but most of them were bare from the waist up. All the men wore dirty shorts and torn shirts of some kind or other. The kids ran around naked.

We figured out they really wanted clothes to wear, but they had no way to buy them. It was hard for them to take garden produce or a captured creature all the way down river to trade at the government post. Whenever anyone worked for us, they always requested their pay in used clothing. Dan's clothes proved a hard match for any kind of a deal because they were oversize on an Auyu. My tops worked for women and for men.

Dan arrived in four days with our supplies and they unloaded the boat right away. There was no time to rest because the first thing on his agenda was to present his ID and travel papers into the nearest government office, which was at Kepy. It was an all day trip there and back in the outboard. Once he was checked in, Dan was permitted to go to settlements outside of Nohon, as long as they wrote an official letter inviting him.

The Catholic Church also worked in the South Coast and the government did not tolerate any disagreements between them and the Protestant missions working in the same area. If a village already had Catholic teachers, for example, they could ask our mission to come in, but it had to be in the form of an official letter sent to the government post and to the missions involved. We were careful to follow the government regulations on this because local officials also held power and could make trouble for us if we didn't follow the rules. We wanted to be on their good side.

When he got back to Nohon, Dan told me I missed a good trip "Kepy town is beautiful. There's sandy ground all around. And the palm trees arch out their trunks in a row all along the river banks." I was sorry I didn't go with him, but I couldn't with Marie. Besides, I was busy with Aunt Margaret teaching me about the medical work before she left on furlough.

Beginning Medical Work

Although Margaret was not a nurse, our mission doctor trained her in the most common illnesses and the medicines needed for treatment. The village built a small clinic made of split bamboo and thatch roof, which was just outside the mission house beside the path. Clinic was twice a day, in the morning for people from other areas, and in the afternoon for the local Nohon people. I unpacked and settled us in and went out to the clinic. Marie made me happy because by that time she loved to have Pu'me carry her around. That way I didn't have to take her with me everywhere.

I watched Margaret work at the clinic, and she gave me hints on what to look for in certain conditions. Even though I was the nurse, she knew a lot more than I did about tropical ailments. Still, she turned the medical work over to me that week. I didn't speak the Auyu language at all. Fortunately, the south coast people had a broader knowledge of Indonesian and I could use it. If I got stuck, there was always someone around who could interpret for me.

Opening clinic twice a day was too much for me. So I told Yah-ya, the Auyu clinic worker, that I would take the mornings, and he could do the afternoons. Dr. Ken had also trained Yahya and he knew how to give shots and treat most common things. He was also faithful in coming to work every day, which was not a tribal characteristic. They prefer to be on their own time. Our medicine was supplied by the mission doctor. The people were supposed to pay for their meds by bringing sago, fresh fruit, shrimp, fish, or even money, if they had it. Yahya collected any of this as his payment. In reality, we actually paid for the greater share of the medicines with station funds set aside for that purpose.

I liked working in the clinic and could have done it full time, except language study was a priority. The people knew when clinic was open, but many tried to come at off times so they could get preferential treatment. Sometimes they came from a distant village after clinic hours. I felt like I had to take of care of them, especially when they traveled so far. And of course, there were always the emergencies that came any time of day or night.

Some of the most repulsive things I had to deal with were the terrible tropical ulcers or infected sores from old wounds. There was no such thing as a simple sore in the tropics. It's hard to describe what they're like with flies all over, sticking like glue to the flesh. The smell was beyond putrid. I gagged, or held my breath, when trying to clean them. I prayed a lot too. Thankfully, our cleaning, cleansing, and bandaging was usually enough to keep the flies off. I used nearly all of the rolled sheet bandages from the doctor's supply, and then dug into my own store when the others ran out. I silently blessed the ladies from our supporting churches for making bandages rolled out of old sheets for me.

Simple penicillin was truly a miracle drug in those days. Of course, the people thought that one shot was a cure-all and many of them never came back again, after their first shot of penicillin. We had water-based, short acting, penicillin, which was used for pneumonias and other infections. But more than one shot was needed for it to be effective, and the people didn't want to make return visits to clinic. There was also penicillin in oil, which absorbed slowly. For long-lasting effect, penicillin in oil was best, especially for tropical ulcers. I also used it, regardless of the diagnosis, if I thought the patient would never come back again.

Lepers

One day a group of ten lepers rowed down-river in their canoes, asking for treatment. They were all from the same village and promised me they would be faithful to come for their medicine.

"Are these people like the ones in the Bible?" David wondered. The kids knew about lepers from their Bible stories.

"Yes, they are. You can see their sores and their whitish skin. We'll talk about them later, after clinic." That night we had a long discussion about lepers and how Jesus healed them, even touching them when it was forbidden in the Jewish Law.

The lepers had horrible, deep sores, which took a long time to heal. Some had missing digits on their hands, or feet. True to their promise, they came every few weeks for medicine. There was one young boy, a teenager, and he really touched my heart.

I wrote to my mom, *"We have a group of ten lepers coming to clinic from a nearby village. There are nine adults and this one young boy, who is an advanced case. I feel so sad and sorry for him. He has open sores that don't heal, and his feet are deformed from burns, and he can barely walk. His fingers are also twisted, and several are cut off at the knuckles. Those were burned too, since he can't feel with them. It's pitiful, and yet he comes faithfully for his medicine. He always brings something to clinic, like a coconut, or a fish, to pay for his medicine.*

David is worried about him and has asked me a couple of times, "Can't you do something else to help him?"

I wish there was more that I could do.

The government has tried to get the lepers to go to the hospital in Merauke, which is a government town further south along the coast. I don't think they can get there by boat. The only way to go would be by plane. Someone from the health department comes every once in a while to take them and they run off into the jungle. You can't blame them for not wanting to leave their own people. They probably would never get to come home again. Some of the medicine for leprosy has to be taken without fail for two years. The problem with staying in the village is taking their medicine for such a long time because if they miss a treatment, they have to start over.

I have never seen a leper before, but treating them made me think of the Bible and how Jesus actually touched them and made them whole. Their skin is dry, and scaly, and is like tough leather when you give them a shot. It doesn't feel soft and warm to the touch. They also have those sores that won't heal. Most of them come with burns on their feet because their nerves are damaged, and they can't feel heat and cold, or pain. The young boy I mentioned had his feet in the fire, and they had to wake him up to tell him that his feet were burning! He is such a sweet boy and never complains. It's so sad to see him."

The two weeks with the Hyatt family went by quickly. The plane that came to fly them out for their furlough to the US was the same one that brought Lorraine home for summer vacation. She was a day early, but no one complained about that. David and Jonathan were excited to see her and show her around. She was thrilled to get home, even though she had no idea what *home* at Nohon looked like. Of course, little sister Marie who was eighteen months old by then, pushed her way into the middle of things and squealed with delight when she saw her big sister. We were family, whole again, which was enough for all of us

I felt bad that I didn't have time to fix up the house and bedrooms before Lorraine came on vacation. But now that the house was officially ours, I could get into our barrels and unpack. I put down scatter rugs, hung up curtains, and got out our own towels. Up until then we had been living with other people's furnishings.

The boys watched as I brought out each new item. Some of the knick-knacks were old and familiar. David, especially, remembered them, "Now it looks like our house."

The supply drums were accounted for, but we were still missing three of the foam mattresses. The new generator arrived on the plane that brought Lorraine from school, but we couldn't use it because we needed tools and wiring to hook it up.

Airstrip Repair

One not so welcome letter came from the head of MAF. The word was that they wanted the hump at the bottom of the Nohon airstrip taken off and leveled out. Effective immediately, MAF was closing the airstrip for about six months. What, we'd only been there for two and a half weeks and now the airstrip was closed down? We were new and inexperienced missionaries and we had no clue how to get people to work, let alone how to go about leveling a lump on the airstrip. Dan and I felt totally un-gifted for such a huge project.

(The feelings of inadequacy assailed us many times in the future, as we were assigned or called on to do a job that we had never done before. But God always stepped in and gave Dan and me what we needed to do it. More often than not, God used other missionaries to help us.)

After reading the letter, I started to worry about what it would mean being without a wheel plane for so long. There was something about going out to the airstrip to meet the plane and talk to the pilot. I could pump them for the latest news and gossip of what was happening on other stations and in Sentani. The pilots were sensitive to our isolation and stopped in for coffee and a visit, if they had time. I knew I would feel it more than Dan because it was harder for me to go out on the river and meet the float plane. That was a trip for Dan and his kids, more than me.

Hiring villagers to repair the strip was also an expense and we had no idea what to pay per day. Dan got on the two-way radio and checked with a couple of our veteran missionaries, asking them how to begin the project. Uncle Chuck Preston, who knew tribal customs, suggested a fair wage and told Dan to try using crews of workers, including some from the other villages around. That arrangement allowed for the work to be spread out among more people, not just one station. They could all earn some money that way. The tribal leaders agreed it was culturally acceptable to have men and women working together. Dan planned to buy sago, the starchy food staple that most south coasters eat, so they could have a meal once a day and keep on working. It proved to be a good plan for all.

The airstrip closed, and I endured, until it was finally fixed and approved with a trial landing some five months later. Dan went out early every morning for roll call and got the crews started on their sections of the measured hump. He never knew from one day to the next who would be coming to work because the people had no idea of staying the course. It was grueling manual labor, using shovels and gunny sacks to haul clay and rocks. They quit work whenever they felt like it. Dan also went out a couple of times during the day to make sure no one was sitting out and just collecting wages. Our kids were not affected at all because they could still play on the airstrip, as long as they avoided the lower part where the people were working.

About that time, the field council sent us a note and reminded Dan and me that our first priority was to be learning the language.

"Yeah, right! We know it's supposed to be our first priority. But…" I had plenty of excuses as to why it wasn't first place with me.

Besides the airstrip project, it took so many hours a day just to live and care for my family, even with the house-help. Other duties and immediate needs always seemed to interrupt the planned schedule. I was still burdened with finishing the rest of my Indonesian course before I could begin Auyu language study. It took self discipline and great motivation to study when there were no classroom hours and I was the only student. I also felt discouraged with the kids and Dan so far ahead of me in communicating. They used Indonesian if they got stuck in Auyu, and were easily understood by the men and boys. It was too bad for me because the women only spoke Auyu. It was easier to let the kids interpret for me, rather than figure it out for myself. I was greatly relieved when I eventually finished the Indonesian course and started with Auyu.

Meanwhile Dan cleaned out his office, which was a cute little bamboo hut outside in the yard. He started Auyu study before the Hyatts left. He also found a few linguistic papers in a storage drum, which were left from an earlier missionary who went home due to illness. Dan used those papers to help him get started in Auyu, and to work out his first lessons to teach the pastors. But he mainly wanted to start from scratch and learn it for himself. So he enlisted the help of a man from the village, named Tamaiy, to work with him. In speaking Auyu, we had to wrap our tongues around our tonsils, and clear our throats for some of the hard to reach sounds. The clearing of the throat and growling part was easy for Dan because his native German growled a lot too.

My hopes of studying together with Dan were also dashed. Not only did our schedules conflict, but we were never studying the same thing at the same time. I was destined to always be trailing him in the language learning department. He set his pace and ran with it, while I lumbered along behind, forever the tortoise. How I envied Dan his ability to catch on so fast, but that must be the reason he was the linguist, not me. I learned to lower my expectations for myself because it was impossible for me to keep up with everyone else. (Looking back, I can say I managed to learn several languages by going along at my own pace. It took my whole lifelong to do it, but I kept at it.)

Dan also picked up every day speech when he went out on the boat a couple of times a week, visiting in the villages. He wanted to get to know the people in their own setting and the boys loved going out on the boat with him. I tried to go down to the village several times a week to visit with the women. Mostly I just sat and listened to them talk. It was a small beginning in developing relationships and getting to know the Auyu in a more personal way.

We went to the village church every Sunday. The Auyu church was new and they believed so simply, trying to follow what they knew. One of the church elders got himself into trouble for his eagerness. He went into a Catholic village and told the people that since their teacher wasn't doing them any good, they should throw him out. The church leader was arrested instead, and he was thrown in jail. They kept him without charge, forced him to work for the police, beat him several times, and finally released him. He never figured out what he had done wrong.

He told his pastor later, "I don't know why they arrested me and put me in jail. I don't understand it all. But I know that God was with me. And now I can still keep telling others about Jesus." He knew what he knew in his heart, and he clung to that.

Summer in Nohon

It was so good to have Lorraine come home, bringing her upbeat attitude with her. She played outside with her brothers nearly every day. Their favorite places were the swimming hole and the airstrip. She also loved taking care of Marie and teaching her new words and activities. Try as she might, Marie still wouldn't put her words into phrases and talk.

Lorraine had her own list of things she wanted to do at home that summer, "Mom, one thing I want to learn is how to bake and cook."

That was a tall order for only three months at home. We baked cookies first, then a cake; both were from scratch. Lorraine's first egg-cracking experience ended up a disaster, but who hasn't cracked an egg and dumped it on the floor, at some time or other? She was glad that the oven on my new kerosene stove actually registered the correct temperature with a thermometer set in the oven door.

Of course, the sibs, David and Jonathan, were skeptical of her baking. "Did Lorraine really bake it herself? Is it any good?"

It took some coaxing, but their sweet teeth won out, "Hey, this does taste good. Can we have more?"

Lorraine was pleased that her baking passed her brothers' taste test. She was proud of herself too, for baking and decorating her first batch of cookies without my help. I was more than willing to let her bake because then I didn't have to do it. Her crowning achievement that summer was an early birthday cake for her baby sister, Marie, whose real birthday was in September.

"Mom I want to make it in the shape of a heart. Can you show me how to cut it out?" Then she made powdered sugar frosting and decorated the cake, all on her own.

Another project was the little bamboo playhouse from the Hyatt boys outside in the yard. The house was up on stilts, about five feet by feet in size, with a thatch roof. It became a tea house when Lorraine took her play dishes and hosted tea parties, inviting Dan and me. The brothers came too, usually laughing and giggling their way through cookies and cool-aid, and then running off to play elsewhere. Dan and I couldn't get into her house without crawling up the narrow pole ladder and squeezing through the three and half foot high doorway. So we stood outside and Lorraine served us through a two foot wide window, instead. It was a fun little house and gave many hours of entertainment.

That summer we unpacked the book drum. Besides our old familiar read-aloud books, I had new titles in chapter books. Lorraine devoured them so fast that I worried about where I could get more for her to read. David and Jonathan caught the fever and even asked her to read aloud to them. I was glad she had the books because it was the same old story in Nohon, no girls to play with. Auyu girls assumed their duties of food gathering, working the gardens, bringing in firewood, hauling water, and sibling sitting almost as soon as they could walk and talk. They didn't have time to play. I admired Lorraine for her acceptance of the situation, never complaining, and she didn't let it get her down. If she wasn't out with the boys, baking in the kitchen, or watching Marie, she was reading a book, or two, or three.

Fresh Food

The local food supply was varied and more plenteous than in Agats. The people brought whatever they had right to our door. They carried a bamboo pole between two people with pieces of fresh wild pork strung across it. The purchaser went out and chose what he wanted. I couldn't believe the jungle hen eggs when I first saw them. They were three times the size of normal eggs, with a hard shell and viscous white inside. The villagers had skinny, free-roaming chickens too, and they sold the small eggs to us, if they found the nest. Other villages grew sweet potatoes and fruit such as: papaya, bananas, lemons and pineapples. There was also a long, thin green bean that I learned to cook. And we were introduced to lots of green leaves, like chard and Chinese greens, all of which had to be cooked. We rarely got any fresh-water fish. I'm sorry to say that I still couldn't bring myself to deal with a crocodile tail when it was offered. We continued to order our staples like rice, flour, sugar, salt, powdered milk and cooking oil from the MAF base in Sentani. And the highland veggie run came about once a month.

Marie liked all the fruit, but it didn't always agree with her. She sucked on lemons, which gives me goose bumps to even think about it. She loved bananas and papaya and I let her eat all she wanted, until I noticed she was having frequent bouts of diarrhea. One day she cried and fussed and wouldn't stop. When I changed her diaper, she not only had diarrhea, but her bottom was red and raw. This was more serious than a simple rash. I couldn't contact the doctor because he was gone. I was on my own.

First of all, I stopped the fresh fruit with the vitamin C content. Then I slathered zinc oxide all over her bottom. It helped some, but she cried every time I touched her. Would it be better if I let her air-dry? She loved the freedom of having her diaper off. Her older siblings thought the whole thing was hilarious, when they saw her exposed to the wind, and weather, and their view. Her skin was extremely white compared to the bare brown behinds of the Auyu babies that we saw every day. It took several weeks to get Marie all cleared up and healed, and the air-dry method proved a success.

Early in the summer, we heard that Uncle Don and Aunt Carol were officially cleared to move to Nohon to supervise the village Bible School. Uncle Don would also evangelize in the villages around us. That kind of work was right up his alley. He couldn't go anywhere without telling someone about Jesus. There was an empty Bible School teacher's house across the airstrip from us. It needed repairs and that was one job Dan didn't mind doing. We were all eager to have them come. Dan checked regularly on the workers and made sure they were doing a good job and the house was ready by the time the Spencers arrived by river boat.

While Dan and I got into the routine of living, station work and language study, the three older kids had adventures of their own. The Hyatt boys left their old bicycle for David and Jonathan. They weren't satisfied until they practiced, fell, and practiced some more, and finally learned to ride that rickety bike up and down the airstrip. One day, they proudly called Dan and me to show us their riding skills, without falling over, of course. After their success with the old bike, they felt justified in asking us to order new bicycles for them to ride when they went to Sentani School for first grade in August.

The natural pool out in the jungle seemed to beckon the kids in the heat of the afternoon. They weren't allowed to go and swim by themselves because I couldn't see them. No problem, there were plenty of volunteers from village friends to go with them. Dan and I took Marie out and got her feet wet, which she loved. Jonathan had really progressed in diving. David struggled with getting his arms and legs coordinated in swimming, but that problem disappeared as he practiced. Lorraine was a natural in the water. I felt more secure, knowing that if the kids ever fall overboard out I the boat with Dan, they would stay afloat long enough to get scooped out of the water, before a crocodile got them. Only a mother would consider all those "what ifs" of living on the south coast. My children certainly had no thoughts of any dangers.

One day, the kids were out playing and came home barely eating anything for dinner. I knew something was up. I persisted in my questions, and finally they came clean.

"Okay, Mom, we went out to the edge of the big garden, by the jungle, with some of our friends. They were teaching us how to shoot their bows and arrows, and we saw a *tikus (tee-koos)*. We shot it and then the other kids started a fire and burned the fur off. But don't worry, Mom, after they skinned it, we took it down to the stream and washed it real good. Then we cooked it again, right over the fire. We divided it, and ate it, and it was really good."

So, what was my problem with them not being hungry? Well, *tikus* is Indonesian for a rat. My kids killed, cooked, and ate a rat! Granted it was not an ordinary rat; referred to in higher class terms, it was a rodent. They're larger, with more meat on their bones. Talk about going native. I warned the kids about eating from the people with dirty hands, poor water, germs and everything else. But I guess this was something they just couldn't pass up.

The roast jungle rat was only the beginning of the kids feasting on native food. As I recall, there were rumors of roasting big, shiny green beetles over the fire, locusts and grubs, which are nothing but large sago-palm maggots, were also thrown into the fire and blackened to a delicious crispiness. There might have been a snake too, possibly a python?

Somewhere along in there, they also ran into a poisonous snake, "We were playing in an empty teacher's house with our friends, and we saw this snake. One of the boys chopped its head off with his machete."

Thankfully, they didn't try to eat that one. They strung it over a pole instead, and brought their trophy home for us and the rest of the village *oooh* and *aaah* over. I'm thinking it's probably just as well I didn't find out about all the other things that went on in the jungle that summer.

Village Dancers - Nohon

Barbara and teenage Auyu boy with leprosy - Nohon

Jonathan, David, Lorraine and friends with snake - Nohon

Chapter Eight: "How about a story?"

Tadpole Tales

Life was never dull, or boring, for any of us in the jungle. Shortly after the jungle rat episode, we had another happening, which I wrote to the Grandmas:

"The frogs in this end of the world not only croak, but they go 'croak-groak' in a voice twice the volume of our normal frog population in the good ole US of A. We always hear them starting up at nightfall out in the jungle. A few weeks ago, we heard them closer to our house. One night it was so bad that Dan got out of bed and went in search of an especially loud and obnoxious one, making such a racket, we couldn't sleep. Nope, he couldn't find it, and that frog continued singing solo. Our house helpers were in their little house next to us and they weren't sleeping either. Seruwi also went out frog hunting, in the dark of darkness, but with no success.

A few days after their nocturnal searches, I went to get a drink from the faucet. Fortunately, I glanced in the glass as I was about to take a sip. There were little black specks swirling around. They looked like little bugs with tails, and they were wiggling. Sometimes we have gotten mosquito larvae in our water, but this was different.

I called Dan and after consideration, he gave his verdict. 'I think they look like tadpoles!' I checked the lemonade I had just made, and sure enough they were swimming around in it too. Ah, ha!

Seruwi went out back and climbed up to the rain barrels under the eaves, and lifted the huge aluminum lid up. There sat our nightly entertainer. He dumped the frog on the ground and we haven't had a concert since. I don't know how the frog got in there because the coverings on the water drums are heavy, and flush with the rim. Maybe he was croaking to get out, since his youngsters had hatched. Heavy rains came after that, and I think most of the tadpoles are now out of the water. We drank the water anyway, only strained it first. I guess that's part of the adventures, or hazards, of living out in the jungle."

The next thing was Lorraine's eighth birthday. We knew a couple of packages were coming via boat mail from our churches, but alas, they hadn't arrived yet. Cards from the grandmas and supporters had come in the mail sac and were stashed away. I dug deep into our storage drums and found a pair of shoes for school, how exciting is that! There was also a rattan set of doll furniture that Lorraine could take to school with her. On her day, I baked a cake and whipped up the recipe for sweetened condensed milk ice cream with the hand egg-beater. A special treat was several cans of soda from Sentani. Soda was a rarity then.

I felt bad that it was so little, but Lorraine was again accepting and philosophical, "Oh, don't worry, Mom. I'll just have another birthday when the packages come." How true, she happily opened her packages in August and in September.

Packages from the US were fun and exciting. They took months to arrive via boat. It was also risky because customs often inspected them and things disappeared before being delivered to us. I urged people to wrap the box in cotton cloth and sew it shut, which kept them safe from sticky fingers. As much fun as it was to get them, I rarely asked for the extra things because of the uncertainty of receiving them.

The boys continued to monitor Marie's development and their latest worry was that she didn't talk yet. I found out the reason for the anxiety when Jonathan asked, "Mom, what language is Marie gonna talk? What if we don't understand her? It might be all mixed up."

What a relief it was when she finally uttered her first word, "bye-bye". She remained sparing with her words; two favorites were ma-ma and cookies. Otherwise, she preferred jabbering to talking and everybody knew what she wanted anyway. She eventually spoke in the three languages she heard every day.

Besides not talking, Marie wasn't walking yet, either. At ten months, she wouldn't even try. Why walk, when she loved being carried around on Pu'me's shoulders. The boys were relieved and cheered her on, when they saw her pull herself up to stand beside a chair. "Oh, look, she's going to walk, just not yet."

Dan gets sick

About that time, Dan got an ear infection or a bug bite in his ear canal. I wasn't sure which one. It was extremely painful and eardrops weren't helping. Then his ear canal swelled shut, with just a little drainage seeping out. I tried penicillin shots, and called a mission doctor on the two-way radio. The pressure inside the ear canal was building up and affecting Dan's hearing. Of course, he was sure he would be deaf for the rest of his life.

With no improvement, the doctor told him to come and get it

checked out. That meant calling for an airplane, and Dan flew to Mulia in the highlands. Doctor Jerry Powell put a drain in the canal and gave him stronger antibiotics. It was over a week before the swelling went down and Dan could come home. We still aren't sure of what caused it, possibly a reaction to a bug bite? It never occurred again.

Meanwhile, Aunt Carol and Uncle Don arrived just as Dan was leaving to go to the doctor. The kids and I were glad to see them again.

David put in his vote, "I'm reallly glad Aunt Carol can come live here, Mom. Remember how she always let us lick the bowl when she was baking in Agats?" I'm sure my kids anticipated being right there to lick a few more bowls from Aunt Carol in Nohon too.

As soon as they settled into their little native house, Uncle Don fired up the motor boat and went out for several days and nights to get acquainted in the villages.

It's a Party

With the men gone, Aunt Carol and I were left alone on the station with the kids. It was okay, we weren't afraid or anything. But we were surprised because that was the week the village decided to have an all night party. Why then? What for? We had no idea, and we didn't have enough of the language to ask for details.

We found out about the festivities when several men came to the house in the afternoon with a request, "Can we borrow a lamp for tonight? We are going to have a dance. You are asked to come."

"*Ma'af,* I am very sorry, but I can't loan one to you. One of my lamps is broken. I have only one for my house. But we will come to watch the dancing." I regretted that I had to tell no. I was sorry I couldn't let them have an extra lamp, but I needed mine for the kids in the house.

Village life was bustling with noise and activity all that day. We could hear them calling and yelling to each other. In the late afternoon, Carol and I decided to go down and see what was going on before it got dark. I carried Marie and we all trooped down the path to have a look. Marie quit jabbering and became shy at all the noise and drama. Lorraine, David and Jonathan were wide-eyed, hardly speaking a word, as we watched everything and everybody. Their questions came later, when we got back home.

I noticed right away that it was a colorful costume gala, a dress up affair. The men and women painted and decorated their faces and their bare chests with white *sago* powder and another red powder from a jungle fruit. The men stuck gloriously brilliant feathers from the Birds of Paradise, cockatoos, and other jungle birds in their cork-screw curls. They kept their decorative nose bones and ear pieces in. Some were wearing dog-teeth, or other animal teeth, necklaces. Most of the men had draw-string tie shorts on, but a few wore only the shell penis coverings. The women made circular halos out of dried, rustling leaves and they had on several grass skirts, which bushed out, and swished to and fro as they danced. Women also wore nose pieces of bone. Carol and I saw a couple of women wearing old cast-off bras, which also looked fashionably chic.

The drums beat continuously. The men beat on them with their fingers held together, palms resting on the outside edge. They appeared to be made of decoratively carved hollowed out tree trunks. Crocodile hide or pig skin covered the ends. One man danced with a plastic bag over his head and sang himself into a frenzy until he suddenly passed out in the middle of the circle of dancers. No one paid any attention to him.

When I asked if someone shouldn't help him, they said, "Oh, no, he gets that way from singing." I kept my eye on him and it wasn't long before he recovered, stood up, and returned to the party.

The women were the main dancers, forming a circle and facing each other to the inside, while they rhythmically jumped up and down and around, chanting and singing. The beat of the drums kept them on track and at a steady pace. I was concerned about the reaction of my kids to the bouncing breasts of the women within the dance circle.

But their only remark was, "How come they don't have any tops on?"

I guess I was the one who was more embarrassed than my kids.

While we were there we didn't see any eating or drinking. That must have come later? We don't know because we only stayed until dark. Then we walked Aunt Carol across the airstrip and followed the beam of our flashlights up the path to the lamp light of our house. We actually slept okay because the steady drumbeat lulled us to sleep. The partying kept up all through the night and they quit around six the next morning.

The incessant drum beat, with the dancing and singing, was just like what you see portrayed in the movies. The big difference from a Hollywood story was that the Auyu weren't going to war, nor were they putting a huge cooking pot on to boil. Their old ways of head hunting, head shrinking, and cannibalism, at least in the village of Nohon, were over because the gospel came into their land and hearts. We never did find out what the occasion was for the dance party, but they enjoyed it and we awoke to an exceptionally quiet village in the morning.

It was also during the week that Dan was gone for his ear problem that news came on the radio about another MAF plane accident, but no one was hurt and the plane wasn't seriously damaged either. The pilot experienced engine trouble and was forced to make an emergency landing on a sandy river bank, not too far out of Sentani. They were able to go in, get the plane out, and fly it back to base for repairs. Even though the accident was not life-threatening, it still gripped my heart and my stomach, as I was reminded again of the uncertainty of life in Papua. This time the kids and I prayed, thanking God for taking care of the pilot and the airplane. The kids prayed nearly every day for the planes, like they were people. I guess the call letters made them sort of human, when you come to think of it: Papa Mike, Charlie Papa, Papa Lima.

I feel another story coming on. This one happened while Dan was gone. What an eventful week that was.

Agata wants you now

Agata and Bono were students at the Bible School and they were from Nohon. Agata had already lost two babies, both died as newborns. When she knew she was pregnant again, she came to me about her fears in losing another baby.

She understood Indonesian and I re-assured her, "Yes, I would like to help you. But I will call our doctor and ask his advice too. I need you to promise that you will follow what I tell you to do."

Both husband and wife agreed to allow me to help Agata when she started into labor. She came to the house several times for a blood pressure check and fetal heart rate and everything seemed normal.

Meanwhile, I cleaned out an empty student's house at the Bible School, which I planned to use for the delivery. Our mission doctor sent me extra meds for possible complications. I prepared a delivery pack and kept it handy for whenever. The Auyu usually went to the jungle to have their babies, but Bono promised me he would make sure Agata stayed in the village.

"Mama, Agata wants you now." It was early one evening, while

Dan was gone, and I heard a voice through our screen window.

By the time I collected my things and went across the airstrip, Agata was already at the empty house accompanied by two other village women. She was definitely in labor with regular contractions. The Auyu usually stand up to deliver, but I wasn't sure I could handle a dropping baby. She agreed to lie down on her back with her legs bent so I could help her. We prayed together and within the hour she delivered a beautiful little boy. Agata did all the work, I just stood there. It was a normal delivery, and when I checked the baby over, he was fine. I cleaned up and waited another hour to make sure everything was alright. The new momma got up and walked on home with her baby in her arms and the two friends at her side.

"Thank you, Lord, for helping me with my first delivery on the mission field. Thank you that it was so easy, and there were no complications. Please be with Agata and her new baby."

The two were doing fine until another problem surfaced. Uncle Don was starting Bible School and he came to tell me that Agata didn't want to move from their house in the village to the empty Bible School house she delivered in. The rule was that all students live in school housing, where they could study better and be away from the distractions of normal village life.

I saw her up by our house the day that school started, "Agata, why aren't you moved yet? All the other students are moved in already."

"Oh, Momma, *saya takut,* I'm afraid."

I asked a few more questions and found out that the old women of the village were scaring her. "The old women are telling me your baby will die if you live in that same house where he was born. The evil spirits will make him really sick. He will surely die."

Ah, so that's why the women have their babies out in the jungle, away from their homes. They're afraid of the evil spirits.

Bono and Agata were known as a Christian couple among the Auyu. In fact, Bono became one of the first graduates of the Nohon Bible School. Dan was back from the doctor by then, and he called for Bono to come and talk with him. I talked to Agata separately. As we talked together, Dan and I tried to encourage them to be good witnesses to the unbelievers who were watching. We reminded them that everyone wanted to see what they would do in this situation. But the village women kept putting pressure on Agata, and she was terrified that her baby would die. Her own mother was scaring her the most.

Dan and I talked it over with Uncle Don. There might be a solution to satisfy the old women and to make Agata feel better too. I gave them a bucket of water with disinfectant soap and a scrub brush. The disinfectant smelled strong and medicinal, which impressed the old ladies.

"Bono, take this bucket and go over and wash out the house, especially scrub the floor where Agata had her baby. Remember, this is not a magic formula to scare away spirits. It is like soap with medicine in it. It will wash the house from bugs that we cannot see."

They nodded agreement and seemed satisfied with the explanation. After washing and fumigating, Bono and Agata moved into the house with their baby. As far as I know, the old ladies quit heckling them. Finally, all was well.

Baby Clinic

That summer I also started a small project, a well-baby clinic. The main purpose was to show the mothers how to keep their babies clean and healthy. Babies were brought to me all the time with infected sores, especially on their heads. The mothers splashed water on the babies' bodies, not their heads. They were afraid of the soft spot and covered it with 'goop' and 'gunk' so they couldn't see it pulsating.

The first session, five mothers and babies came. The Auyu didn't have any taboos about me holding their children, and I was allowed to take each baby and bathe it in a little tub in front of the class. Demonstrating helped, since my vocabulary was so limited. They were various ages, one month to about ten months. Several were quiet, most of them cried, loud and long. It was okay though, the moms loved it, telling everyone which baby was theirs. Of course, the women already knew which baby was which. I gave each of the mothers a bar of soap and a small towel. It was hard to get soap and even a small piece of it was a treasure to them.

While bathing each one, I showed them how to hold the baby, bracing it across the back, supporting under the arms, and holding its head so it wouldn't slip into the water. I actually used soap to soak and gently clean off their crusty heads. That brought gasps from the audience. We talked about keeping the skin clean so that if the babies were bitten by flies or mosquitoes, the bites wouldn't get infected. The idea of bugs carrying infection was all new to them.

The class was well received, and the women were eager to learn about taking care of their babies. We met several more times during the summer, with the first group telling others to come. It was only a small start towards better hygiene and health for babies, and we were getting to know and trust each other, as well.

End of Summer

The month of August came before I was ready for it. It was also our one year anniversary of arriving in Irian Barat. Wow, the things that had happened in our lives and on our island. I thanked God that He kept us well and safe, and at the same time I couldn't believe that I was still there.

Another school year was about to begin, and this time David and Jonathan were going with Lorraine. It was hard enough telling Lorraine good-bye when she left for school in January. I didn't know if I was ready to let three of my four kids go now. I argued with myself that the boys were too little, not mature enough, and that they would not be able to take care of themselves without me around. Yet I got clothes out of barrels and Pu'me and I were sewing on name-tapes all summer long. I knew this day would come, just not so soon.

My feelings aside, David and Jonathan were getting more and more excited about school. They wanted to play with boys from America who came from their own peer group, which was only natural. Not that they weren't having a great time with village friends. But Jonathan especially was getting tired of being surrounded and the center of attention every time he went outside. "Oh, mom, the kids keep touching me and pulling my hair."

David didn't have as much of a problem because his hair was darker and he loved gabbing with any and all who crowded around. Lorraine was lonely for her girl friends and she was ready to go see them at school. It was me, I was the one who wasn't quite there yet.

The plan was for a float plane departure on the river because the airstrip hump removal was still a work in progress. It took a long time for the gunny sack brigade to haul sand away and fill in elsewhere. Dan and I talked it over and decided he would go with them for the first few days. As it turned out, it was a good plan because something else happened just before the kids had to leave, which leads me into one more missionary tale.

A Rotten Floorboard

More supplies came up river from Yawsakor and Dan was out on the boat helping to unload. He stepped on a weak board, and plunged his right leg through the floorboard, badly scraping his shin bone. I washed the blood off, bandaged it up, and thought nothing of it. But a few days later he developed a fever, then chills, followed by acute pain in that leg. The scrape on his shin felt hot and was a bright red color. I saw a distinct red line running up his leg to the groin area. Dan had blood poisoning a couple of times as a young man, while working on the farm in Germany. We knew that's what he had again. I gave him a shot of penicillin and double dose of aspirin for the pain and to bring his fever down. It was after sundown and I couldn't call the doctor on the two-way radio until the next morning. We had to make do through the night by ourselves.

Other than a red, slightly swollen shin, it didn't seem so bad at first. But Dan gradually became more restless as the hours passed and he spiked a fever again. He became delirious and started talking nonsense. Then he thrashed from side to side in the bed, and I couldn't make him stay down by myself. I sent the kids across the airstrip with their flashlights to ask Uncle Don to come over and stay with us. As Dan's temperature increased, so did his restlessness. During the night, Uncle Don physically forced him to lie down, and then held him down on the bed. I decided to go ahead and give penicillin shots every four hours, plus aspirin. We tried putting cold washcloths on his forehead and wet packs on his leg. But he would not lie still, and he kept brushing the packs off.

The children could see and hear all that was going on. Lorraine helped out by taking Marie into her bed that night. Jonathan got scared and came crying, "Mommy, my leg hurts too."

It was a long night, but towards morning Dan gradually became calmer and his fever went down a little. He still had the telltale red line up his leg.

As soon as it was daylight, I called on the airplane channel to see if I could get in contact with the doctor. YES, he was on! We switched to the medical channel and I told my story. Dr. Ken, our TEAM mission doctor, was recently back from furlough. First of all, he calmed my fears, saying I had done the right things and there was nothing else I could have done. He ordered me to continue the penicillin shots, four times a day, for another few days. The wet packs were to be continued, and I was to give Dan a shot for pain from the station emergency box. The box contained prescription meds and were to be used only with a doctor's order. Dan felt better after the pain shot, but told me he also felt like a pin cushion from all the penicillin shots. Whatever, I was glad that he was alive and able to complain about it.

It was scary to see someone I love so sick, and then have to be the one to rationally decide what kind of treatment to give. As a nurse, I was supposed to know what to do. And I had my medical books to look things up. But when it's one of your own, it's hard to be objective and think clearly. I know the Lord helped me to at least act like a nurse and do what I needed to do for Dan that night. (But diagnosing, prescribing, and treating my own family was one of the hardest things I had to do on the mission field.)

Dan was laid up with his leg the last two weeks before the three older kids left for school. He could barely hobble, and the pain was much worse when he did try to walk. At one point I thought there might be a sliver of wood under the skin because the wound kept draining, and it wasn't healing as fast as I thought it should. Since Dan was already planning on going out to school with the kids, I called on the radio to see if he could go to one of the mission doctors while he was out there.

Did I mention that Marie chose the last week before her siblings left to get the measles? A number of babies and young children had come to the clinic with them. I knew something was up because Marie was fussy and crabby and ran a low-grade fever long before she broke out. After she got the spots, her fever went down and she was much happier. There were no worries about Lorraine, David, or Jonathan because Lorraine already suffered the measles in the US, and the boys were inoculated against measles.

Lorraine, David, and Jonathan go to Sentani School

Departure day for school was coming up fast. Aunt Carol and I collaborated, deciding to have a picnic party before the kids left. We made paper decorations. Uncle Don got in on the act and made mortar board hats with tassels for each one. On their last evening, we ate outside until the mosquitoes chased us back inside. For the rest of the evening, we played games and read aloud, one more chapter of a Sugar Creek Gang book. I gave each of the kids a little pillow that I stitched for them. Lorraine's was shaped like a flower, David's was a tiger, and Jonathan was a little bear.

"These are little prayer pillows that I made for you to put on your beds. They will remind you that Daddy and I are at home praying for you every day."

We lay down together until everyone was asleep. Then Dan and I went to bed ourselves, knowing what the dawning would bring.

The next morning the kids were up and ready to go at five AM. But Papa Lima, the call name for the float plane, was behind schedule. We ended up waiting all morning for the plane to come. Since it was a water landing, we walked down through the village to the riverbank and packed ourselves into the boat to go out to the big river. With a full load, the plane needed a longer take off space and the river by us wasn't straight enough. It took us about thirty minutes to get out there.

"Daddy, we've gotta go pee." Jonathan whispered. "Can you ask Uncle Don to stop somewhere?"

Don obligingly steered to shore and let them out near a native lean-to on the river bank. "Nobody look!" Both boys ran up the bank and came back to the boat in a matter of minutes with a swarm of huge mosquitoes buzzing behind them. Whoops, the next time we go out on the boat we'd better take repellant with us.

The plane came, they loaded luggage first and Dan and the kids climbed aboard. David almost cried, but I saw him suck it up. I didn't cry in front of them, but the tears came in buckets as I was sitting in the boat with the plane flying overhead. Marie, of course, couldn't figure out where everyone was going, but she knew it was a sad because I was crying. Uncle Don didn't say anything as he took Marie and me back to the Nohon landing.

(Years later, when the twins were leaving for college in America, David wrote me a letter. He talked about that first goodbye and going away to school.

"Dear Mom, I remember that first day that Jon and I left for Sentani School. Dad came with us, and I remember leaving you and Marie in the boat with Uncle Don. We flew over you when we left and I remember you crying in the boat. I was crying too. It was hard for me to understand why you were crying. I guess it's been hard to understand all along. But this last time now it isn't so hard to understand at all. Way back there in first grade you knew this day would come. So it hurt. I guess now I'm just realizing that this day has come too. Our family is no longer really a family in the sense that we were then. I love you, Davey"

I don't know how other moms took it when their kids were leaving, but it was hard for me every time. It never got any easier. I knew in my head that keeping my kids at home in the village was not a good situation. But that didn't help the empty feeling there was in the house and in my heart when they left. I knew that I could commit them to the Lord's care, but it still hurt. I literally cried out to God for His help every time my kids left. And God was there, watching over my children, His children, in the same way He watched over the unseen jungle creatures and the birds in the sky. Even with my tears, I knew that many in America were praying for me, for Dan, and for my kids as they went to boarding school. Some of those dear friends prayed for our family through the years, until God called them home to heaven.)

As soon as I got back to our house, I started putting away the kids' things. That became my habit whenever the kids left for school. It was therapeutic for me to get in their rooms and put things in order. And it was also a good idea to pack things away, especially the toys, keeping them dry and clean in the drums, out of sight from the visitors who came into our home.

Government people and school teachers often stopped by for this or that request. If they saw something that they liked sitting out, they had no hesitation in asking for it, our kids' toys included. It was a cultural thing because they thought we, as white people, could always get a new one of whatever they wanted. It became a balancing act for Dan and me to know when to give, and when to stall, and say no. If the toys were not seen, then there wasn't any problem.

A couple of days later, a message came over the radio from Sentani; Dan had gone to see Dr. Powell in the central highlands. The next day Dr. Jerry called to tell me that Dan's resistance was low from the ear infection he had earlier, and then he developed another infection from his fall through the deck on the boat. He still couldn't walk without pain. The good news was that the wound was healing and there was nothing inside, like a sliver. As a result of that accident, I became a dragon about treating minor sores right away, lest any family member develop a major infection overnight.

A week later, Dan came home and I went out in the boat with Uncle Don to meet his plane. This time I noticed how lush and green it was along the river. We saw several white egrets silently gliding over the treetops. There was a small village on a bend in the river, situated on the curve of a sand hill. It was lined with palm trees all along the banks and looked just like a picture postcard from some tropical isle. Wait a minute, I was living on a tropical isle and didn't even appreciate it.

There were a few mangrove tree clusters, with their tangled roots growing up out of the water. I always thought they looked kind of spooky, like gray tentacles reaching out to grab you. But out on the water, the jungle was not as dense and felt less oppressive. In fact, I thought it was a tranquil scene, quiet and peaceful, one where I could collect my thoughts and enjoy what God had made.

When the plane landed, the men unloaded and Dan was in the boat in a matter of minutes. As soon as the pilot took off, I couldn't wait any longer and wanted to know right away how my three kids were doing. Dan told me about settling them into their dorms. One day he went to class with the boys, but otherwise, he let them go on their own. They already made friends with the other boys, as well as a couple of the girls who were the same age. There were twelve or thirteen in the class and Mrs.Hazelett was their teacher.

(Several from that class went all through school together. Today there is a network of MKs who can contact each other at any moment, anywhere in the world. If something is going on, they let each other know. Those bonds of boarding school days continue to remain strong, and firm, and unbroken.)

After we got home and into the house, Dan reluctantly told me the "rest of the story," about leaving his three children at school. It was a traumatic parting. Early in the morning he went down to school to tell them goodbye, before school started. They hugged and kissed, but the parting was much harder for Jonathan. When Dan drove in the car to meet his plane, he looked in the mirror, and Jonathan was running after the car. He stopped the car and got out, but Mr. Hazelett, the school principal, was already there.

He took Jonathan in his arms, hugging him, and yelled at Dan, "Just go. Get back in the car and leave!"

"I was so mad at Mr. Hazelett for what he said. But I knew he was right. I couldn't prolong it and make it worse. So I got in the car and left without looking back. Driving off like that was the hardest thing I have ever done in my life. Leave my son behind, and leave him crying!"

Jonathan was safe in Mr. Hazelett's arms, and we knew he was in the arms of God too. But how could soft-hearted Dan turn away like that? We both believed it was the right thing to do, despite the heartache. What other options were there for schooling our kids at that time in history? Sentani School was a wonderful place for them to be.

But oh, how that separation hurt, gouging right into our hearts. I could hardly stand thinking about it as I heard Dan's story, and I wasn't there. We both cried tears, and cried out to God.

After such a terrible good-bye, Dan and I could hardly wait to hear from the kids. It was two whole weeks before we had a plane connection from Sentani. That was one of the longest waits of my life. The boys wrote through their appointed older brothers who put their words on paper. Jonathan talked about how he liked numbers in school. He was most excited about being the only one in first grade, besides David, who was allowed to swim and to dive off the diving board in the deep end of the pool. David was the teller of tales, and he told about the class being noisy for rest period, so they all had to go back and take a rest after school. That was, according to him, a great injustice. Lorraine and David both told on Jonathan, that he got the can of peanuts I sent and ate most of them before they knew they were there. That was also not fair. But the amazing thing was there was not one word from them about Dan's leaving and Jonathan chasing after his car.

Aunt Pat was the school nurse again that year, and she also included a short note to us, saying that Jonathan did fine after his dad left. I felt better hearing a good word from an adult who knew how hard it was for Dan to leave his kids. Once their letters came, I could envision happier times at school, rather than dwelling on the parting scene in my mind of our boy crying for his Daddy. We both knew that if our kids were not content and adjusted at school we couldn't do our work in the tribe, either. We would never leave them in school if we thought they were genuinely unhappy there.

David told us later, "It is hard when we first go. We always have at least one time when we feel really homesick and want to go home. But then we feel better, and we're okay."

(We entrusted our kids to their teachers and dorm parents who watched over them, taught them, loved them and mentored them well. The MKs had an even larger mission family outside of the school staff. The parents of the other kids, and many pilots and their families also came alongside to help when needed. How blessed our kids were for that greater family of aunts and uncles in the mission community, family that they remember and love to this day.

I know there's been a lot of debate about boarding school, with both sides having pros and cons. Missionaries worked in many tribal groups in Papua, places where it was isolated, sometimes hostile and dangerous, and physically and emotionally unhealthy. That's the way it was then. Our children learned to be independent and to trust God to take care of them when they were away from us. Thank you, God, for the mentors and counselors you sent along the way.)

Above, Jonathan, David, Lorraine to school
Below, Sentani Missionary Kids' School

Chapter Nine: "Are we moving again?"

Pirimid, our second Annual Conference

A couple weeks after Lorraine, David and Jonathan went to school in August 1969, Dan and I attended our second Annual Conference in the highlands.

Marie was all eyes looking at the crowd when we landed. She hid her face in my shoulder when we got out of the plane. The Danis must have looked more forbidding to her, with their glistening black skin and muscular bodies. Some wore their thick hair in string nets and others had bones through their noses, which made them look even more threatening. Dan carried Marie down to our cabin from the airstrip because she wouldn't let go of either one of us.

At eleven months, I was about the only one Marie would let hold her. What were we going to do at Conference? But she ended up loving the young Dani girl who watched her during meetings and afternoons. She was most happy when the girl carried her around on her shoulders outside. In the mornings, Marie played on the floor with toddlers in the conference nursery. She sat and watched more than she played because she had never been with kids her own age before.

A bug and a prayer

Another "bug" went around that year and a lot of us were sick, including me, of course. It was the usual vomiting with diarrhea, and I ended up staying in bed in our room near the outhouse, while Dan went to the meetings. The vomiting continued, so I took a pill for nausea, and a little later I felt the urgency to go to the bathroom. It was noon time and everybody was in the dining hall. When I got out there, I started to feel dizzy and light-headed, and my hands felt numb and cramped up. I must have fainted. Out of my fog, Aunt Pat Fillmore appeared from somewhere and she sat me down, or was it up? She asked for help from the two Dani men who were tending the hot water fire nearby, but when they couldn't understand her, she left me and ran off to find Dan.

The door to the outhouse was wide open and the Dani men by the fire could see that I was sick. They came over to the door and I heard them jabbering away. One of them stepped in and put his hands on my head and began praying in Dani. He didn't know what to do otherwise, but he prayed. As disembodied as I felt, I realized what he was doing and thanked God for him in my heart. By then, Dan came running with someone else and they carried me to our cabin. I've never forgotten that experience of having those Dani men, naked savages as the world would call them, pray for me. They believed God and knew He would help me. How wonderful for me to be the recipient of their faith and trust in the Lord.

Change of Direction

Little did we expect it, but we were singled out for another life-changing move at Conference. The Council interviewed us and asked for our agreement. The Field reassigned Dan and me to the Bird's Head station of Anggi to begin a translation ministry there among the Manikion tribe, now called the Sougb. The placement was effective immediately after our conference, as soon as we could get there.

Anggi station was where we were originally assigned, but because of the tribal rebellion and fighting against the Indonesian government our first visa application was refused. Our second request for a visa was granted on the basis that we go to work in a south coast location. We thought that maybe someday, in the distant future, we might be allowed to go the mountains, but certainly not in our first term.

The reason for the about face of our field council was that the missionaries at Anggi, Hank and Margie Bock, were returning to the states with serious medical issues. They were leaving in six weeks. The Bird's Head area tribes had recently signed a peace agreement with the government. But the churches of the three tribes the mission worked in were scattered, and some were closed. With the peace settlement, the missionaries were trying to rebuild the churches.

The Field believed it was vital to keep Anggi station open. A few years before our arrival in West Irian, the Sougb people turned, en masse, and threw away their *fetishes,* and other symbols of witchcraft to indicate they wanted to follow Jesus. Then the rebellion against the Indonesian government erupted and many left their churches and joined the rebels. A few of the church leaders were trying to gather the people back together, but they were new believers and they needed a missionary to help them.

Another problem at Anggi was that the Indonesian military was still occupying the area, with a small post set up at the lower end of the airstrip. The local people were afraid, and many of them were living out in the rain forests near their jungle gardens. It was still a volatile situation, which made it all the more important to have the station occupied to help maintain the peace and regain stability in the tribe. Dan and I were the only ones available who could move to Anggi immediately.

Hank Bock told us one interesting thing, "The Sougb people have prayed for you, by name, ever since you applied for a visa that first time. They haven't given up praying that you would be allowed to come to them."

In a way, that was a word of confirmation that God might be directing us to go to Anggi sooner, rather than later.

It was unsettling for me to think about another move, especially since we had only been in Nohon four months, and we moved from Agats before that. My thoughts and feelings were mixed. We accepted the field placing us on the south coast with the Auyu tribe to learn their language and translate the Bible for them. I felt good setting up the medical work there and I liked working with Aunt Carol and Uncle Don. Now, suddenly, all that was changed and we were to transfer to Anggi, away from the jungle and into the mountains?

However, we couldn't move until the central government in Jakarta gave a stamped letter of permission because Anggi was still a restricted area. The inter-mission director had recently visited Irian Barat and told our field leaders that restrictions for missionaries in the Bird's Head were relaxing. After conference, the field council immediately submitted a formal letter of request for our relocation and approval was granted within a couple of weeks.

The rest of the conference remains a blur to me because my mind was in turmoil as I thought about packing and moving again before Christmas vacation, when the three kids would come home. My heart was divided, feeling guilty about leaving the Auyu people, and being glad at the same time about moving to a cooler climate.

Dan and I planned go to the Bird's Head after Conference for the normal first time station visits. Now the plan included that we stay in Anggi for a full week so the Bocks could orient us to the fractured ministry with the Sougb tribe. After that, we would go back to Nohon and pack. We set early December for our move to Anggi.

I wrote to my kids from Conference telling them about another move to Anggi. Their only mention of it was to ask, "Are we moving again? What's it like?"

Otherwise, their letters contained all the news from school. Dan and

I decided to wait and tell them more about the move when we went to see them later in the fall.

The Conference also reconfirmed Spencer's placement in Nohon. They would run the Bible School, work with the Auyu church, and do village evangelism. I felt bad that Aunt Carol and I would be miles north and south of each other. She would be alone at Nohon, and I would be alone at Anggi for over a year, until Aunt Pat was reassigned to the Sougb tribe.

Good-bye Nohon

With us leaving Nohon, it also meant that there was no other translator on the field to work in the Auyu language. The one saving factor for them was that the South Coast-ers had a better grasp of Indonesian than the mountain people. The few missionaries working with them were able to use simple Indonesian in their ministries over the years. Our mission never got the personnel needed for evangelism and translation in the south coast tribes. A few church leaders had opportunities for training and study in the Nohon Bible School and in other Indonesian speaking schools later on. The national Christians are the evangelists for the South Coast, even today, which is a good thing.

Packing up was bitter sweet. The *hotter* season was right then and we were totally exhausted after a long day of packing and doing other station duties as well. Sweat dripped off our bodies as we repacked the drums I had emptied a few months previously. It took several weeks, but finally everything was stored and we were ready, at least physically, for that final move to the north coast. We planned to stop and see our kids at school on the way.

Of course, I couldn't help but think about the advantages of moving to the mountains where the weather was fresher and cooler. But it was still an emotional time for me, especially when the Spencers began moving their things into our house. Life in Nohon was good, despite the heat and humidity. The Auyu people were winning their way into my heart. They were so disappointed when Dan told them we were going somewhere else. Their displeasure showed even more when they were reluctant to help us move our drums down to the river into the river boat.

(As I look back, I'm not sure I could have stayed on the south coast and lasted, physically or emotionally, for a lifetime. It took so much time and energy just to live and do daily chores. To this day, I greatly admire those of our missionary friends who spent their lives on a jungle station. They persevered with stamina and strength that I didn't begin to possess. I trusted God to help me, wherever He put me, and I was committed to do His will. But God knew me, and He is the one who moved us to Anggi. But I'm ahead of myself again.)

We left Nohon early one morning and the weather was beautiful. A clear day was welcome because we had flown in stormy weather several times already. I was beginning to dread flying, getting tense and fearful if there was the least little bump or dark cloud in the sky. My nervousness and anxiety about flying were developing into full blown panic attacks, pressing hard at my heart and making it hard to breathe. One time I nearly fainted when I got out of the airplane after a bumpy flight.

The fear and panic increased, until one day I begged and cried out in prayer, "Oh, Lord, I can't do this anymore. I can't stay here and be afraid every time I get on an airplane. Even the pilot knows when there is fear in the plane. Please Lord, help me, I don't want to be afraid anymore."

It didn't happen immediately, but over time, God calmed my fears. I recited Bible verses for reassurance, and I eventually had peace in my heart, or a sort of truce, about flying. I wrote about my fears and anxieties to a couple trusted friends in the US, and they prayed long and hard for me, too. But on the day we flew out of Nohon, I was just thankful it was a smooth flight and we were going to see our kids.

When we arrived at the school, I think the kids were glad to see us. I say that because I recorded in my journal that Jonathan hid when he first saw us. David cried. Lorraine ran up and hugged us. I guess we all had plenty of emotions to go around that first time we visited the three of them at school. From August to November was a long three and a half months since they left Nohon. Marie was the one who was spontaneously delighted and excited to see the kids as she squealed and gabbed away to them in some unkown tongue. It was all of ten minutes before the three big kids were back to their normal selves. Everyone started talking at once, telling Dan and me about school, activities, and their friends.

Birthdays

We arrived just before David's and Jonathan's seventh birthday, which was on November sixth. Their birthday was the time we aimed for every fall for our vacation, as long as they were in Sentani School.

That year it was mid-week and the dorm parent, Aunt Wilma Ross, baked each of them a cake. They were allowed a full table in the school dining room and could ask whoever they wanted to sit with them. Of course they invited their first grade class to come and eat cake. One of their classmates, Steven Powell, had some balloons, and he gave them to the boys to help celebrate. In following years, we invited friends up to the Guest House for birthdays, and I made the ice cream and baked the cake myself.

The boys were never overly concerned with presents. The important thing was to have something new, and something to unwrap. That year I found a couple small toys, and I bought new shirts and shorts in the MAF trade store. The clothes from MAF were what the missionaries bought to use as trade items for the tribes' people. But some of them were nice enough for the boys to wear at school. My mom also sent them small packages of birthday and Christmas gifts those first few years. Birthday cards from supporting churches usually came in time for the actual birthday, which was nice.

(Lorraine always missed celebrating her birthday with friends at school because she was born in June when it was summer vacation. She lucked out in another way though by celebrating several of her birthdays around the world: Germany, India, Thailand and Papua. Our furloughs usually started in June and she benefited from travels to other places in the world.)

The main story from the boys that first semester was all about the spray caterpillars that hatched in great numbers in October. They inhabited the big tree beside the first grade classroom. David could hardly wait to tell on his brother, "Mom, Jonny got sprayed by the caterpillars. He turned red all over, with huge hives. He was itching and scratching a lot too. Aunt Pat sent him home from school to take a shower, and put calamine lotion all over his body. He gets to go home and shower every time. Aunt Pat says Jonny's was the worst of all the kids."

Jonathan proudly bore the admiration of his school friends in David's telling of his "Horrendous Hives" story. The school finally had to cut the tree down, which was sad. It was a giant of a tree, spreading its shade over the entire central section of the school yard.

Marie took a notion to start walking just before we left Nohon. Her siblings were delighted to see her toddling around; or should I say running? She no longer wanted to be carried, there was too much to do. The kids also tried to get her to say the few words she knew because they loved the way she pronounced them. Of course, she wouldn't open her mouth to say one thing, when she knew they wanted her to talk. She was definitely a native girl, going barefoot and peeling her clothes off if she was hot. The three older kids were delighted with her antics and waited to see what she would do next.

The school swimming pool was a big attraction for all the kids. We went down nearly every afternoon. I watched Marie closely, or else she would jump right in and come up sputtering. Dan was finally elected to hang on to her because she wiggled and squiggled herself out of my arms every time. At the beach, she was fearless too, heading straight for the waves and never looking back.

Honk Kong Flu

That semester was also the semester of the Hong Kong flu. There were sixteen out of 120 kids with flu, while we were there. In fact, when our flight to Anggi was delayed, Harold Catto, the head of the C&MA mission, asked if Dan and I could help the house parents out for a few days because they were also sick. So Dan and I moved from our little Quonset hut by the pool up to the girls' dorm wing and slept in one of their rooms. We ended up staying an extra week until the house parents were back on their feet again.

Our kids were excited to have us as house parents for those days. And Marie was thrilled about the move to the girls' dorm. There was so much to see and grab in their rooms, although I tried to keep an eye on her so that she didn't take things. She ran around enjoying the company of everyone and I had to go find her when it was bed time.

Aunt Pat was busy as school nurse, keeping fevers down from those who were sick. She gave lots of sponge baths that week. David was the one who got sick in our family; he had vomiting and a high fever, which I recorded at 104 degrees F.

"Sorry Davey, but I have to sponge you down again. Your fever is too high."

They moved all the sick kids to one end of the dorm near Aunt Pat, where she could watch them. The mission's office radioed for another nurse to come out and help. Dr. Ken Dresser labeled it the Hong Kong flu, and everyone who hadn't been sick yet was to get a flu shot. I remember the sight of all the MKs lined up outside the clinic. Most of them sucked it up and acted brave in front of their friends.

Little sister Marie was another story. She was also included in the shot brigade and she cried, loudly. Her shot didn't do much good because she came down with the flu later in the week. In fact she was sick right up to the time we had to leave Sentani and go up to the Bird's Head. I took the flu vaccine in a thermos for the missionaries in Manokwari, when we left.

Besides the flu, the kids acquired another tropical problem that semester. Lorraine and David tested positive for amoeba. We can't figure out why Jonathan didn't get a positive report too. It was their first time, but not last, with parasites in their systems. (In fact, on furlough, when we had to do those awful stool exams, if any two of us tested positive, the doctor figured we all had it and ordered that we all take the cure. Fortunately, none of my kids were ever seriously sick from the bugs, or from the cure! We jokingly counted it as a badge of honor from living in the tropics. Dan, on the other hand, has struggled with amoeba and intestinal upsets all of his life, on the mission field and at home in the US, as well.)

After our extra week in Sentani at the dorm, the good-byes to my three kids were not nearly as emotionally traumatic for me as when I had to leave Lorraine alone in school. For one thing, I knew the three were together. This time I felt less guilty, the kids seemed to really like school and were happy with their new friends. It was also late in the semester, and Christmas vacation was in a few weeks.

Flight to the Bird's Head

Dan, Marie, and I, flew to Manokwari, the coastal town in the Bird's Head, which was the take-off station for interior flying. The TEAM Bible School was located in the Sowi area, near the airfield, outside of Manokwari. We stayed in a cement block house, waiting for our flight to Anggi in a couple of days. Some of our outfit drums were already there, and Dan went to the storage barn to prioritize which ones were to go into Anggi first. I wasn't much help with lining up the drums because they were heavy to move.

Worse still, it was my turn to come down with the flu that everyone in Sentani was getting. I went to bed and stayed there for several days, not caring whether I lived or died. The few missionaries who dared to come and visit were barely acknowledged by me. I ran a high fever and then sweat it out, but it was so hot outside that I couldn't tell much difference, even after my fever broke. The memories of my first sights and sounds of Manokwari remain hazy to this day. My journal pages remain blank too.

Since I was incapacitated, Dan went by himself, again, to check in with the local government officials. He took our paperwork to the district immigration offices on the island of Biak, which was our first port of entry to Papua. The trip required a flight across the bay, but Dan was able to go and come back, after an overnight with our friends, the Hanas. The officials in Biak said our permits had not yet arrived from Jakarta, but all was okay otherwise. Dan left a bunch of passport pictures with them so they could process the forms when they arrived from Jakarta. We were both thankful they didn't require him to come back again when all the forms were in hand.

After the delay from my sickness, the plane was finally coming up from the MAF base at Nabire, which was farther south, down the coast from Manokwari. I was still tired and weak, but it was time to look forward and exert my energies on getting to Anggi. I didn't have that much time to unpack and set up house before the kids came home for Christmas. Flexible, elastic, stretchable, adaptable, that describes us in those early days.

Anggi Station

Chapter Ten: "What's her name?"

The flight into Anggi signaled our third move in less than a year's time. We didn't know it then, but this one would be for the rest of our Papuan lifetime. It was Thanksgiving Day, 1969, when we three flew on a Mission Aviation Fellowship Cessna airplane to Sururei Village, at Anggi Lake.

The View

It was a twenty-five minute flight and we flew the scenic route at sunrise. The plane climbed up the coastal side of the ranges, without a ripple of wind, and we picked our way through huge cottonball clouds that were scattered on the mountains tops. There were dense forests on the topside of the Arfak Range, and below us were the mission houses of Minyambou, beside the grass airstrip. Several Hatam villages stretched along one side of the airstrip in the narrow valley. Individual thatched roof houses were nearly hidden from view in the trees on the mountainsides. We flew through what looked like a skyway between two ridges, with the clouds ballooning up on the mountain tops on either side. It was like going through a tunnel, and at the far end was the sparkle of water from Anggi Lake.

As we neared the water, a great plain spread out below us. A number of villages were scattered in tall grasses and marshes. Several streams glistened in the sunlight, meandering their way out to the lake. We flew lower and glided over the end of the five-mile long lake, which was as smooth as mirrored glass. The water reflected the forested mountains so well that there was little difference between reality and the image. The black shadow of our little Cessna looked like a great, silent bird with outstretched wings, flying along the shoreline.

We banked to the right, and climbing up and over another mountain, a great circular valley opened up, showing patches of gardens scattered everywhere. Directly under us was an airstrip with Sururei village lined up along one side. About half way up the airstrip was a fenced in section surrounding the shining aluminum roofs of the mission buildings. Near the bottom of the airstrip, on the opposite side of the village, we saw several tents, which belonged to the Indonesian military group stationed there. Miniature people were running from all directions to the grass airstrip.

We circled round, soaring out and over the lake once more. The pilot lined up for landing and gradually lowering altitude, we flew straight in and landed. The prop sputtered to a stop right outside the front gate of our new home. Talk about a door to door delivery. Were we there yet? Yes, NOW we had *arrived at our final destination, all ready to* stay.

The large group of people gathered at the edge of the airstrip hung back, murmuring in the Sougb language, of which we didn't understand one word. Pastor Baysee came out to the airplane and welcomed us in Indonesian, *"Selamat datang, nama saya Gembala Baysee, welcome, my name is Pastor Baysee."*

The soldiers, with loaded rifles slung across their backs, came up from their encampment and boldly walked out to the airplane. They knew we were coming from military authorities in Manokwari, who passed along word of our arrival to the group at Anggi. Dan politely greeted each one of these men with a *selamat* and a handshake. Then he turned back to help the pilot unload the airplane.

The Sougb people overcame their reticence of mingling with the soldiers and approached the plane to grab suitcases and boxes, and bring them inside the fence for us. Marie had her face buried in my shoulder, suddenly shy. Dan followed us with the key and opened the padlock to our corrugated aluminum house. I went inside with Marie to receive our luggage and supplies, hoping to sort everything into piles on the cement floor as it came in the kitchen door.

Dan went back to finish unloading outside and waved the plane off. Before coming into the house, he made the compulsory rounds of shaking hands and greeting the Sougb people who were by then eagerly crowding closer to welcome him. The military guard ambled back down the airstrip to their tents, apparently realizing that we didn't pose any kind of threat.

Home at Anggi

My most immediate need was to set up our kitchen, so we could eat. The Bocks sold their household things and we had dishes, silverware, and pans from them, already stored away in the cupboards. Our food staples came in with us, and Dan asked the crowd if anyone had potatoes or vegetables to bring to us. The wood box outside the kitchen door was full of wood. The basics were there, ready to start up housekeeping.

There was a small kerosene refrigerator, with narrow freezer, which ran across the top of the fridge. The kitchen sink was hooked up via plastic pipe to the aluminum rainwater tank under the eaves behind the house. The water was strained as it ran off the roof, catching fallen leaves, but that was about it. It was safe to drink directly from the tap.

I managed to start a fire in the cast-iron wood burning stove, despite the initial smoke wafting into the kitchen. I lit the kerosene soaked kindling sticks first, the wood burst into flame, and with a poof the smoke ran up the chimney. What a wonderful stove. It was great heating up the topside for cooking and the oven for baking, both at the same time. The oven on the woodstove lacked a temperature gauge, but I guessed at it, and if I kept the fires going steadily, everything baked evenly.

After setting up the kitchen, I unpacked suitcases and started on the four priority outfit drums that were flown in before our arrival. I still felt weak from my recent bout with the flu. But the higher altitude and cooler climate kicked in as soon as we landed and I was feeling more energetic. About half of our stuff was over 500 miles away in Nohon and it would be a while before all of it was delivered to Anggi. One of the first things I dug out was our Christmas decorations because December was upon us, and my kids were coming in less than three weeks.

When we moved from Nohon to Anggi, we decided to let our househelp go back home to their highland village. As a result, those first months, Dan and I did all the housework, including laundry. We discovered that the art of living can take all of your time, if you let it. I eventually got another couple to help me because I wanted to do something else besides housework.

Dan scrambled to get the kids' room ready. We bought two camp cots from the Bocks for the boys. The plan was to make Lorraine a bed out of scrap lumber, but hammer and saw were new to Dan. He quickly learned that a diagram on paper didn't always work out in practice. I'm happy to say that his carpentry greatly improved over the years. The bedroom space was only about ten feet by ten feet, and so we lined the beds up side by side.

I sewed spreads on the treadle sewing machine that Margie Bock left for me. The treadle was old, but new to me, and I learned to sew quite well on it. I dug deep in our drums and found sweaters, long pants, warm pajamas and put them in the storage cupboard in the kids' room. It was ready.

Of course, there were a couple of problems in setting up the house. We later learned to expect difficulties, if not disasters, every time we went away and came back to our station. Something or other always broke down or wouldn't work, when it was perfectly fine before we left. Our arrival at Anggi was no exception. To start with, the battery for our two-way radio for air traffic and contacting other stations was dead. We didn't have a radio until the kids came home from school, which meant no contact with fellow missionaries. Nor did we have a way to listen to world news; it was total isolation from all that was familiar.

Dan sent a note over the trail with a couple men to the Minyambou station, telling them our radio was out, would they please send back information about when a plane might be coming. With the radio out, it meant that we wouldn't be able to give weather conditions when the plane did come. That was also part of our job, to give the station weather report, when the plane was due. I'm the one who felt the isolation more, but we were very busy and that helped.

Not Again!

In the process of cleaning our house, I made a disconcerting discovery and I immediately called for Dan to come, "Look at this rat dirt. I should have known. We have rats in this house too!"

Rats; a long-tailed rodent, resembling, but larger than, a mouse. I engaged in battle with those pests in Sentani, Agats, Nohon and now in Anggi. It's not that I'm afraid of them. Well, I am, a little. But it was also the idea of running into one in the middle of the night, --a dark, whiskery creature, sneaking around in the shadows, running around over-head, or knocking things down in my cupboards and making a racket.

Dan got out the rat catchers, which were a huge version of mouse traps, and set a couple in our pantry. We soon found out that our rats were not the common western variety because they wouldn't eat our pieces of dried bread, or our peanut butter, or our canned cheese. No, they had tribal taste buds preferring sweet potato, or a piece of pig fat, according to the wisdom of a Sougb person who Dan asked. Talk about native taste buds.

"Dan, please leave a *pelita (pe-lee-ta),* a little kerosene lamp, lit in our bedroom and out in the kitchen. I want the one in the living room on too. Maybe the light will scare the rats away. At least I won't be worried about running into one in the dark."

The rats were hard to catch, even with a special menu to choose from. I heard them night after night running above my bed, overhead in the rafters. I had no problem waking Dan up to accompany me to the bathroom. Even with flashlights to show us the way, I wasn't taking any chances. Finally, we caught one. We heard the trap go "snap" in the night. I couldn't face it, wouldn't handle it, and didn't want to look at it either. One peek told me the body was about four inches long, with a tail that looked even longer.

I heard Dan in the early morning as he made the kitchen fire and then hollered out the door to a man on the airstrip, "We got a *tikus.* Where should I throw it?"

"Oh," the man yelled back, "You can give it to my daughter here."

I was up by then, and watched out our kitchen window as Dan gave it to the little girl. She joyfully danced around our yard, swinging her breakfast by the tail, before she took it home to roast over the fire. Talk about a double take. The Sougb people not only ate rats, but they ate just about any creature that had meat on its bones. The sight was enough shock to my senses.

Then Marie beckoned with her hand, "Mommy, kitty, kitty!" She was perched on my hip, looking out the window, when she saw the little girl and wanted to pet the dead rat.

A New Name

After helping me to set up the house, Dan was out and about with the people every day; making friends, listening and repeating Sougb phrases. I wanted to get out of the house too, but I struggled to make time for it. My days were full with cooking, housekeeping, and taking care of Marie. The temptation was to stay busy inside because I honestly was busy. Marie was unimpressed with my busy-ness and she begged to go outside every day. If we stepped outside the kitchen door, the people came flocking in from the airstrip. I know I wasn't the one they came to see. Marie was the main attraction. Everyone wanted to get near her. They were fascinated with her almost white hair, and reached out with their fresh-from-the-garden hands to stroke it. Marie didn't care, nor was she afraid. She just grinned and jabbered away to whoever was listening or watching. She loved the little kids who followed her around the yard.

As soon as the Sougb people saw her, they wanted to claim her as their own. They decided to adopt her by giving her a Sougb name. Of course, such a momentous decision required careful thought and more than a little bit of arguing among themselves.

Some wanted to call her *Dou-maria-Sururei,* which means "Maria-from-the-village-of-Sururei," where we lived.

But no, that name was not broad enough, nor big enough because they said, "All of the Sougb should claim her."

In the end, they chose *Dou-maria- anggiji*, which means "Maria-the-one-who-belongs-to-Anggi-Lakes". That name was more inclusive and satisfactory to everyone. (She is still referred to by that special name and they say she is one of them, belonging to the Sougb people.)

The Learning Bench

Whenever we were outside, the women and I played a sort of getting-to-know-you game. There was a pole bench out in the yard beside the house and, unless it rained, I went out to sit on it for a while in the afternoons and Sunday mornings after church services. The women came into the yard and sat next to me on the bench, while we watched Marie toddling around in the yard with a trail of kids behind her. The women chatted away and I could at least hear the language, if not understand it. I did catch a word now and then.

The women were very serious about "studying me," or "learning me," to talk Sougb, except I never got anywhere with their method. Someone would say a word or phrase, the others repeated it, then it was my turn, but I had no clue what I was saying. Usually one of the younger women in the group who knew a few words of Indonesian interpreted for me.

On Sundays, I took Marie to church across the fence from our house. But she was such a distraction that most of the time I had to bring her home. Everyone was looking at her, instead of focusing on the preaching. Dan did not tolerate anyone's toddler weeping, wailing, or otherwise talking during the service. So I spent a lot of time out on the bench waiting until church was over, while Marie played outside.

The more we sat together, the less shy my visitors on the bench were. They started asking personal questions.

"Did Dou-Maria drink breast milk when she was a newborn baby?"

"Does she still drink it?"

"Can she eat sweet potato?"

They were natural questions because Sougb women nurse their babies until the next one is coming, often for two to three years. Sweet potato, which the mother chews and then spits into the baby's mouth, is the first solid food introduced.

I answered in Indonesian, "Yes, I gave her breast milk when she was little baby, but she drinks from a cup now. She eats a little food if it is mushed up, but I don't chew it first, like you do."

I think they needed to know that we white women were like them, we nursed our babies just like they did. Maybe they felt safer asking me because I was a mother. Aunt Pat told me they never asked her anything like that.

Another afternoon while sitting on the learning seat, one of the women stroked my legs and pinched the calf, murmuring something that got a chuckle out of everybody. I immediately asked, "What did she say? Tell me, what was it?"

One lady reluctantly admitted, *"Nyonya ada kaki besar."*

Well, thanks a lot! I guess it was supposed to be a compliment. The translation, "Mrs. has fat legs." Maybe it wasn't a compliment to me, but it was to them. How come? The Sougb were hungry most of the time and they were all thin and skinny. Their idea was if you had money, you had enough to eat, and gained weight to prove it. Since we white-skins were definitely bigger than them, we must be rich. (I noticed in later years when a few Sougb had government jobs they ate rice, instead of sweet potatoes, and they took some kind of black market shots, maybe cortisone, to get fat. They wanted to impress their people that they had moved up in life.)

Marie and I were definitely bonding with the people. I noticed little red bites all around my waistline and wrists, and around the tops of my socks. And they itched. It was cooties! Like the Danis of Pit River, the Sougb also had people fleas and pet piglet fleas. They carried their little pigs around just like we would carry a puppy. With our arrival, the fleas merely changed residence and were living on us.

Once I noticed the bites, it wasn't long before I detected little red specs all over Marie's body too. And of course, Jonathan was the one of the older three who got totally bitten up when he came home from school. There wasn't much you could do about the fleas because they were hardy souls and they multiplied faster than rabbits, I believe. I often watched, fascinated, as a woman sat on the bench beside me and captured a jumping speck of a flea, and then crushed it dead between her two fingernails. I eventually learned to see the fleas and even annihilated one once in awhile. But that was rare. We white-skins learned to endure their presence, just like everybody else.

Anggi Station

When I told our kids about the move to Anggi they didn't show much curiosity. They took a third move in stride, "It's okay, mom, we can see everything when we get home for Christmas."

However, I waxed eloquent in my letter to the Grandmas:

"Anggi is 6,000 feet plus in altitude. You can look on a map and see two small lakes, near the town of Manokwari. The village of Sururei, where we live, is right on the edge of the biggest lake. It is a lot cooler than the coast and the swamps. The water is cold and deep, and the land on either end of the lake is marshy. There is only one area where we saw a sandy shoreline. On the rest of the lake there is hardly any shore, only rocks beside the water's edge and the mountains rise up out of the water. I doubt that the kids will want to swim in the lake for long because the water is so cold. The people are afraid of the water and none of them even know how to swim because they believe evil spirits live in the lake.

There is a grass airstrip which runs uphill, starting from just above the marsh area. The two mission houses are alongside of the strip, about halfway up. There are higher mountains all around, with the villages of Sururei, Sagwameba, and Kofo scattered at one end of the bowl shaped valley surrounding the airstrip. The scene makes me think of rural northern Minnesota with tall pine trees all around, and cabins nestled in the woods.

A reed fence surrounds our mission property. Right now, the yard is all overgrown with tall grass. We have enlisted some women to bring their machetes and cut it, and they can earn a little money. The buildings are made of corrugated aluminum, nailed onto tree pole frames. The houses are on cement slabs, not on piles like the south coast. Our house is divided in half with two small bedrooms on one side and a kitchen-living room combined on the other side. Out back are two storage sheds. One is for fire-wood, another is divided in two with a laundry room on one side and work-storage on the other.

The outhouse is up in the back yard. One of the first things on my list is adding an indoor toilet to the house. With aluminum walls and no insulation, it's drafty inside and listeners outside can easily hear all our conversation; good thing none of them speak English. I hope we can eventually put inside walls up to buffer the noise and block the draft. We have two wood-burning stoves; one is to cook on. The other one is a pot-bellied stove in the living room, and it will be warmer for Marie when she crawls around on the cement floors.

About the people, this is the tribe that we were originally assigned to. Then our visa was refused because of the rebellion of the tribes in this area. Peace has been negotiated, but there is a military encampment at the bottom of our airstrip, near the fresh water spring. The people are scattered around because they're afraid of the soldiers. I don't really like knowing they are down there with their guns, either. They enforce travel restrictions, and Dan can't go out to other villages like he wants to. But the church leaders promised they would come to Anggi for teaching.

Several years ago there was a great fetish movement among the tribes, where they burned their charms and witchcraft items, indicating they wanted to follow the Lord. But with the rebel movement, many broke away because of the pressures of the tribal culture. The Bocks, who just left because of illness, felt so bad to see them return to their old ways of magic, poisons, and witchcraft. Right now there are only a few churches meeting regularly. But the elders are trying to gather them together and restart teaching the scriptures. It won't be easy for us because we have to maintain our relationship with the military, and at the same time try to encourage the people to come back to their villages and to their churches."

The Sougb People

One of the first things we noticed about the Sougb was that they wore western dress and used fabric for loin cloths. This was totally different than the Dani, Asmat and Auyu, who used some form of natural dress, like grass skirts and gourd or shell penis sheaths. The Sougb were familiar with cloth as one of the two main elements for their bridal payment system. In generations past, trading ships reached the shores of Papua in search of the brilliant feathers of the Birds of Paradise for ladies' hats back in Europe. The Sougb traded feathers for colored cloth and glass beads, which were the second item used in payments and dowry settlements.

The other issue was that under Dutch rule, the Bird's Head area tribes were shamed and pressured into wearing clothes. When we arrived, nearly all of the adult people around the station wore at least one piece of clothing. The Sougb men dressed in ragged shorts and dirty tee shirts. The women wore the wrap-around sarong, which were introduced generations ago by Malaysian traders in ships. Men and women wore the loin cloths when they were out in their gardens or on the trail. The little kids ran around bare naked, or they wrapped a piece of cloth around their shoulders for warmth.

The Sougb were definitely dirtier than the south coast people because they rarely bathed. We met a few that I'm sure had never bathed in their lifetime. The climate was cool and windy, with the average rainfall of six feet a year. The mountain streams and the lake were too cold to bathe in. From earliest times, the people were afraid of the stagnant mountain pools and the lake water, believing the spirits dwelt in them. They walked around the ponds from a distance, and only ventured to the lake shores at risk of their lives, or so they thought. One advantage to not washing was that their pores remained closed and they kept warmer.

Beyond the dirt, their normal skin color was a dark reddish-brown. They had curly, wooly, black hair, but many of them had a reddish, almost blonde highlight in it. At first I thought the red coloring was from malnutrition, but I decided it was hereditary because it ran in clans. Some of the men wore their hair long and bushed out, with who knows what, most likely head lice or bed bugs, living in the mass on their heads. They had bamboo pick combs sticking out of their hair too. The women had different styles of little braids all over their heads. The Sougb weren't as big and muscular as the Dani people. Yet they looked healthier than the south coast people. I was glad to see that their teeth appeared whiter and there were no toothy, decaying grins from the adults or children, unless it was a child who had lost his baby teeth.

Starting Out in the Clinic

Out behind our house there was a small bark and tree-pole clinic, about twelve feet by twelve feet, three sides, with a hard packed dirt and gravel floor. The roof slanted from front to back and was made from corrugated aluminum, like the rest of the buildings on the mission property. It was open in front, and there was a pole bench attached to one wall with a table made of small poles and tied together with vines. Through a doorway, across the back, was a small supply of medicines and bandages, which were kept locked.

The Sougb were excited when they found out I was a nurse and could give shots. They asked if I would open the clinic right away. I wanted to wait until my kids came home from school and open in the

New Year, after they went back to school. But due to popular demand of those who were genuinely sick, I opened clinic the second week we were there. At that time there was no trained national aid to help me. I officially opened three mornings a week, but there was always the unscheduled knock, or cough, at my kitchen door with someone asking for medicines. I was scared and worried about understanding the language well enough to know what the complaints were, and even more uncertain about giving the right medicine. But Pastor Baysee came to the rescue and acted as an interpreter, using Indonesian. He was there most days when I opened clinic.

Aunt Pat came to visit Anggi our first Christmas. She helped me by writing out several language lessons using medical terms. I studied the list and carried it with me to clinic, feeling more confident with the vocabulary words. As it was, I learned more medical phrases in Sougb than anything else. It bothered me that I could tell someone to wipe their snotty nose, *"Barges ban abes,"* but I couldn't tell anyone how to come to Jesus. I felt guilty, thinking that I wasn't a real missionary because I only worked at the clinic. It didn't seem as spiritual, saving bodies and not souls. (Over the years, I realized that medicine opened many homes in villages, which allowed us to share the gospel message.)

The clinic was crowded out at first with everyone asking for one of those magic shots of penicillin, the miracle drug. The Sougb people were convinced that sticking something into their body was more powerful than pills. We located the glass syringes and stainless steel needles in Aunt Pat's house and sterilized them in the pressure cooker. Nothing was disposable then and we used them over and over again. I learned how to sharpen needles on a stone and to smooth out a burr on the tip. Contrary to government medical practices, I used one needle, one syringe per person, setting them aside to clean and re-sterilize later.

The Sougb remained eternal optimists, and nearly every adult patient asked for a shot. That's funny because who in America asks for a shot? What a disappointment it was to the general populous, when I didn't automatically "shoot em," one and all.

The second day I opened clinic, a group of government people suddenly appeared, marching across the bottom of the airstrip. Without greeting us, they filed into the elementary school building and set up medicines on a table. I walked over to introduce myself and to see exactly what they were doing. A few people received colored pills, maybe vitamins? I also noticed they used the same syringe and needle repeatedly, giving every adult a shot. No wonder the people thought that injections were the answer to everything. Some people developed abscesses from the dirty needles and I had the privilege of treating them afterwards. The only word I can use to describe their infections is "awful."

The list of common ailments of those who came to my clinic narrowed down to four main categories: malaria, upper respiratory problems, tropical ulcers and sores, and parasites. I felt very inadequate deciding and treating people by myself, although I could always call our mission doctor on the two-way radio for advice. He was on duty for medical traffic once in the morning and once in the late afternoon, and I often listened just to learn the recommended treatments. Eventually, Aunt Pat taught me more about village nursing when she moved back to Anggi. We only practiced general medicine because pregnancy and childbirth were taboo subjects for the Sougb women, who tended to their own deliveries. (It was years before we were allowed to teach anything about pregnancy, childbirth, and early childhood.)

Many Hats

Meanwhile, Dan was busy fixing everything in sight, supervising yard work, and getting the airstrip cut. He measured for the living room addition that we were going to add on to our small house, and he got a crew together to carry rocks to fill in for the foundation. Besides the living room, we eventually added the indoor bathroom, another bedroom, and offices in the back of the house. Station supervisor, carpenter and repairman were only a couple of the extra hats that Dan wore in his missionary career. He also bought fresh vegetables to send out to other stations, when we knew the plane was scheduled for the next week. Anggi was known for its white potatoes, green beans, squash, leafy greens, garlic, and small onions.

Sougb language translation was Dan's main job and he wanted to get at it. Hank Bock, who preceded us, left ten basic language lessons, telling him that he should be able to speak Sougb within five months. But with all the other work that needed doing, Dan felt discouraged that he didn't have more time to study the language. I think he learned more than he realized in that first month because he was outside talking to the people all day long. His problem was that he had to put off serious linguistic and grammar study until the New Year.

The pressure was also on because the pastors were scheduled to come in January for the next set of church leader's lessons, right after our kids were to go back to school. Dan worked out the Lessons, but he ended up teaching them using about ninety-five percent Indonesian and five percent Sougb. But he did it, and we even remember the very first lesson, "Moses on Mount Sinai."

The soldiers came into our yard several times a week just to see if anything was interesting. They didn't do much all day, except guard the local people. I don't know why they set up their sentry post in the village when the ones in rebellion had the guns and were hiding out in the jungle. With time on their hands, the soldiers were curious about us and what we were doing.

"Why do you live here with such savage people?"

"What do you do here?"

"Who is there to help you?"

They liked to stand outside the shed and watch us wash clothes. The wringer wash machine captured their attention, since they scrubbed their own laundry on a rock in the stream. It was even more surprising for them to see a white man doing what they perceived to be women's work. It didn't bother Dan to help me and I was thankful for his help.

Dan was also glad to talk to the soldiers because he wanted to keep up on his Indonesian language skills. As a woman, they didn't expect much conversation from me anyway. A couple of the soldiers asked Dan to teach a Sunday afternoon Bible lesson for them. He felt torn between using the time to prepare for a class in Indonesian and the greater time he needed to study the Sougb language. He ended up teaching a weekly Bible lesson for a couple of months, until someone complained that they were too simple. That gave him the excuse he needed to quit. It was taking more time than he thought it would because he didn't have the vocabulary to teach in-depth like they wanted. Shortly after that, they were transferred out of our area, and I'm glad to report they took their loaded rifles with them.

Home for Christmas

After the big rush of moving in and fixing up, my three came home for Christmas, for a three week break. After the kids got off the plane at the gate, they rushed into the house to check things out.

Lorraine was actually excited to be sleeping in the same room as her brothers. They shared a room in Agats too, but not in Nohon. The boys liked their camp cots, but Lorraine's bed promptly fell down when she plopped down on it. No problem. Dan added more nails, two more boards to support the bottom, and the bed was good to go, or should I say good to sleep. Dan eventually used thick plywood from our shipment crates to make a bed with a headboard shelf for Lorraine. The boys got bunk beds out of the same plywood a little later.

"Hey, guess what everybody? I'll need you to be my helpers during this vacation because we don't have any house-helpers right now. Seruwe and Pu'me went back home. Lorraine, you can help me in the kitchen. We'll all take turns washing dishes and sweeping the floors. Boys, you'll have to keep Marie entertained. I'll also need you three to carry the firewood down from the shed. And for wash day, you'll have to haul water from the rain drums to the laundry tubs and help me hang up clothes on the line. I'm sorry, but I know you guys can do it." The kids were great sports that vacation and they learned to appreciate how much time it took just to live, without extra conveniences.

One fun job and family tradition, depending on who you talked to, was baking Christmas cookies. I didn't have time to bake before the kids came home that vacation. But since you can't have Christmas without cookies, I enlisted everyone as bakers, except Dan, of course. Toddler sister, Marie, had to be in the middle of everything and she ended up totally dusted with flour. She loved getting her hands in the dough and grabbing globs of it to eat. The kids were great, taking turns keeping her out of mischief. However, when it came time for serious clean-up, I got no volunteers, zero, zilch. I wonder why?

All our cookies that Christmas were for us to eat. In later years, when the kids were home early enough, we baked several batches and varieties, and sent decorated cookie tins out to the neighboring mission stations. The risk was that flights might be canceled, due to weather or other emergency, and then the tins wouldn't make the connections for each station.

Aunt Pat Fillmore flew into Anggi on the same plane with the kids. She had been gone for a couple of years because of the uprising and the people were excited to see her back. I was glad to have her, too because she spoke Sougb and she could explain things about the culture and help me with the language. She was also a great cook and did a lot of baking and cooking, which we benefitted from. Aunt Pat came into our hearts and family that first Christmas at Anggi and she's been there ever since.

The kids wanted to go outside and explore as soon as they'd

checked out the inside of our house. But they didn't get very far because the yard was full of people, and the military came back up and were walking around with their guns too. The crowd closed in to get a better look at the white kids, quickly invading Jonathan's space. They touched his white-blonde hair and rubbed his arms. It was too close and the boys grabbed Marie's hands, swinging her in a "u-turn" and came trooping back inside. "We'll go out later. Too many people are out there, and they're up in our faces."

There was no *later* that day because in the early afternoon it rained. They ended up staying in the house and unpacking their suitcases, instead. What fun!

The reason the crowd was still in the yard was that we were having four flights that day, bringing our outfit drums. On the second flight in, Dan flew out and down to the small coastal town of Ransiki to show our immigration papers at the district police office. Wonder of wonders, he landed at the coast, walked into town, checked in, and made it back to Anggi on a return flight before the mountains closed in with clouds and rain.

The next morning the sky was a brilliant blue, and the lake beckoned the kids. "Daddy, will you take us swimming at the lake? Pleeease, Dad."

The so-called *path* to the lake was a mucky, muddy, swampy walk down to the shore. Marie and I stayed home, but the big kids got their wish. They swam in the icy waters of a mountain lake, ending up with goose bumps, blue lips, and chattering teeth. They weren't gone for very long.

The Sougb kids trailing along behind them couldn't believe their eyes when our kids jumped into the lake. They grew up with tales of evil spirits, and were terrified of the ones they thought were in the water. We later heard of people crossing the lake on one of their balsa wood rafts and falling into the water. No one tried to rescue them, nor did they make any effort to save themselves. They were hexed and it was no use. They just sank and were gone. The story of our kids swimming in Anggi Lake was repeated far and wide for many years.

Grandfather's Bones

One day before Christmas, Aunt Pat asked if we'd like to go over to the gardens where the big trees were standing. The attraction was to get a closer look at the monstrous sawed-off tree trunks that we had seen when circling Anggi for a landing. They looked like grey giants in comparison to the normal trees on the mountains.

"They are burial trees." Aunt Pat explained. " In the old days, when a man died, the Sougb left the body in the house by the fire until it was all dried out. The widow stayed in the house by the corpse and kept the fires burning. When the body was all shriveled up, the relatives came and gathered it up and dropped it into the hollow trunk of those giant trees."

The kids were excited with the ghoulishness of the story and wanted to go into a garden to get a closer look at one of the trees. They were hoping they could see a skeleton, or at least a few bones. The immense giants were bare of branches, but a few green sprouts grew out of their cut off tops. The trunks grew straight up into the sky, and we couldn't see even one bone sticking out.

"Let's measure the tree and see how big it is," Lorraine suggested. The six of us held hands and circled the trunk.

With arms out-stretched and face against the trunk David gurgled, "Hey, we still can't reach all the way around. Dad should have come with us, then we could do it. My neck hurts from trying to look up the trunk to the sky."

Aunt Pat mentioned a smaller burial tree on our side of the airstrip and the kids wanted to go see it immediately, but it was cloudy and we didn't make it until the next day. That barren tree trunk was in someone's garden way out behind our house. It was narrower and shorter than the giants over in Sagwameba village. We spotted a large, round knothole, way up high.

"Hey look," David pointed. "I can see bones up there. Wow! I wonder how long they've been there, and who put them in the hole."

Sure enough, the "grandfather" was sitting in the hole with his head down and his chin resting on his bent knees. The kids were delighted to see real human bones.

We watched that tree for years as it leaned and listed in the wind, until it finally fell over. Then there was a big to-do about what to do with Grandfather's bones. They put them in a great, great grand-daughter's house, temporarily. After several months, the extended family gathered for a proper burial in the ground. Grandfather's bones were finally laid to rest. That was the only time that we ever heard of the bones falling out of a burial tree. When we arrived at Anggi, the trees were no longer used as bone depositories because the Dutch government had long since ordered the Sougb to bury their dead. The giant trees had to be cut down because they were too tall and interfered with the small plane on landing. I don't know what they did with the bones of their ancestors, but am guessing they buried them.

Plane Landing at Anggi

Lunows' Aluminum House - Anggi

Chapter Eleven: "Where are your marbles?"

First Christmas at Anggi

When the kids came home, they were excited to see the familiar, handmade Christmas ornaments from America, which had been stored away for two years in our shipment.

"Now it looks like we're really home for Christmas. We even have our Christmas stockings hanging up on the bookcase." David was the one who noticed things like that, and he looked around with pleasure. The red felt stockings he talked about traveled back and forth with us whenever we went on furloughs. I embroidered the kids' names on them, and hung them out every Christmas.

We didn't have a Christmas tree, so Dan took the kids on an expedition up the mountain to look for one. They found a cedar tree, but it was too tall for our house. They simply pulled it over and cut the top out and brought that part home. The branches were thin and sparse, but they filled out when we hung our colored paper chains and other ornaments on them. We also had a few shiny glass balls that didn't break when we shipped from America. It didn't matter that there were no electric lights; we thought the tree was beautiful. With the pot-bellied stove fired up, the glow of the candles around the house, and Christmas records playing on the battery powered player it felt like an old-fashioned Christmas.

The thought of the military at the bottom of the airstrip was bothering me. The day before Christmas, I baked a cake on a cookie sheet, frosted it, and sprinkled it with fresh shredded coconut. The kids and I loaded up a big tray with tea, sugar, and Christmas cookies, and bagged up a couple of bottles of cooking oil. Dan carried the loaded tray and we took the rest and trooped down the airstrip. The soldiers were speechless, seeing our whole family. But their leader stepped forward, bowed, and accepted our goodies, murmuring, *terima kasih,* thank you.

Going back up to the house, Dan told us, "They were surprised because it wasn't cultural for us to bring the cake down to them. A servant would do that. But I'm glad we did it ourselves."

There was a constant stream of people at our door the day before Christmas. They were all asking the same thing. Did we have any canned fish, sugar, tea, or salt to sell? Dan felt bad because he didn't know we were expected to order extra things for our little trade store. (The following years we ordered salt, sugar, tea, ramen noodles and cooking oil as early as October. We eventually took orders from the churches and tried to get rice flown in before the holidays, depending on space available in the plane.)

But that first Christmas, all Dan could say, was "*Ma'af,* sorry, we don't have any extra supplies to sell."

Christmas Eve was our family time, again. Aunt Pat and I made it a candlelight buffet, with pastas, salads, homemade herb and cinnamon breads, and we opened a small canned ham from one of our packages. I even went out to the village to handpick Swiss-chard leaves for a fresh salad. This was chard that was NOT growing close to someone's outhouse, or the toilet stream. I also made fruit soup from dried fruits and a cinnamon stick.

After supper, we gathered in front of the pot-bellied stove and sang a few carols. Our family was not a great singing group, especially when David and Jonathan got to giggling. The carol singing became a tradition only because I said so. Then Dan read the Christmas Story from Luke, chapter two, and prayed. Presents were next, the ones for Dan and me were gifts that Lorraine, David, and Jonathan made at school. That year we received several small packages from America, just in time to open them for Christmas. I also shopped in our barrels for new clothes, games, craft kits and books to give as presents.

Marie didn't bother anything under the tree, until we started opening presents. When she figured out there was something inside the packages, she came alive and grabbed one and started tearing the paper off.

Christmas day was the big one for the church. Around mid-morning we heard singing and chanting, coming from several different directions in the distance. As it got louder, we went out into the yard and saw long lines of people streaming down the mountain pathways, carrying bundles of wild flowers to decorate the church. They brought pale yellow and purplish mountain orchids, green fern branches, white and yellow rhododendrons, and stalks of yellow, red and coral wild gladiolas that were blooming out in the villages. Vines were already strung back and forth across the church, and they draped the flowers and small fir tree stems over them. The gloomy bark church was transformed into a fragrant flower garden of color. It was beautiful.

The elders set up their version of a Christmas tree, which consisted of a couple of thin fir tree branches stuck in a bucket of dirt. The school kids used tree sap as glue to make colored paper chains and looped them around the tree. Men carefully tied small candles on the tips of the branches. Other ornaments included shiny tin lids from Milo-cocoa tins, and red cellophane paper from Marie Biscuit cookie wrappers, which they tied with string and hung on the tree. In following years, I sent out a plea for old Christmas cards from our supporting churches. They punched a hole, added a colored string and we gave them out to the Sougb churches. My favorite decorations were the fresh flowers and branches hanging down because they seemed so natural in the bark church. I thought they were culturally appropriate and totally honoring to the Lord.

Aunt Pat and I cooked a big meal together for noon on Christmas Day. The table was fancy and formal, with Oma's tablecloth and napkins from Germany. I had ordered a small frozen turkey from MAF, which arrived when the kids came home. They came, already frozen, from Australia via Papua, New Guinea. The bad news was that even though it was a small turkey it was still too big to store in my little freezer. What to do? I let it thaw, roasted it, cut it in half, and stored the halves in the freezer. It didn't look as good when displayed on our table, but it tasted just as good and we even had dressing and gravy. We bought green beans and squash locally, and I used pumpkin pie spice for a squash pie. I had saved a package of Dream Whip, the powdered mixture that you add milk to and whip up into snowy white peaks with an egg beater. The kids loved putting a big glob of that on their pie.

Sougb Christmas Services

By mid afternoon, the procession to our kitchen door increased, as the pastors came, one by one, "*Tuan*, mister, will you fix my lamp for the church service?"

"Tuan, my lamp won't light. Can you fix it?"

"Tuan, can you let us use one of your lamps tonight?"

The service was set for dark, between six and seven PM. Dan went looking in his shed for spare parts. He provided what he could find, replacing broken mantles and filling the empty lamps up with kerosene. My job was to wash and clean the grimy, smoke-filled chimney glasses. As each one was repaired and lit, the pastors took it over to hang in the church.

Night was falling and people were slowly gathering. We stood out in the yard, watching the mountains as fire brands came streaming down the pathways to church. The wind carried the sounds of chanting and singing. I got goose bumps realizing that these people who lived for centuries in darkness were now coming down the mountains singing praises to God for sending His Son Jesus. What a transformation in their lives.

The little bark church, with its dirt floor and pole benches, was crowded out. The women and girls sat on one side and the men and boys on the other. The scent of fresh flowers and fir branches filled the air, almost overcoming the smell of all those unwashed bodies gathered together. The tree was up front, in the middle of church, and they lit the candles among the branches during the three hour service. My kids watched intently as each new candle was lit, wondering if any of the paper decorations would catch fire. Too bad, none ever did.

We sat through pastors, church leaders and even government people who got up to preach or give a speech. The multitude of speakers made for general restlessness. It was too much and too long. Dan eventually worked with the church council to cut down the holiday services to no more than four speakers, plus the occasional government person who might want to add his political two *rupiahs'* worth to the program.

During services, the usual procedure was to go outside for a potty break any time the urge came upon them. But that Christmas service was different because the military came to guard us while we were in church. They proceeded to check everyone in and out who went to the bathroom. That scared the young girls especially, and so they stood in the back and waited to go outside, at the same time getting more and more fidgety as the service drug out.

Finally, the last prayer was prayed and we were all more than ready to go home. The various groups took the remaining candles off the tree and lit their dried bundles of fire brands. Everyone headed home, chanting and singing as they disappeared into the darkness.

The flower decorations and the tree were left for that week until the New Year's Service, which was mainly a repeat of the Christmas celebration. Once again Dan repaired broken lamps, and filled and lit them for the pastors. The Christmas and New Year's Eve services were the only nights all year that the Sougb had evening church. The New Year's program was shorter, with fewer speakers, and no government propaganda commercials given. The main stories were the "Flight into Egypt" and the "Soldiers Killing All the Babies in Bethlehem."

Again they lit fire brands and headed home afterwards, but several young men hung around and came coughing at our kitchen door a short while later, asking, "Is it midnight yet?"

This continued every half hour, until Dan finally gave up, "Yes, it's midnight now."

The boys went out into the yard and hollered out into the darkness *"Selamat Tahun Baru, yen yaugwan!* Happy New Year to you, every one of you!" Other voices echoed the announcement as it was carried on the wind, spreading out and up the valley.

The kids and I were asleep long before midnight, but we woke up with the hollering. When the people started getting their own watches, we really missed the New Year's Eve enquiries at our door. They still woke us up with their loud shouts of *Selamat Tahun Baru*, and they eventually discovered fire crackers to blast off at midnight, too.

On New Year's Day, after the sun came up, we were surprised by a large crowd marching around our house, chanting and singing. Dan went out to ask what was happening, and was informed it was time to shake hands with the missionaries. The clapping crowd lined up from our kitchen door all the way out the gate and onto the airstrip. Dan called me, and Aunt Pat came out too, and we made our way down the line, shaking hands with adults, as well as the children. It was especially significant that year after several years of rebellion and fighting against the government, and now there was peace. (It became a New Year's ritual, a sign we were all united, of one heart.)

Exploring

When the holiday activities were over, we decided to get out and do some exploring together. Besides our walk over to see the burial trees, I had only walked down through the village once. This time, we went up valley following the rocky banks of the creek. The water was numbingly cold, coming from springs in the mountainside and from rain pelting down at higher altitude. Climbing up, we often walked in the stream with our tennis shoes on because it was easier than skirting or stumbling over the many boulders along the edge of the stream. The mountains were steep and narrow as we progressed up the ravine. The creek nearly closed off with the trees and heavy underbrush.

Along the embankment we could see a lone house here and there, almost hidden back in the trees. We climbed up to one that was easy to reach and Dan called out. A man came to the door, but it was obvious he didn't want to invite us in. He stood blocking the doorway so we couldn't see inside. His body was dusty with ashes and his face was nearly covered with a musty beard, and he had long matted hair. He glared down at Dan, not even glancing at the kids or me.

He greeted us in a brusque voice, *"Mei-ji-re-so.* Greetings to all of you.*"*

Dan returned the greeting, *"A-bi-re-so. Our hearts are happy to meet you.* I am Tuan Lunow and these are my wife and children."

The man stood not saying another word.

Dan looked at us and quietly said, "Let's say good-bye and go now. He doesn't want us here."

We waved, "Abireso," and stumbled our way back down through the underbrush to the creek.

After we were out of his sight, Dan explained, "He might be one of the rebels still hiding up on the mountain. He doesn't have to be afraid of us. I'm not going to tell on him. But it's better to leave them alone. We want them to trust us, not be afraid of us."

(That was one of the few times that we ever felt unwelcome among the Sougb people. It was a strange and slightly fearful experience. Many other tribes of Irian were hostile to missionaries, but no one considered the Bird's Head tribes as fearsome as those in the central highlands and the south coast. I never felt really afraid of any of them, even when Dan was gone and I was alone on station. It took years, but those very ones from upstream eventually ventured down off their mountain and were welcomed in church. Dan and I got to know them personally and grew to love them.)

Sougb Houses

Another day we walked over the creek to Sagwameba village. The bark houses were scattered, seemingly with no rhyme or reason to where they were located. Some were built in sweet potato gardens and others were higher up on the mountainsides. The government wanted them to build their houses in two straight rows on either side of a village pathway, but neatly lined up villages hadn't arrived yet for the Sougb people.

The houses were at least seven to eight feet off the ground. They said it was for protection against evil spirits getting in, or attack from their enemies. Building materials were all natural, a tree pole frame with bark walls and palm frond roofs. Inside, the roofs were covered in a blackened pitch, which came from the smoke of the open fireplaces. The pitch effectively sealed the roof from rain, but the smoky air was also bad for their lungs. I think many Sougb people died of respiratory diseases, not unlike ailments of coal miners in the US.

At one house, a man came out and called to us. There was no mistaking his welcome. The kids scrambled up the notched tree trunk to the door with no effort at all. Dan had to take my hand and help me up. I never was good at the balance pole, notched or not. The only light inside came from the doorway to the entrance, and there was a small doorway at the far end. We waited a few moments for our eyes to adjust to the gloom and darkness.

On the right side, the men's side, it was wide open with an ash covered fireplace extending the length of the house. Above the fireplace there was a pole rack where they slept or stored a few belongings. There was also a larger pole laid across the floor about five feet away from the fireplace, which they used for a pillow as they stretched their feet across the ashes to the fire. The flooring was of thick sheets of padded bark, slightly rounded because it wouldn't lie flat. The cracks in between the bark were wide enough for peelings, kernels of corn or other dropped seeds to fall through to the grunting pigs and clucking chickens, eagerly waiting under the house to catch anything edible. The rafters were strung with bunches of bean pods and garlic, with bark-string bags of small potatoes drying there as seed for the next garden. With only a thin layer of bark siding and open doorways, the men's side of the house felt cold and drafty. At night they blocked the doorways with another piece of bark and bamboo sticks which criss-crossed to hold the bark against the door frame.

The left side of the house was always for the women. It was divided into cubby-hole rooms with a fireplace in each one. Those little eight by eight foot spaces were closed in, making them warmer and almost cozy. Each cubby had a small six inch square cutout piece of bark for a window, but the women usually kept them covered over. As a result, the inside of their rooms were dark and shadowy. The women cooked for themselves over their own fires because it was taboo for a woman to eat anyone else's food, except what she had cooked for herself and her young children. Older sons, five years or more, moved out to their father's fire to cook and eat on their own.

Whenever I went inside a little room, I had to sit down and let my eyes grow accustomed to the dark, in order to see who was sitting there by her fire. If I wasn't invited in, a disembodied hand might reach out for me and Dan to shake. For several wives, each wife had her own personal cubby hole on the women's side. Otherwise the extra rooms were for extended family members, like mothers-in-law, or other female relatives, who might come to visit.

The house at Sagwameba was the first house we went into, and it followed the basic plan for all Sougb houses. At another place, an old chief hailed us from his house and invited us in. His first wife was in her cubby and they let Aunt Pat and me go in to see her. She was literally all shriveled up and couldn't walk anymore.

Aunt Pat talked with the dear old lady, "Is your heart ready to go to heaven? Jesus is getting your room ready. Let me pray with you."

I didn't understand any of the conversation, but she told me about it later. We prayed with the grandmother and left her in her little room.

I found out later that it was the custom when an old woman could no longer work in the gardens, she would go into her little room, gradually stop eating, and wait to die. To them, their life-worth depended on how productive they were in the gardens, or in caring for children and grand children. When they couldn't do the work anymore, they believed their usefulness was over and it was time to die. The old men did the same thing, except the sons made a cubby for them at one end of the men's side of the house.

When we left that house, the men and boys started trailing behind us because they were so interested in David and Jonathan. One man insisted on making them bows and arrows right then and there, but please come to his house first. He gathered the bamboo sticks, which were growing in a cluster right beside his house. We all watched him make the bow and a couple of arrows. He used vine string that his wife had made. When they were done, he proceeded to take the boys outside to show them how to shoot the arrows.

"Now you, now you," the men demanded a demonstration from each of the boys to make sure they really knew how to do it.

David went for it, but his brother, Jonathan, was too shy to try it in front of everybody. None of the men would let that go by. "Now you, now you," they chanted Jon on.

He finally took the bow and arrow, aimed, fired and made a good long, straight shot, which of course made everyone happy.

After living in the jungle, the mountains fascinated the kids, "Dad, we want to see the lake and our house from on top of the mountain. Can we go up there today? It's not raining now."

The kids were asking to climb a mountain that was at least 7000 feet, making it 1000 feet higher than our airstrip. They were rightfully proud of making it to the top. "Oh, man, mom, we could see all of Anggi Lake, and right over the pass to the other lake. It's smaller, but higher up than our lake. And the water looks real blue. Anggi Lake is black. We saw these pools on top of our mountain that had sort of dark, greenish water. Dad said the people are afraid of them."

(I'm glad their dad took them for the grand view because I never did get the hang of going up the mountain. The paths were about as wide as a bare foot imprint. They were often slippery from the rain, and sometimes they went straight up, as in nearly perpendicular. Fortunately, Dan eventually trekked all over the mountains visiting churches. He was the one to show the kids.)

New Friends

After that first climb with their dad, a favorite pass time of the kids during vacations was to climb the mountains with their Sougb friends. None of them had any trouble hiking. They hauled along some rice and canned mackeral fish and cooked it all in a pot over an open fire on the mountainside. They acquired more friends as word spread about the rice and canned fish for picnicking on the mountain.

Most days the kids played outside on the airstrip until the afternoon rains started. The village kids loved playing with them and came running when they saw the boys were out. The game for that vacation was marbles. Jonathan got a bag for Christmas and they were beautiful. But the marbles started disappearing and his bag got lighter and lighter.

We couldn't figure it out, "Mom, I'm not giving them away, honest."

"Well, something is going on."

I was determined to solve the mystery. "Don't worry. I'm going to check it out and find out what's happening."

The next time Jonathan took his marbles outside I went out and watched them play. By shrewd observation, I discovered the answer to the puzzle. The village boys played a fair game, but come time to quit, a couple of boys quietly scooped up a marble between their toes and simply walk off with them. From then on the game was up, literally.

Jonathan counted his marbles as he put them into his bag. He made sure nobody went home with a marble between their toes. The three kids felt challenged by the between-the-toes marble trick. They practiced until they could carry away marbles between their toes, just like the best of them.

The Sougb boys invited the three older kids down to the village, where they started talking Sougb with such ease that I was jealous. It was Agats and Nohon all over again. My own kids interpreted for me, when I didn't understand what was being said in Indonesian or in Sougb. I was grateful for their help, but I hated it too.

Ye-sa-ya and U-gwe-se-bei became special friends to David and Jonathan. There were no girls for Lorraine to play with. At the ripe old age of eight years, she was too old. Like the Auyu, the Sougb girls didn't have time to play. They had already assumed their roles and taken on duties of the women with garden work, carrying firewood, hauling water, and watching over younger siblings. Lorraine just shrugged her shoulders and went outside with her brothers and their friends. Otherwise, she entertained herself with crafts, reading, baby-sitting Marie, or baking inside.

Marie, on the other hand, started out younger than Lorraine. She became almost a native, identifying herself with the women's work. She loved to run around wrapped up in a sarong, carrying a doll, with a string bag containing a few sweet potatoes slung over her head. Imitating the other little girls, she hauled water in a cooking pot from the stream, dug sweet potatoes from the garden, and cut grass with a knife. Yes, I let her have a small knife because one day I saw her taking a bigger, sharper one away from another child. I figured she could just as well learn how to use one from me that wasn't so sharp. Afterall, she saw Sougb kids carrying knives around, why not her too? As far as I remember, she never cut herself.

A-day-mu, or his Christian name is Abraham, was Marie's lifelong friend as she grew up. His mother died when he was a baby and his older sister, Dessy, raised him. She became our house-helper and often brought him to work with her to play with Marie because they were about the same age. Adeimu learned to play house, play dolls, look at pictures in a book, and to generally play anything else Marie coerced him into doing. He taught Marie how to climb trees and pretend hunt with bows and arrows. The two of them managed to get into mischief together too, like stealing cookies from the cookie jar in the kitchen. It ended up that when one got a licking, the other one did too.

(Abraham is a government teacher now, but he still calls Marie his little sister. Last time I saw him, he was chuckling about the spankings the two of them got from *Nyo-nya,* the Mrs., which is me.)

There were a couple of huge old cedar trees in our back yard. The boys had a grand idea for one of them and their dad was a part of the plan, "Can you get some help and make us a tree house up in that tree behind the house? It would be really neat to sleep up there."

Two villagers enthusiastically made a long pole ladder, tied with vines. They built a platform with four bark walls high up in the long needle branches. The older kids climbed up and played in it, even before the side walls were put on. All the while, little sister was at the bottom of the tree longingly looking up, desperate to play up there too.

One afternoon, just after her siblings went back to school, I heard a pitiful cry, "Mommy, Mommy."

I ran out back and there she was, halfway up the ladder to the tree house. Of course, she was stuck, but only a little bit scared because she couldn't go up or down. After the rescue, I moved the ladder, not trusting my number two daughter that she wouldn't try it again.

Night-time

At night, when *the feet of the sun* dropped over the mountains, everything closed down. The people climbed into their bark houses, closed their bark doors, and no one ventured out again until dawn the next morning. The Sougb were afraid of the possibility of getting hexed by the Surer, someone they said was a real person in the daytime and changed into a shadowy figure at night. He supposedly walked around in the darkness, doing witchcraft and evil deeds. Because of their fears, we had the evenings to ourselves, unless there was a medical emergency and someone came to the door.

Some of our fondest memories are the nights at home with our kerosene lamps lit, the rain pounding on our tin roof, and the warm fire in the pot bellied stove. Without electricity, we didn't have TV or other electronic entertainment. The lamps brightened up whatever room we were in. Our entertainment was simple, like reading books out loud, or playing board games. The kids especially loved hearing their dad read because of his pronunciation of certain words, which came out in a heavy German accent. The Sugar Creek Gang books were favorites at Nohon. Lorraine found out about Narnia and Aslan from her Aussie friends at school before they were published in the US. Later, we discovered the "Hobbit" and the Tolkein trilogy. A favorite devotional book was "Little Pilgrim's Progress" and Ken Taylor's "Bible Stories for Little Eyes."

While we were on the south coast, we started subscribing to our favorite magazine, National Geographic, and it actually came through via boat mail, still wrapped and uncensored. As pre-schoolers, the kids looked at the pictures. But they read them over and over again, when elementary and high school students. We subscribed to *NG* from 1968 through to 2000. In fact, an article about the Asmat people and a detailed map of New Guinea came out while we were on the south coast. I was so impressed with the accuracy of the article and map that I sent a letter to Dr. Melville Grosvenor, the editor, and he actually responded with a personal letter.

When we played the board games, Dan loved cheering everyone on to the finish line or home base. In our family, we never quit the game until everyone made it home. Dan was also the inventor of our special *Winner System*, where nobody was a loser. We had first winner, second winner, third winner and so on down until everyone who played got a winner tag.

The kids loved it, and that system lasted until one day when David, about second grade, came to Dan and asked, "Dad, I didn't really win that game did I? You just said we were all winners?"

"Shhh, don't tell the other kids about this," and so the secret was kept. We shared our Winner System with other missionary families and they adopted it for their young kids too.

Railroad Train was another Lunow invention. Everyone, except me, snuggled under the blankets on our big bed with a flashlight. "All aboard," Dan called out the stops in German and the kids went on an imaginary trip to who knows where. The fun part of it was not leaving anyone behind, traveling on the rails, and watching out for the fast-closing of those automatically sliding doors on the train. What an exciting adventure those trips were, under the covers, in the shadows of the flashlight.

Then there was *Tickle,* with the kids hiding all over the house and Dan roaring loudly as he found them and proceeded to tickle them to death. This was the most hazardous game to play, especially when one of the kids got tickled so much that he or she had to call for a time out, "Stop Daddy. Daddy, Daddy, please stop. I gotta go to the bathroom.

Now!"

Dan only made it worse by bellowing, "No, no, you can't go," and then hanging onto them.

Batman was another riotous game with the three older kids assuming the roles of Batman, Robin and Batgirl. Dan was the Joker, out to foil the good guys. It, too, ended up on our bed, with the Joker subdued, then suddenly breaking free and gleefully tickling our heros.

Back to School

January 1970 came too quickly and it was nearly time for my three big kids to go back to school. It seems oh, so long ago now. What fun it was to search in our storage drums for new clothes to replace outgrown ones. Sewing name-tapes on didn't seem such a chore anymore. Aunt Pat was heading back as school nurse, which helped me to let the kids go and made it easier for them to leave too. Of course Marie didn't get it. She kept looking from suitcase to suitcase, knowing something was happening, but was unable to ask us.

When the plane finally came and Lorraine, David and Jonathan flew off, Marie stood at the gate to our yard and looked and looked down the airstrip. It was very hard for me to see her so distressed, and I couldn't explain so she would understand. All she knew was that they went bye-bye. I was with Marie on the good-byes; I didn't do them very well, never did, never will!

That semester the first letters from school took several weeks. It seems like I was always in a state of waiting to hear from my kids. We knew the school would notify us if there was an emergency. Otherwise, MAF-airmail to the interior remained our major means of communication.

When the letters finally arrived, the news was all about Jonathan getting sick on the airplane and throwing up. He had looked pale before they left and I had distinctly asked him about taking some medicine.

"I feel okay, mom," he had assured me.

The other exciting topic from the kids was about the games the pilot played with them. "He did tricks in the air. One was making the pencil float. It was neat." David told on him.

That story made me wonder if Jonathan got sick before, or after, the air-obatics. No matter, I know the pilot was trying to take their minds off leaving home. They went on to tell about their friends, and all the school activities, never mentioning leaving home.

And so we have the beginning of a new year, 1970, and another semester at school for the MKs. Now that my story has brought us to Anggi, our final destination, I'll skip blow by blow details and share memorable events as they happened.

Burial Tree-Anggi

Mud path to Anggi Lake

Chapter Twelve: "Did you say he has a sliver in his foot?"

After all the excitement and flurry of moving to Anggi, followed by the kids' Christmas vacation for five weeks, I was hoping to settle down into a quiet routine of learning the Sougb language and working in the clinic. I started by making a schedule for the coming months and dividing it down into a weekly To-Do list for myself. We had already reserved two weeks during the semester to see the kids at school. (Every time we visited them we set our dates for the next semester. My calendar schedule and lists revolved around Sentani vacations twice a year, and the dates Dan had the church leaders coming for their teaching sessions, which were every three months.)

Bags of Mail

Weekly letters to my kids weren't on my To-Do list. I didn't need reminding that Sunday afternoon was my time to spend with them, writing letters. The activities were on my calendar and I used daily notes from my journal, lest I forget something they might want to know. As I wrote, I visualized telling them in person. I know my letters helped them to feel like they were a part of our work in the tribe, even though they were away at school.

The kids told me, "Mom, we always know that you write us every week, even if the plane is late and we don't get the letters right away."

"Mom, I get the most letters of anyone in school. My friends don't hear from their parents nearly as much. I know I will get a letter from you every week. They make me feel like I'm at Anggi." Lorraine wrote that to me when she was in high school.

For other correspondence, I wrote bi-monthly letters to my mom and grandma, and quarterly letters to our supporters and those who prayed for us. Dan had to write home to Germany because I didn't know German. In between times, there were personal letters to answer mail, plus many thank you notes for financial support. I kept an old shoebox of received letters and blank air forms beside my chair and tried to answer several every evening. My early letters were all hand-written.

Then I started using a manual typewriter, typing general news on onion skin paper with four to five carbon copies. I added personal notes at the bottom of each one. We received so many cards and letters at Christmas that I mimeographed a letter in January in order to respond to everyone. It was wonderful when computers came along and I could print out my letters. I'm sure that I kept the post office solvent, buying so many stamps. Of course, everyone liked receiving the colorful stamps from Indonesia.

(It was hard to remember who I sent letters to and so I kept a notebook with monthly lists of letters written. Not counting weekly letters to our kids, I mailed an average of 600 personal letters a year. The Nebraska church friends sent out our prayer letter listing of 350 names, four times a year. A concerned business man in our Minneapolis church later challenged us to better market our ministry by sending monthly letters to a more intimate group of some 120 supporters. That was the beginning of the Lunow's Logbook. I sent copies of our prayer letters and the Logbook to our mission, resulting in the editor of publications asking me to adapt a number of articles for TEAM's mission magazine, Horizon. I became a published author.)

Writing was important to me, meeting an emotional need within me. It meant connecting and conversing with my kids, family, and friends, even though we weren't sitting across from each other. A more practical benefit was that letters kept our supporters informed and aware of what was going on with us and the ministry. When the plane brought a mail sac, I picked it up at the airstrip, went home and settled down with a cup of hot tea, and had a long read, chat, with my children and the rest of the family who were out there praying for us.

The Toddler

When the older kids left for school, the house was quiet, except for Marie. I took her everywhere with me since I was her main baby-sitter. Her company brought great blessing to me because I learned to see the Sougb through her eyes -the eyes of a toddler exploring the world. I was naturally reticent about going out and talking to people I didn't know, preferring that people make the first step towards me. Marie was the opposite, rushing out to meet and greet everybody with joy and spontaneity, chattering the whole time. She shortened my get-acquainted time by welcoming everyone into our yard and then running off to play with their kids, leaving me to practice my language skills with the women.

The Sougb were Marie's adopted people from the beginning. They crowded around her, got up in her face, touched her, pulled at her shiny blond hair, and it didn't bother her one bit. She was un-phased by their body odor, dirty hands, snotty noses, native dress or undress, or their calloused and cracked bare feet. It was all the same to her.

Everyone tried to get Marie to talk to them in the Sougb language, but she steadfastly ignored them and wouldn't say a word. One day someone tried a new idea to get her to talk. A lady took Marie's wrist and patted her chest, then patted Marie's chest back, all the while saying, *"Dou-maria-ang-giji, Dou-maria-ang-giji."*

After repeated chest pats back and forth, Marie joined in the game, patting her chest and then her friend's, still without uttering a word.

The women erupted into cheers, exclaiming to one another, "Hey, look at Dou-Maria. She did it! She's one of us now."

The meaning of the chest pats? It was a greeting they teach their children, "You're my friend. I'm your friend." They decided that Marie's love pats were the same as talking in Sougb.

When she finally started talking, she repeated words in Sougb to her outdoor buddies, words in Indonesian to her friend the teacher's wife, and English words to us at home. No wonder it took her a while; she was learning three languages at once. She instinctively knew which one to use in response to the person she was talking to. When I wasn't being green with envy, I heard how Marie kept imitating and repeating the new words and phrases, until she had them down in memory and on her tongue. I challenged myself to follow her lead in language learning, except for one occasion.

Marie and her friends were sitting out on the grass airstrip, laughing and having a good time; or so I thought. A Sougb woman came into the yard and coughed at the kitchen door to get my attention.

"It's me. I came to tell you that Dou-maria is talking with her friends, but they are teaching her bad words that we cannot use. I don't think you want her to talk like that."

Upon further enquiry, I found out that the kids were teaching her swear words! They thought it was hilarious to hear her say them, speaking perfect Sougb, at that.

I had no clue about forbidden words in Sougb, but I remained vigilant for other dubious habits. Although we were living in a different culture, I wanted Marie to learn western customs and courtesies too. Of course, she preferred the life style of the Sougb, rather than practicing manners from an unknown, far away country.

At least, she appeared to be following my admonitions of how to act when she played outside. One day a mom and her bare-naked baby came into the yard. Marie toddled over to them and squatted down to get eye contact with the little boy. I'm sure she wanted him to play with her, although I couldn't hear what she was saying to him. I saw her lean in and look closer at her unsuspecting playmate. Then she got up and pulled a handful of grass and went back and wiped his runny nose with it.

I chuckled to myself, *"That's good. I don't have to worry. She doesn't let it run and now she'll come to me to wipe her nose."*

Not so fast, mom. The very next Sunday Marie came toddling down the aisle in church with a big dried up leaf in her hand. She stood by my bench and proceeded to blow her nose all over the leaf!

I tried to keep Marie in the yard with our gate locked so that I would know where she was. If the gate was ever left open, she made a beeline for the airstrip and freedom. The path to the village ran off of it and Marie liked nothing better than to go into someone's house, sit by their fire, and eat sweet potatoes. Oh, how the people loved to feed her and she loved to eat.

When I protested, a woman told me, "Oh, but we're taking care of Dou-maria. We feed her when she is hungry. And we're teaching her our voice." I gave up, but did ask the lady to please tell me where Marie was if she showed up un-announced at her house.

Most of the regular visitors understood that Marie should stay in the yard, but one afternoon I looked out and the gate was wide open, and no Marie. What happened? A young boy came down the airstrip, "She hollered at me with a loud voice, begging me to let her out. I opened the door for her."

On that occasion, she went down to the village and scaled a notched pole that went up about eight feet into a house. I was calling for her when a man stuck his head out the door and told me she was in his house. Of course, they had already filled her up on sweet potatoes by the time I got there.

I might not know where to find her when she escaped from the yard, but I did know the Sougb people loved and protected her when she was with them. I had to relax and learn to trust them to watch out for her. Besides, she opened doors for me to meet women who were otherwise very shy and would have never ventured to my house to meet me. Marie had already gone ahead into their houses.

Househelp

When the older three left for school, I tried a couple of young village girls for sweeping, washing dishes, stocking up the woodbox, and watching Marie. What I considered simple cleaning didn't go very well with them because they simply couldn't see dust and dirt. Baby-sitting Marie was a mutual love affair, and I'm sure they would have loved to watch her all day. But after a month's trial, I let them go when I found out they worked double-duty by going directly to labor in their gardens the rest of the day, after they had worked all morning for me. It was back to doing my own chores, with Marie as my sidekick again. Dan helped some, but he was building the new living room addition, plus studying for church leaders' lessons, and trying to learn Sougb.

We decided to ask for a Dani couple who were already trained in housekeeping to come and help us for a while. It took a couple months to get them there. But when they arrived, they started right in, and rarely needed any supervision from me. I set up a daily routine for myself, clinic work in the mornings, language study in the afternoons, plus time for Marie and my other duties. Ling-gay, the husband, and War-i-neek, the wife, lived in a wood-hewn, grass-roofed Dani hut, which Linggay built behind our house. The Sougb people were amazed because it was on the ground, and was round, instead of rectangular, like their houses. I was thankful they lived close the year they were with us, especially when Dan was gone overnight visiting in other villages.

The first year at Anggi, my medical vocabulary increased daily, but I wasn't learning every day words and phrases because I spoke Indonesian with our Dani helpers. My religious vocabulary was also non-existent, although I recognized certain words and phrases that were repeatedly used in church sermons. It was so nice having Linggay and Warineek work for us, but I knew the best way for me to learn to speak Sougb was to have someone from the village helping me in the house. As much as I appreciated their help, after a year, we decided it was time to send our Dani couple home.

When they left, the search was on again for local help. This time, Pastor Yonaden told me about a young married couple, Dessy and Yunus, from the village at the top of the airstrip. He encouraged us, "Ask them. They are Christians. You can trust them."

I asked, they answered, "Yes, we will."

When Dessy and Yunus came to work for us, they had never been inside a western house before. They were clueless, not knowing how anything in our house worked. I remember them that first day, standing by the kitchen sink, turning the faucet on and off, watching the water run out. It was a simple set up with one inch plastic pipe hooked up to a rainwater tank out back, under the eaves of the house. The wood-burning stove, the kerosene refrigerator and lamps were all great mysteries to them, too. Oh, my! They had a lot to learn, and I had to go slowly.

Basic cleanliness was relative with Dessy and Yunus. My request that they wash hands when they came to work each day was a novel idea. Learning to sweep the floor and wash the dishes took a long time. They liked using our broom, but oh, the dust clouds whirling around, especially with Dessy.

"How do you sweep it into a dust pan?"

"Why do you sweep it into a dust pan?"

"Isn't it easier if we just sweep it out the door?"

"Oh, did you want me to sweep down the spider webs too?"

I don't think they actually saw the dust and dirt on my cement floor, or the cobwebs hanging from the ceiling. Thankfully, they took my word for it.

The dishes were another story. Dessy told me, "We wash our dishes in the stream, without soap. Why do you want us to wash the dishes in hot water?"

I showed them how to wash my windows, and they wiped the spots out, but left the smears. Fingers were rolled into the wringer on the wash machine a couple of times, before they learned how put the clothes through. Using the wash machine was a great delight for them because they got to wash their own clothes after doing ours. I suspect that extended family had their clothes washed from time to time, too.

Each new task took a great deal of patience, but I was definitely learning the Sougb language. Explaining housekeeping the way I wanted it done required a lot of words. When words failed me, I relied on showing them how to do it. In all the years they worked for me, I don't think that Dessy and Yunus ever really understood why I wanted things cleaned in certain ways. But they were faithful, they did it the way I asked them to, and they stuck with us for the rest of our years in Anggi.

(Dessy and Yunus, with their four kids, and Dessy's baby brother, Abraham, became part of our family and we were an extension of theirs.

Letters to the kids at school always included tales of Dessy and her gang, or she had messages for me to write to them. Our kids were their kids. During school vacations, the kids always went up to Dessy and Yunus' house, or trekked over the mountain and spent the night in their garden house. Those memories remain etched in the hearts of our children: hunting tree possums at night with bows and arrows, and eating by their fireside out in the wilderness.

Dessy actually cried real tears, mourning for her chicks, my kids, every time they went off to school, "Oh, *Nyo-nya*, I miss them so much. I watched them grow up. I cooked for them. I washed their clothes. They came to my house and sat by my fire. They played with my children. They *are* my children! My heart is heavy and grieving for them. I am crying for them.")

Anggi Clinic

I started opening clinic every morning, Monday through Friday, and only as needed on Saturday and Sunday. Marie loved going out to the clinic, where she became my little hypochondriac, telling me how sick she was, experiencing the same symptoms as my patients. She was thrilled with my stethoscope, listening to her own chest thumping.

The otoscope was equally exciting, "Look in my ears, mommy. Turn the light on too." Marie had a lot of earaches growing up. They developed into ear infections, requiring courses of liquid penicillin, which Marie hated taking. My druthers would have been to keep her away from all the sickly bugs and walking pneumonias that came to clinic. But since that wasn't possible, I hoped the exposure would help her immune system.

Even with my list of medical terms from Aunt Pat, I struggled to communicate in Sougb and usually ended up mixing in Indonesian, with a little English, as well. Instead of a simple question and answer, it was a great challenge to find out who was sick and what their symptoms were. Clinic conversations went something like this:

"A-bi-re-sou, ban ar-e-ba da-gi-ro? Your life to you, how are you sick?"

The one who looked sick stood before me, but said nothing.

Another woman stepped up, pointing with her chin, saying, *"She is sick."*

"How is she sick?"

"Her head hurts."

"How long has it hurt?"
"It has hurt for many days now."
"Did she get hot?"
"Yes, she is hot, mostly in the afternoon."
"Did she go down to the coast?"
"Yes, she went there and she is back now."

All this time the patient remained mute, looking down at the ground, letting her companion divulge one clue at a time. The most obvious thing was her recent trip to the coast, where malaria is rampant. I checked her forehead, yes, she had a fever. Her chest was clear of pneumonia and bronchitis. Pulling down her lower eyelid, it was very pale, indicating low hemoglobin. It looked like malaria to me.

Laying out four days' worth of pills, I pointed to each little pile, "These four white ones and the red one are for malaria. Eat them right away with sweet potato when you get home.

This next pile you take when the sun is falling in the sky.

These are for when you wake up again, for two mornings.

You must take them all as I have told you, and don't share them with anyone else." I wrapped each little pile in separate old envelopes, and sent her and her informant on their way.

(It took years to catch on to the nuances of the culture and figure out the grammar. But the main issue for me in the clinic was that the Sougb don't answer direct questions, they need a middle man to do the explaining. I also had to be sure of who the patient was because the spokesperson was also willing for me to examine them, even though they weren't sick.)

I found out that medical work was much more than simply passing out pills or giving shots. The Sougb belief system didn't allow for an ordinary illness without a cause. It had to be black magic or a hex. They believed that only old people and babies died naturally. Could they trust me and my western medicine, if they were hexed and going to die anyway? And they did die, sometimes without an apparent illness. But as long as they came to clinic, I gave medicines, ministering with my limited knowledge, and people got well.

Sure, I felt like a failure as a nurse more than once, especially when I misunderstood something. For example, one afternoon a couple of people came across the mountain to report about a man in their village, "He has a sliver in his foot. It is in the top of his foot."

That sounded simple enough to me, so I gave them an empty five pound margarine tin with a washcloth and told them, "Take this with you. Fill it with clean, warm water, put the cloth in, and then put it on top of his foot. If the sliver does not come out in two days, bring him to me."

A few days later there was a big ruckus outside in the yard. A crowd of people was surrounding a man on a tree-pole stretcher. I went out and discovered it was the man with the sliver in his foot. But it was not a simple little splinter. It was the tip of an arrow with barbs on it! The point had broken off and was sticking all the way through his foot, bottom to top. I felt terrible that I had misunderstood and caused the man several more days of agony.

"My heart is sad for him, but I can't help him. He needs to go out to the doctor in town. We will pay for him to go on the airplane, but someone who speaks Indonesian must go with him."

The family talked it over and agreed the patient and a relative could go to the hospital in the coastal town of Manokwari. Word spread and relatives living in town hired a taxi to take them to the hospital, where and Indonesian doctor took the arrow tip out surgically. The wound healed quickly and the two men returned to Anggi in about a month with many stories to tell of their life in the big city.

The Death Wail

It was especially hard for me if I was treating someone and they died. I wrote a letter to my mom about it. *"One of the little babies I've been treating for pneumonia at the clinic died. They sent word from the house that the baby was dying and asked us to come. Dan and I went up to the house and found the mother in her little room, holding her baby. Other women were sitting around talking softly. The baby was struggling to breathe, its' little chest pumping up and down with the ribcage showing. The mother told me that his hands and feet died the afternoon before, which was their way of saying that his extremities were cold and he was near death. I sat with the mother for about ten minutes until the baby died.*

"Is the baby dead?" The women sitting around already knew the answer.

When I said, "Yes," they started to wail. If you've never heard such a cry, it sounds so desolate and hopeless. I cried too because I felt sorry for the mother. She already lost two babies before I came, so I didn't know why they died. She came to me right away when the baby got sick. I started on daily penicillin shots, plus aspirin for fever and cough syrup. She came faithfully to clinic and gave the medicine in between. It's hard to understand why the baby died.

Meanwhile, the father was sitting out in the big room by his own fire. He was dry-eyed until some of the men came to cry with him. This man was in the rebel movement and he left the church. But when his baby was unconscious, he asked for a pastor to come.

Pastor Yonaden arrived just after the baby died. He let the people in the house cry for awhile and then told them it was time to pray. After the 'amin' other village people came in to mourn. I think the mother's crying was for real. But I wonder about the others. They see death so often in smaller children that I think they get hardened to it.

This was our first experience of being in a home when someone died and hearing the death wails up close like that. We heard the crying all through the night as the wind blew the sound across the valley."

The death wail, we heard it again, soon after the baby died. Pastor Baysee was sick for a month or more and I called the doctor on the two-way radio about him. (Baysee was the one who met us at the plane when we first landed, and he interpreted when I opened clinic.) Dr. Ken thought it might be his gall bladder, and there wasn't much we could do. One night Baysee got very sick and suddenly died. Dan and I were in shock and the people simply refused to believe it.

They came asking us, "It isn't true, is it?" Baysee was one of their first pastors, surely he would live forever.

His old mother was still living then and she had an even harder time. She came and cried to us, "I know he is in heaven with Jesus. But my heart still hurts. He is my son. He is a gembala, a pastor!"

She was so proud of him for being a pastor in the church. For months after his death, she walked up and down the airstrip, wailing and calling his name. On windy nights especially, it was an aerie, desolate cry, echoing up the valley and over the plain as she walked back and forth to the airstrip. Her cries were far more pitiful than the wails for the baby that died. One of the pastors finally went and tried to console her and help her to stop, but she cried for several more months.

Marie began waking up when she heard the wailing. She called for me, always asking the same questions, "Who is crying? Is it the old lady? Why is she crying?"

Each night I tried to reassure her, "Yes, it is the old mother, crying for her boy. She is sad because she misses him. But he is with Jesus in heaven now. You can go back to sleep. She will stop crying soon."

Others died and the death wail followed. It must have weighed on Marie's mind because when she was about four years old, she unexpectedly announced, "I don't want to go to heaven."

A moment of silence from me, then I asked, "Why do you think you don't want to go to heaven?"

She took a big breath and in typical Marie fashion blurted out, "Because you have to get dead to go there."

(I know these death experiences were in her thoughts at school too. Her first grade letters home always asked, "Has anyone at Anggi died yet?")

Departure of the Military

In the New Year of 1970, the word on the jungle vine was that the soldiers were leaving. It sounded like wishful thinking to me. It was another six months before rumor became reality and they were transferred to the other end of Anggi Lake. Even though they moved across the lake their presence was still felt, especially when they called for bags of rice to be dropped by airplane. The bags barely missed houses and people when falling from the sky. Military patrols still marched around to villages searching for arms. They usually burned down a house or two, just to intimidate the people.

Meanwhile, the government inducted Sougb men into service as local militia. The ones selected were mostly from the rebel movement who had turned themselves in. With much whistle blowing, the soldiers trained them in the art of marching on the airstrip and carrying long sticks over their shoulders, like guns. Eventually, they were sent to another island for a year and trained as guardsmen. Others from the group were inducted into the army and never came back to Anggi again.

During that brief time, the church pastors were required to carry letters of identification and permits to travel around to their churches. Pastor Sario and his assistant were arrested by a patrol looking for guns. They took them to jail, roughed them up, and threw them in a cell. Sario was a new believer, but he remembered his Bible stories.

He waved his arms, dramatizing his story for Dan, "We sang and sang, with loud voices, just like Paul and Silas did when they were arrested. We prayed and prayed, using loud voices again. We two slept that night and the next morning the soldiers let us go because we didn't do anything wrong. Our hearts are truly glad because God chose us to suffer, just like God's people did in the Bible."

Speaking the Sougb Voice

Meanwhile, it took me over a year to understand simple, daily conversation. The native speakers talked so fast, I couldn't keep up with them. Even though I had a thick tongue for speaking, I could read the language and understand simple conversations. Besides the medical terms, I learned Bible verses and studied the Sunday church lessons. Religious vocabulary seemed easier to memorize, maybe because it was repeated more often. Once in a while, I went to Dan's office and listened when he was working with his translation helper, called a language informant. I always learned a lot, but didn't have time to go sit in his office very often.

(Both of us took yearly vocabulary tests, a thousand new words each, plus a big test in grammar and conversation. Dan was my teacher and I remember taking those annual tests from him for years. The field language supervisor sent Dan his tests and he tested out long before I did. Pat Fillmore was the one who helped me learn more practical speech in Sougb.)

I felt discouraged about language learning most of the time. I remember my first break-through in communication came one Sunday afternoon. I was sitting out on the bench in the yard with Marie, when some women came to sit with us. I wrote to friends about it. *"Usually the women talk while I listen. This time one of the women asked me about the memory verse for the week. I got my lessons out and read the verse, and they practiced it back to me. Then I hesitantly asked the women if they understood the story for the week. It was about David and Bathsheba. They looked blank. Remember this is the first time they've heard the story. With the help of a woman who spoke a little Indonesian, I read it in Sougb and then explained the main points in simple sentences. Hooray, we understood each other. It seems like a small thing, but it was a huge encouragement to me. This was my first time to tell a Bible story and it felt good."*

Over The Mountain

Dan's goal was to visit all of the Sougb churches and see each village with his own eyes. Since the rebellion, churches were struggling along with less than half the men they had before. Dan thought it would encourage them to return, if he came for a visit. Our first term, he made shorter trips, less than a week because I was alone on station. (Later he made extended treks, some as long as a month, until he visited in all of thc churches at least once. Plus he went out for several baptisms in the early days. Pastors traveled alongside on every trip, learning to examine for baptisms, and to teach and preach.)

On the other hand, I was no good at the hiking thing. One time, I managed to walk halfway up the mountain near Anggi to see the layout of our station and the lake. It was beautiful up there, so peaceful and restful. But going up halfway was about my limit for climbing. Except for one day when several people came from a village two mountains away from us. They were asking for help because a number of babies were sick, and several had died.

"Could you come over to our village and give them medicine," they asked me.

My first reaction was to tell them no because I knew I was not a mountaineer. I was in a quandary about trying it. There was a whooping cough epidemic on the coast at that time, and I thought it might be what they had in the village. After talking it over, Dan told them we would come, but to pray for me to be strong. I wrote about that monumental trip to my mom.

"Well, I had my first mountain hike, or a better phrase for it might be that it-had-me. We started early morning and the people assured me they made it there in about one hour. It took me three hours and then I had my doubts. Dan said it was a wonderful trail and he had no trouble. Marie got a ride on someone's shoulders all the way. One side of the mountain was a gentle slope up. But going back down on the other side, it was straight down. I know now what they mean when they say the spirit is willing but the flesh is weak. My knees were rubbery and my feet just didn't want to go anymore.

The view from the top of the mountain was spectacular, though. You could see both lakes from up there. Breath-taking and beautiful.

When we finally made it down, we went directly to the preacher's house. They had cooked white potatoes, sweet potatoes and corn-the-cob together in a pot. We opened our water bottle and sat down to eat. Everyone came in to watch us. It was quite an occasion.

Marie loved eating in the native house, sitting around in a circle on the floor and grabbing out of one pot. She also had a passion for checking out the bathrooms, wobbling out from the house on a pole walkway to the thatch outhouse over a stream. The toilets have narrow bamboo flooring, which make it easy to squat and do your business through the slats. The pastor's outhouse doorway had only a palm leaf covering and Marie absolutely had to go potty several times.

After eating, the crowd lined up for medicine. You should have seen my clinic, right out in the open. I spread my medicines out on three logs. Someone brought a pot of water and with my one drinking glass, we were in business. First, I checked all the babies with my magic stethoscope. At least the people think it has special powers. Several babies had pneumonia and needed penicillin shots. Some had a fever and were obviously sick, but I didn't find any that I thought had whooping cough.

The adults were after the babies. One shriveled up, toothless old lady said she was just tired and ached all over. There wasn't much I could do for her, except give her vitamins. One young fellow had been shot in the leg by the military several years ago. His leg was swollen and draining pus from a little hole near the knee. They said he took several pieces of bone out when it first happened. Now he can't walk and probably has a bone infection and will eventually die. Really sad, but I couldn't do much for him.

I sat on the logs giving out medicine for over an hour. Then the rains started and we ran for cover. While waiting for the rain to stop, we rested on the floor of the preacher's house. Then we started the return trip, going back up the steep side. It was awful with the wet path, and I felt like my lungs were going to burst. Dan took my hand and literally dragged me up to the top. I was almost crying when we finally got there. Then again, there was that spectacular view with the lakes spread out before my eyes. It helped calm my frayed nerves.

On the downward side, Dan carried Marie on his shoulders. He went on ahead with her and I slid down in my own time. Marie really enjoyed the ride, as she bent over Dan's head and whispered his ear, giving him all kinds of advice. 'Be careful. Don't fall.' She murmured, 'Whoopsy,' when he stumbled. You miss out on the full benefit of this because she was talking to him in two different languages.

We all made it back before dark and I was especially overjoyed to be home because I had blisters on my feet."

Top, Barbara teaching Sunday School

Bottom, Barbara with a patient on a pole stretcher

Chapter Thirteen: "What will happen next?"

School life in Sentani

As soon as the kids left for school after a vacation, I immediately started planning our next trip to see them, which was usually about two and a half months into the semester. Anticipating the visits to school helped me get over the loneliness of their leaving. Meanwhile, our letters traveled back and forth, along with my goody-tins of home-baked cookies, roasted peanuts, and candies from America. The pilots were always careful to look out for the mail sacks and see that they were delivered to the MKs as quickly as possible.

After their first Christmas break in Anggi, David wrote home about several calamities. "Lorraine sprained her wrist and ankle. Aunt Pat wrapped them up in ace bandages. She's okay now."

Then, "Jonny got bitten by a spider and it swelled up. The next day he got sprayed by the spray caterpillars again, and this time he was covered with hives and itching. He got to leave school and go up to the dorm and take showers."

David was also very homesick that semester. Every letter he asked at least once, "When are you coming out to see us?"

When we finally did go out, the kids greeted us with great news, "Guess what? The rules changed and we can sleep with you every night now."

That was a major change for the better. It was more like being on vacation. I cooked, instead of the kids eating at the dorm. They ran home for lunch and after school snacks. The best part was having our evenings together and no dorm schedule.

We checked in with their teachers and were glad to hear that all three were doing well. Our advice to the kids about school was always the same, "All we want is for each of you to do your best. You're each different. You don't have to get all A's, just do what you can do."

Lorraine, who actually was a straight-A girl, was very disappointed when she didn't do well in the science fair one semester. It was a misunderstanding because she had never been in one before and didn't know what was expected. I thought they should have given her a break too. But she learned from it and did an excellent job on her project the next year.

The kids never lacked for activities on campus. They were excited about swimming lessons and learning how to dive. Lorraine started piano lessons, which were taught by one of the other missionaries. David also took piano lessons the next year, and he is the one who kept it up and still plays today.

Friday evenings they had "Fun Night" when the whole school played outside games, skits, or sometimes watched old black and white movies on the movie projector. They all remember "The Loony Birds of Wake Island" and "World War Two; The Battle for the Pacific." The school also fixed up the old mess hall from General MacArthur's World War Two headquarters that was down near the girl's dorm. They used it for roller skating and playing basketball. No one was ever bored at school.

Lorraine had one other problem that was a first for anyone in our family. She wrote home that she thought she had head lice. Horrors! When we got to school, I asked her about it and she laughed, "Yeah, I do, mom," and went on her way.

I thought she was joking, until a couple nights later, "Mom, can you check my head, it really itches. I think I do have head lice."

This time I sat her down and actually looked in her long, thick hair and made a major discovery. "Oh, yes, it's true. You're infested, big time. I can see tiny, moving, gray specs in your hair."

Further inspection revealed almost invisible, clear nits curled around many strands of hair way underneath and close to her neckline. How do you treat that? We went to Aunt Pat at the clinic and tried a generic shampoo for head lice. It didn't do anything. Other missionaries knew a sure cure. Lorraine got her first, and last, diluted kerosene soak. It was a drastic treatment, it was potent, it stunk, it burned a little, but it worked. All of the other girls in her room had to go through head inspections with Aunt Pat. The next time I listened when my kids mentioned head lice, regardless of how funny they thought it was.

Marie was thrilled when we went to school and she saw her older siblings. It was even better when we were in a guest house together and she roomed with Lorraine. When the kids were out of school, Marie followed them around like a pet piglet and she squealed like one too. They were not delighted, but they tolerated her tagging along, although I think they secretly enjoyed her adoration. She was a real pain when we went down to the swimming pool. It took all of us to keep track of her at poolside because she was fearless and had no problem jumping into the deep end, not knowing she couldn't swim yet.

When David and Jonathan had their eighth birthday the next fall, they were excited about celebrating with us in a guest house, instead of the dorm. I made their cake and homemade ice cream, and they invited their class. They received their first Bibles that year, the edition with Jesus words written in red letters. Both boys spent the rest of that vacation poring over their new Bibles, dispensing tidbits of information as they read.

"Mom, Jesus really had a lot to say, didn't he?" David was looking at all the passages in red that Jesus spoke.

Besides being able to read their new Bibles, they were excited to participate in the Bible "sword drills" at chapel. The drill is a challenge and a contest to see which team, or child, can find Bible verses the fastest. David was thrilled to write home, one time, that he was a winner in the sword drill one Sunday evening.

Another activity that the older kids did at school was bike riding. After the boys learned to ride the old bike in Nohon, I ordered new bikes through the mission in America. It took nearly a year because they were shipped out in another missionary's outfit. Uncle Frank Ross, the dorm parent, had the pleasure of putting them together when they came. He sent us a short note about them.

"Your kids' bikes are here and running smoothly. It's good to have nice kids like yours in our home. I trust they will have a good year and grow physically, mentally and spiritually. Frank and Wilma"

The kids were thrilled riding their bikes around the campus with the other MKs. Since we hadn't seen them, Lorraine described the bikes in a letter. We discovered that they had the deluxe model with gears and hand brakes. My order was the standard, no frills model. At that point, there was no way we could send them back. Our kids came out on the high end of that deal.

(Sentani School was originally set up as a boarding school for missionary kids. When our kids started, the United Nations was still monitoring the transition from Dutch rule to Indonesian rule. They asked if their children could attend school as day students. Twenty-five UN kids enrolled that year, along with ninety plus MKs. As a result, our kids made friends with children from Western Europe, Poland, Sri Lanka, India and other countries. The UN parents knew it was a Christian school and they agreed to allow their children to attend chapel and Bible studies, even though some were Hindu, Catholic, and other religions. The MKs were not in the least bit shy about sharing their faith with their new friends, either.)

Summers at Anggi

It always felt good, and yet was an adjustment, when the kids came home for their vacations; summer was three months, and Christmas was five and a half weeks. We were a whole family again, going from three to six. I cooked more and baked more. Dan tried to take off time during the day to do things with the kids. The three vacationers readjusted to home-life, instead of dorm-life, and to mom and dad giving orders, instead of house parents.

Marie, of course, was more demonstrative, jumping up and down, squealing, and calling names when she saw the kids getting off the airplane. She could hardly believe her good luck the next morning when she made the rounds and the big kids were still there. Some of the thrill wore off though, when she realized she wasn't the only one and she had to share mom and dad with them.

The first summer at Anggi, three hungry, growing kids came home from school. We bought all our potatoes, greens, and seasonal vegetables locally. I sent out a food order earlier in the spring, but it wasn't long before I discovered that I underestimated the amount we needed for the summer's food supply. Twice a week, I baked five loaves of bread and cinnamon rolls. The cookies kept disappearing, almost as fast as Lorraine and David baked them. We had fresh lemons to make lemonade. But my sugar and flour were down to the last Tupperware containers by July.

I was beginning to worry because I needed my order for the forty pound bags of flour, sugar, powdered milk, and cartons of canned goods to feed the hungry hoards at my house. The plane wasn't coming for another two weeks. What could I do? I called our neighboring station and asked if they had any flour and sugar they could spare. We paid an ax-head for a man from Testega to walk three days over the trail with twenty pounds of flour and a couple pounds of sugar.

All of my back order of food eventually arrived, but on another flight the pilot forgot our eggs and meat. My few cans of meat were also gone. Again I thought of my mom and the "end-of-the-month" meals she used to make us. Trying to be creative, I used mom's recipe of rice in milk with sugar and cinnamon, but it was a big flop. My kids preferred plain rice. One meatless meal consisted of green beans, canned vegetarian pork and beans, and French fries, with lots of ketchup. My kids thought it was wonderful. I was the one whose conscience pricked for giving them such a poor meal. Even though the menus were irregular, we had more than enough to eat, and we're here to tell the story today.

Summer activities expanded as the boys ventured outside with their tribal friends. Lorraine joined them when she didn't have a project or two going on inside. By then Marie wanted to tag along on all of their adventures.

I wrote home, *"David and Jonathan play outside most of the day. David is also the one who rattles off the Indonesian. I think he is doing very well catching onto the Sougb language too. He really likes to be out and talking to the people, and they like him for it.*

Our helper made the boys bows and arrows, and Jonathan sure can shoot. He is also good about playing with Marie. I think it's because he lets her get away with more. Lorraine and David make her mind. Of course, Marie really plays up the 'potty' bit with three big kids to take her. At first Jonathan wasn't so hot on the idea, but now he will at least sit her on it.

Lorraine is a terrific reader and the boys are getting there too. The kids spend their evenings looking at our National Geographics and reading other kids' books. Jonathan found his voice and he can actually sing. His brother David has a clear soprano voice."

The boys also liked climbing the mountains with their friends. They usually took their bows and arrows along to hunt birds. One afternoon they came back all excited, "We shot a bird! It was sitting right on the nest and we got it. Then the guys made a fire, and we cooked it and ate it."

How can you not be glad with them when they hit their target, while at the same time, tell them it isn't right to shoot a mother bird? I tried to explain. "The village boys you were with don't see the difference between a mother bird and a father bird. To them it's just food because they're hungry all the time. But you boys aren't from the village. It's not right to shoot a mother who is protecting her babies. If she was on a nest, then she had eggs or baby birds. You wouldn't shoot a deer with her fawn. Don't shoot a bird on her nest either." They accepted my explanation and, as far as I know, they never killed another nesting bird.

When the kids were home, they were home. We couldn't go anywhere like shopping, or to the movies, or to see anyone else. The only near neighbor was Aunt Pat's house in our yard. Every few years, we had Annual Field Conference in the summer so all the MKs could attend. We all enjoyed that break. The kids met up with school friends and kept busy with planned activities. On station at Anggi, they basically made up their own outdoor games and adventures. I have to admit that after being together all summer, the kids and I were almost glad when it was time for school to start. Of course, I immediately felt guilty for thinking such thoughts, especially when I was standing out there waving good-bye to them as the plane took off for school.

An Adventure

Our second summer at Anggi, I planned a medical trip across the lake. One of the churches asked us to come because the women in their village had large goiters and their babies were born with cretinism, or other severe developmental disabilities. Iodized salt was not yet available, either. The treatment for a goiter was iodine in very thick oil. We used a large needle and a fat syringe and shoved the plunger down with the palm of our hand in order to get the iodine in. The shots reduced the size of the goiter, allowing the women to have normal babies. The pastors of the church promised to meet our medical party at another church, which was across the lake.

Aunt Pat was back in Anggi, and she helped organize and pack up meds to bring with us. When Marie heard we were going in the boat, she charmed her way into the trip, which meant one of her siblings had to keep an eye on her every minute. Dan stayed at home to study, or so he said.

My letter home told the story in greater detail, *"Last week we went across the lake to a village to give goiter shots. Lorraine was appointed official photographer. You should have seen some of the people. They come from an area where almost everyone has a goiter, small or great. Several were so big you couldn't even see their necks. Something even more sad is that the women have severely disabled children.*

We set up clinic in front of the church. Our needles and syringes were clean for the first group. The next set we had to boil needles in a pot of water over an open fire. The people brought water which had some grasses in it. I strained it out, but I'm sure it wouldn't have passed inspection in a US hospital. There were a couple of men in charge of the fire whose job was to boil the needles in a pot for twenty minutes. They had no idea what they were doing and came running every five minutes trying to tell me the needles were ready. Fortunately, I was watching the time myself.

Besides giving thirty-nine goiter shots, we passed out pills for other ailment, gave penicillin oil shots, and bandaged some gross sores. We took our own picnic lunch and ate in the church.

The trip back across the lake was something else. We used the two aluminum boats, and several tribal boys came along to row. Pat's new boat motor hasn't come yet. First, the wind started blowing, the waves were getting high, and then it rained. The kids had on their life jackets and weren't worried. It had been a long day for Marie and she took a short nap. I'm the one who didn't like the wind, or the waves, or the boat rocking up and down. It took a good hour and half to cross. Then we walked up from the shore, right through the mud. All I could envision was toilet waste because the people go to the bathroom in the streams that drain into the mud at the lakeshore.

We looked like a motley crew going up the path. Our clothes were wet, hair frazzled, we were mud up to the knees and beyond, and it was still raining steadily. It would have made a great picture of the terrible hardships missionaries go through. Only we didn't take time for any pictures. We were too tired and wanted to get home by our fires. It ended up being an adventure to write home about."

Getting ready for another school year

With three kids in school, it took me all summer to get their clothes ready. I automatically dumped their suitcases when they came home from school because, after two semesters, they outgrew everything. My first resource for new clothes was our shipment drums, where everything was arranged according to size. Each year they were short on something and I had to sew it for them, extra shirts for the boys, or more dresses for Lorraine. Girls were required to wear dresses to school them, shorts and pants were for play. One summer the boys didn't have pajamas and I ended up sewing six pairs for them. I was proud of myself on that one because I didn't have a pattern, and so I cut one out of paper. The pajamas actually turned out just right. No wonder it took me all summer to pack, between sewing clothes and the multitude of name-tapes on.

The next issue was new shoes and they were always a problem. I packed in full sizes in the states, going one up from each size. (Who knows how fast their kids are going to grow up, let alone how long their feet will be four years into the future?) Oh, joy, this time I found a new pair in the right size for each of the kids. They were leather tie shoes. Yes, that's all they had, one pair each, big enough to wear all year. Once in awhile Lorraine was lucky enough to get a pair of Sunday shoes from other missionaries selling things that their kids couldn't wear or had out-grown. David had new shoes in first grade that pinched his toes and the dorm mother found him a pair from another missionary, and traded his smaller pair with someone else. Sandals and tennis shoes were also allowed for school, after school they wore rubber flip-flops, high top tennis shoes, or they went barefoot.

By mid-August which was getting near the end of summer vacation, Lorraine, David and Jonathan were talking about seeing their friends and making plans for school fun. They had been on station for nearly three months and were getting antsy to go where there was a little more action. The kids voluntarily aired out suitcases in the sun and brought them in to be packed. I still had a few last minute jobs to do before they left.

One afternoon, I called David and Jonathan to come sit on the barber stool out by the clothesline. Our friend, Alton Olson, had shown me how to cut hair with hand clippers, scissors and a comb. I can't say that I was ever great at it, but I did it well enough for the Lunow men to appear in public. David's hair was straight and showed every little nick that I made. He was the fussiest about his hair too. Jonathan had the wave and curls and didn't care how his hair looked. I also trimmed Lorraine's hair and cut Marie's when she went to first grade. I say cut, not styled because someone better than I had to do that. Thankfully, there was always a missionary wife, or teacher at school who could trim and cut when the kids needed it.

Lorraine asked for a permanent before going back to school the first summer at Anggi. It was a Gentle Toni perm, which I bought from another missionary. I nervously followed the instructions for each step, to the second because I'd never given one before. To my relief, and surprise, the perm looked great, and Lorraine was proud to show her friends.

We didn't exactly broadcast the other two standard preparations for school. Each kid got a worm cure the last week home. I included Marie in the pre-school treatments because she and Dan had already tested positive for parasites. I figured since Marie was the one out in the village, eating who knows what, she should get the worm treatment as well. Another afternoon the kids had to sit on the bench in the yard, while a couple of the Sougb women checked for head lice. The boys barely required a glance. Lorraine and Marie took some time, since both of them had the long hair. The women always found a few head lice and nits when they checked the girls.

The school cycle began for another year. Marie cried hard when her siblings boarded the plane and took off, and I felt like bawling my eyes out, too. Instead, I went into the house and cleaned up their rooms. It was a couple of weeks before any letters came. This time David and Jonathan printed theirs, and Lorraine wrote in cursive.

Jonathan said, "School is hard and I wish we could be outside more."

David was happy, "All my friends are back at school too. I really like my class."

Along with letters from the kids, we got encouraging notes from the school staff. Elfeida Toews was the new school nurse, replacing Aunt Pat. She wrote, *"Thanks Barbara, for your info on your children. You sure have a sweet family. I especially enjoy Lorraine as she's in my dorm this year. She's so helpful and a joy to have around! I can count on her when I need her."*

Aunt Dee Sunda wrote about David and Jonathan, *"Just a word about your boys. They could not have been better, nicer boys than they've been the last two and a half days. They are so lovely to have here in the dorm that I could wish for a whole room full of them. I don't say this to flatter them, but to make your hearts rejoice and be thankful for what God has accomplished in them through you, their parents. Keep praying that the Lord will continue perfecting the work in their characters and personalities, and I know they will grow to be men that you will always be glad to call your sons.*

I don't see much of Lorraine, but she appears to be well-adjusted and content. There have been no tears or frowns from the boys either! They're glad to be back in school. David told me about the lovely going-away meal you prepared for them. They're counting the time till you come, of course.

Thanks for your prayers. We really want to be good parents to the kids and to keep each one of them close to the Lord. We have thirty in our dorm this year. Love, 'D' "

Plane Down Again

We heard via two-way radio that MAF had another plane crash in the central highlands. It happened about noon, when pilot Martin Kehle was overdue on his second trip into a mission station. The weather was closing down, with cloud build-up on the mountains, and limited visibility. When Martin didn't answer radio calls, MAF knew something was wrong, but they couldn't search that afternoon because of rain and cloud cover.

We followed all the radio transmissions, praying and hoping that the pilot would be found alive. Martin was a new arrival, only three months on the field. He was thirty-four years old and had many hours of flying experience in other parts of the world before coming to Irian Barat.

The terrain where they thought the plane might have crashed was steep mountains, with dense trees, and narrow water sheds for streams. MAF called for two helicopters from Papua New Guinea to help search. Despite careful searching, it was two days before they found the accident site. It was located in a mountain valley which looked similar to the station the pilot was returning to. The plane was resting on top of the forest canopy. It was such steep and dense terrain that the helicopter couldn't get close. The recovery party had to hike for two days to reach the crash. They decided to bury Martin's body on site and have a memorial service in Sentani later. The plane was a total loss, as well.

Although we didn't know Martin personally, our hearts still grieved when we heard of his death. MAF's loss was our loss. It was the second major accident in West Irian in less than two years.

A Boating Accident

Only a week and a half after the plane crash, there was another tragic accident. We in the mission community didn't hear about it until after it was all over, when a full report was given over the two-way radio to our mission field chairman.

The accident this time was a boat capsizing on the south coast with a missionary family on board. Larry and Shirley Rascher were on a boat trip from their jungle station to villages which were 125 miles down-river. The passengers included a teenage native boy, Moses, and the three youngest Rascher children, Chip, who was eleven, Gregory was four, and little Karen was two years. Their teenage twins, Keith and Kathy, left the week earlier for high school in Manila, Philippines. Uncle Larry is the one who showed Dan how to captain the river boat when we moved to Nohon.

The Raschers decided on the boat trip because the south coast pilot was sick and MAF was behind in flying, because of search and rescue for Martin Kehle's crash. Besides, they thought it would be a fun trip for the little kids to go out on a boat. The boat had a cabin for sleeping, and they could take several days visiting churches along the coast where there were no airstrips.

The day of the boating accident they were out to sea and following along the coastline. A tropical storm suddenly came up and huge waves capsized their boat. Uncle Larry and Aunt Shirley grabbed Gregory and Karen and hung onto the overturned boat. Chip was a good swimmer and he stayed close to Moses, the native helper, and both of them hung onto the boat, too. During the first hours of their struggle, Chip was a hero, preventing the boat from breaking up by throwing himself over the hull and lifting the anchor up every time the big waves crashed against it.

After about five hours of intense winds and waves, and hanging on, little Karen and Gregory were pulled from the arms of their mom and dad. Uncle Larry frantically fought the waves and swam to them, but they were already drowned. All he could do was whisper a prayer and let them go into the arms of the Lord. He swam back to Aunt Shirley at the boat.

When the waves continued battering the boat, Uncle Larry urged Chip and Moses to swim for shore. The two boys grabbed floating boards and swam towards a little island. After hours in the water, they made it to shore through the mud of low tide and sprawled on the beach.

As the boys disappeared, Uncle Larry and Aunt Shirley decided to try for land, too. They stayed together and finally made it to the opposite side of the same small island as the boys, but they didn't know it. They were exhausted and literally crawled on hands and knees through the mud to shore. By that time Aunt Shirley absolutely couldn't go any more, so Uncle Larry left her lying on the sand right at daylight. He trudged ahead and found a small outpost from a mining company along the beach. The men from there took a boat back down the shoreline to find Aunt Shirley. Just as they found her, they saw Chipper and Moses coming along the beach too. What a reunion that was, after thinking that each other had drowned. It was truly a miracle that they were alive.

The mining company helped them get to the MAF base where Uncle Larry called Hank Bock, our field chairman, to tell him what happened. That was when the rest of the missionary community heard it on the radio.

The story was beyond believable to us; surely it wasn't true? Less than a month ago we had seen the Raschers at our Annual Conference. They were just back from home leave in the US and it was the first time we saw Gregory and Karen. They were such fun, and all the kids were on the lookout for their safety when they were outside. Gregory was a toughie, always imitating his big brothers. Karen was tiny and petite, like her mommy and oh, so feminine. The older siblings, Keith, Kathy and Chip dearly loved and teased them, mercilessly. Aunt Shirley's face radiated joy whenever she was with them, or they were playing around.

Again, we were plunged into immeasurable sadness and loss. My mother's heart wept for the loss of those two precious children. I cried, for Shirley and Larry, for the three older kids, especially Keith and Kathy in Manila. I felt close to them all, like they were my own children. Questions plagued my mind and I thought about them, over and over. What if it were my children? What if it was my family? I thought about myself dying, but not my children. How could this possibly be part of God's greater plan? Why?

I didn't really expect God to answer. For me, it was about facing the reality that God didn't promise a smooth path, or an easy way. He might ask more from some of us than from others. He just wanted my obedience and trust. And He promised His presence to be with us in whatever He called us to go through. I examined my heart again, and I believed that. I knew God wanted me and my family where we were. And until God led otherwise, I told Him that I was still committed to stay headed in the direction He had called me.

Top, Traditional Sough House-Anggi

Bottom, Sough Women by their fireside-Anggi

Chapter Fourteen: "Can you ask for a black baby?"

Feeling Sick

It was getting towards the end of another summer and I wasn't feeling well and it didn't go away. I thought of several possibilities, upset stomach, the flu, malaria, or maybe a parasite? The light finally dawned that maybe I was pregnant. Here I arrived in Papua having a baby and now I was leaving for furlough next year with a second baby. What kind of family planning was that! My heart reminded me that I'd always welcome a baby. But my stomach turned over from morning sickness into all-day sickness. The more nauseous I got, the more depressed I felt.

Summer vacation was nearly over and almost all of the name-tapes were sewn on the kids' clothes. I was feeling so bad that Aunt Pat came to the rescue. She lived in the house just across the yard from us. Not only did she take over meals, which made me gag with the odors, but she lined up suitcases and enlisted the kids to pack their own clothes for school. Lorraine was ten, David and Jonathan were eight, and Marie was almost three years old. She watched the others pack their suitcases.

Aunt Pat practically lived at our house the last few weeks before school started. In fact, Marie began to wonder about that and pestered me with more questions than I wanted to answer. "Is Aunt Pat here? Is she eating with us again? Why is Aunt Pat cooking for us now?"

I tried to shush her, "Marie, Aunt Pat is cooking because Mommy is sick. Of course, she's eating with us? Don't you want her to?"

"Oh, no, I like her to cook for us."

If Aunt Pat happened to get a break and skip a day while the family had left-overs, Marie was right there with more questions, "Mommy, why isn't Aunt Pat eating with us? Doesn't she want to eat at our house? Doesn't she like us anymore?"

By the time Lorraine, David and Jonathan left for school in August, I was in my third week with extreme nausea and I was losing weight. Dan called Dr. Rob Wight, who told us to come to the Pit River Hospital station as soon as possible.

MAF flew us straight from Anggi to Pit River. By the time we got there, I was so weak I couldn't walk down the path to the cabin beside the hospital. Dr. Rob loaded me up for a thrilling ride on the back of his motorcycle. After I got to bed, he started IVs and all kinds of shots, of which I do not know or care what they were. The one that I did know was an iron shot, and it really hurt; but it also made my hemoglobin go back up. Whatever the meds were, they helped, and the constant nausea and gagging stopped after a couple of days.

I felt embarrassed going to the doctor. After all, I'd been pregnant before, what was the big deal this time? Dr. Rob tried to encourage me about coming, pointing out that I needed his help, like IVs and shots, to stop the nausea.

He went on to ask if there were multiple births in the family; to which I answered, "Yes, I already have twins."

"Oh, well, I was going to say that often with such extreme nausea, like this, it can indicate a multiple birth."

Thanks, how encouraging is that? Dan and I laughed about that one, and thanked God for the humor in the situation, too. We stayed at Pit River for a couple of weeks until the nausea was under control and I could go back home.

I was sick to my stomach through the nine months, but nothing like in the beginning. Another complication developed early in the pregnancy, a blood clot in my right leg. Dr. Wight suggested a course of oral antibiotics, wrapping my leg in ace bandages, and walking each day. The phlebitis never cleared up entirely, but lasted through my pregnancy.

We waited to tell the older kids about a new baby until we visited them at school. They were excited and immediately started thinking up names for girls and boys. With Marie's birth, they prayed for a girl, but this time it didn't matter.

Marie didn't catch on to a new baby until I started to get an enlarged belly, and then I was forced to tell her. Her questions were typical Marie questions, "Can you ask the doctor for a black baby? Will you feed the baby like the people do?"

Pit River for the third time

We stayed at Anggi for eight months, then in early March of 1972, we flew to Pit River, with a stop in Sentani to see our big kids. Dr. Rob also wanted me to go into town and get an x-ray at the government hospital in Jayapura. The admissions office insisted that one of their doctors examine me first. Dan used his best Indonesian and explained the x-ray was ordered by a mission doctor interior, and I wasn't able to get a written letter from him. Permission was granted, minus an exam by that doctor.

The x-ray department had no gowns, and so I remained in street clothes, which meant I pulled my blouse up and my skirt down below my navel for the x-ray. The technician took a couple shots, checked to make sure they developed, nope, tried again, and they were okay. I paid for them and took them with me to show to Dr. Rob. Dan and I looked at them too, and were relieved to see only one baby.

The day after my x-rays, we flew in to Pit River. This time we were in a house of one of the furloughing missionaries at the top of the airstrip. Several couples were waiting on babies, and we shared housing. It was our first meeting with Isaacs, Cousins, VanderMeers, Akses and Burkharts, and we all became good friends. The plan was that the one ready to deliver move down to the little cabin near the hospital. The rest of us remained in the houses at the top of the airstrip, until we were ready to deliver. All of us were there a couple weeks ahead of our due dates anyway.

Dan, Marie and I shared a house with Peter and Nel Akse, and Nel's older sister Elsa Stringer. They were from Holland, but spoke good English. Elsa was a seasoned missionary, but Nel and her family were new to the field. Nel's baby boy was already born, but needed to gain weight before going back to their station. Besides the baby, they had a little girl, Ellen, who was about five.

By the time I got to Pit River, my right leg was swollen and painful from the phlebitis. Dr. Rob re-wrapped the ace bandage tighter and ordered a round of penicillin shots. He also told me to get out and walk, which was easy to order, but hard to do. It rained every day and the paths were muddy and slippery. Dan walked with me most of the time. Of course, Marie was ready and willing to go outside any old time of the day or night. The walking helped, but my leg was hot and painful to touch right up to delivery and for several days after.

Dessy and Yunus, our house helpers, came with us from Anggi because Dan wanted them to go with him to see the linguistic consultant Dr. Myron Bromley about Sougb grammar. It was more economical to combine the trip, since air travel was expensive. Tangma, Dr. Bromley's station, was 15-20 minutes by air from Pit River. They flew over the week before my delivery, and Dan came back in a couple of days, leaving Dessy and Yunus there to wait for a second linguistic session scheduled after the delivery. Of course, they had never been out of the Anggi area, and seeing Dani culture gave them cause for wonder and amazement. Each new day was a great adventure for them.

It's a Boy!

D-day finally arrived. We sent a cable through the mission office the day of birth and I wrote a letter to my mom a few days later.

"Latest flash: Matthew Wolfgang Lunow was born March 21, 1972 at 6:53 PM. He weighed about 7 lb. 10 oz., but we're not sure the scale is accurate. He has dark hair, looking very much like Lorraine did as a baby. He's in good health, with a good appetite. The nurse took him for a couple hours the first night because he was crying so hard. She gave him a few ounces of water, which he drank right up and wanted more. Oh, yes, he was also full of poop and immediately filled his first diaper, and his second one, and his third one.

It was another fast delivery. I had light contractions around 6 AM, but when the nurse checked me, they stopped. Nothing more happened all day long, until 5 PM when the pains started again and were more regular. Dan and I walked over to the hospital.

All it took was a couple of hard pains and Baby Matthew dropped down into the canal. I barely pushed, maybe once or twice. I didn't know it, but it happened so fast that I had a cervical tear and was hemorrhaging. The doctor clamped the bleeders and quickly sutured me up. He estimated that I lost about a pint and half of blood, but I didn't feel anything, and had no clue how bad it was. It's funny how you can be so sick and not even know it. Dan was in the delivery room watching, and it was quite traumatic for him. They started IVs and I stayed there all night so the nurses could watch me.

In the morning, Dr. Rob decided to give me a pint of blood. He checked blood types and found one of the other dads had my blood type. Ed VanderMeer gave his blood, but within minutes of starting the transfusion, I re-acted with chills and shaking, and the nurse stopped it.

That whole experience left me very shaken, but by evening of the second day, I was feeling better, but had no energy whatsoever. I'm getting iron shots to boost my hemoglobin. I want to nurse, but don't have much milk yet.

Doctor Rob told Dan that I should not get pregnant again. He suggested that I have my tubes tied as soon as possible. We agreed with him and I'm glad the decision is made. Dan felt awful watching me bleed like that. If I had gone into labor at Anggi, I would have bled to death. That was a sobering thought, and I have to admit the delivery took the kinks out of me. Our friend, Alton, wrote just before we came here to Pit River that he works in a fully equipped hospital in India. He suggested I get surgery there when we visit them. India has an aggressive birth control program and they provide free services for prevention. We will see.

I still have the blood clot in my leg and have to keep my leg wrapped. I'm getting daily penicillin shots for that too."

It was hard to muster enough energy to take care of myself, and the baby. My milk was slow to come in and a couple of ounces of water in a bottle wasn't enough either. Matthew was so distressed that the midwives, Corky Hook and Pat Goodlet, took him for one night each so that I could get some sleep. They ended up feeding him a couple ounces of formula, which he eagerly slurped up. I didn't have any worries about him being a fussy eater. He was starving all the time.

Aunt Corky was new to the field and the Missions Fellowship asked her to fill in at Pit River while other nurses were on furlough. They also needed an extra nurse because there were several missionary babies expected around the same time. Corky was so worried she wouldn't do well as an obstetrical nurse, it had never been her first pick, but she did fine. Matthew was always her boy because he was the first baby she helped deliver as a new missionary.

Of course, Marie didn't want to leave her new baby brother alone. She even watched him sleep, chattering loudly the whole time. Matthew's second day of life, Dan woke up with Marie's eyes staring at him, "Daddy, can I see my baby brother now?"

I had to be on the alert watching her during the day because she kept trying to pick him up. She didn't know what gentle meant. She couldn't lift him off the bed, even though she tried. She kept asking, "When can we go and show our baby to Lorraine and the boys at school?"

"Yes, yes, Marie, we are going to see them all soon. But the doctor says I need to rest at Pit River for a little while longer."

There's something about holding your new baby that dims the memory of a difficult pregnancy, and delivery complications. Even though having another baby was a shock a first, I realized that God planned it all, and the timing of Matthew's arrival was just right. (He was my baby, number five, and he gave me joy and company in the years ahead, especially when Marie went to school. I'm sorry that his entry into this story is so near the end.)

We stayed at Pit River for a full week after delivery to make sure that my hemoglobin was stabilizing, and the phlebitis was clearing up. Then it was off to Sentani where Lorraine, David and Jonathan were jostling in line, waiting to hold their little brother. We were there ten days, long enough to spoil the new baby forever. The kids, and their dad, couldn't stand to hear him cry. If they detected the least little snort, or if he showed a wrinkle on his brow, they were right there to pick him up. Of course, when he continued to cry and was inconsolable, then he was speedily turned over to me. The noise of the household didn't bother him at all, he seemed to enjoy it. Early evening, around supper time, he fussed for an hour or so, but the good news is that he started sleeping through the night while we were in Sentani. None of my other kids had ever slept through so early, but I wasn't going to complain.

Since we were planning on going to the US in June, the rush was on to get a passport and travel documents for Matthew. We took him to town to get passport pictures and I filled out forms for a US birth certificate, which had to be processed at the US embassy in Jakarta. It was complicated because we needed an Indonesian birth certificate before they would issue an American one. Dr. Rob put in a word for us with the local government people, and they gave us Matthew's Indonesian certificate before we left Pit River. After all the paper work was done, Matthew ended up with birth certificates from Indonesia, the US and Germany. He was born, all right.

From Sentani, Dan wanted to go to Tang-ma to finish the language consultation with Myron Bromley. Dessy and Yunus were waiting there, so we flew back interior. It was my first time landing at Tangma, and that felt like an amusement park thrill ride. The mountains were steep and narrow as we flew up and over the southern range. We made a wide circle, then a sharp turn, and the airstrip opened up in a valley before us. The plane swooped down on the bottom of the strip, then climbed a steeper slope up to the flat landing area at the top. Whew! What a ride.

Myron and his wife, Dr. Marge, a medical doctor, welcomed us. Their youngest, Lois, was still at home with them and Marie was delighted, thinking she could play with her. Peter and Nel Akse, and their family were also there that day. They are the ones we lived with for two weeks at Pit River. (Tragically, their family perished in another plane accident at Tangma a couple of years later. Ellen was the only survivor because she was in Sentani School at the time.)

Dessy and Yunus were also excitedly waiting alongside the airstrip. Dessy could hardly contain herself when she saw Matthew, immediately begging me, "*Dan dou-wan de-se-dou-gwo e-ni,* can I watch him?" She was good at holding him and shushing him.

Obviously, Dessy preferred to take care of Matthew, over working on the language team. But Dan needed her input, as well as Yunus'. Dan was still trying to figure out tone, versus stress, in the Sougb language.

Dr. Myron made the investigation almost a game, when he asked them, "Do you think you can whistle the words that sound alike for me?"

"What do you mean?" Dessy asked. "We can whistle. But how do you whistle words?" It was new to them and they got to laughing. They had no idea that their language had a musical pattern to it.

Myron demonstrated by whistling a word or two. They caught on, whistling back and forth, until they reached an agreement with Dan. The team decided that Sougb had both tone and stress, but it was easily understood in context. That meant we didn't have to put punctuation marks on words that sounded alike. What a relief that was to Dan.

During consultation hours, I took care of Marie and Matthew, which expended all of my energies. I sat in on a couple of the linguistic sessions, but only to hear what they were deciding to change, or not to change. Dr. Marge Bromley and I visited during the day. She gave me advice about the new baby and taking care of a toddler. Being a medical doctor, she was a great resource for questions. I got her take on diseases and treatments that I needed help with in the clinic at Anggi. With Myron in linguistics, Dr. Marge in medicine, they were our kind of people.

By the time we finished the consultation, Matthew was nearly a month old. It was a relief to finally go home, after two months of suitcases. We only had six weeks before furlough. I dreaded the job of packing suitcases and drums that was looming on the horizon for me.

Packing Again

After four years and two babies, I was ready for furlough. Back home in Anggi it was time to go through the house. Since no one would be living there while we were gone, I put everything away and only left furniture and some bedding out. I packed as much as possible into the 55 gallon drums, clamping the metal rims down to close them. It took me a couple of weeks, with interruptions to care for Matthew and Marie.

Aunt Pat took over my clinic duties when I was sick during my pregnancy, and she continued with the clinic work while I was packing. Medicine was one less responsibility for me to think about, although I still helped in the clinic whenever I could. Aunt Pat was in charge though.

School was out the middle of May. When Lorraine, David and Jonathan came home their main interest was to play with their baby brother inside, and play outside with their friends. My main focus was to get clothes ready for furlough. I was determined not to drag eleven pieces of luggage back to America again.

"Each of you can have one suitcase and one hand-carry for the airplane. Right now your job is to empty your school suitcases and show me the clothes that still fit. Then we'll try on a few larger sizes still left in the drums."

Marie chattered incessantly, excitedly telling her siblings "We're going on *furlough* and we'll fly in the big plane to America." Of course she had no idea what furlough meant, or how big a jet plane was, but it sounded good to her. She was ready.

Documents, permits, and renewals

Preparation for leaving required renewal for all of our documents and permits for exit-reentry. The mission offices in Sentani and Jakarta worked for months before our departure dates. (It was never a smooth passage through the various departments, and some form or file always got lost or hung up. If anything was out of order, we would not be able to re-enter Indonesia after home leave. Dan also had to get his US immigration status re-instated. He filled out forms and went through the same process every time we traveled back to the states because his green card expired after two years absence from the US.)

We had Matthew's birth certificates in hand and he was stamped in my passport, but we ran into trouble with his information when we got to Jakarta. In order to visit our friends in India again, Matthew also needed a German visa. Don't ask me why because it was complicated, but the gist was that we could only take him to India with us if he was stamped in Dan's German passport. Dan went to the German consulate to fill out forms. That's where a German birth certificate came in, and he was duly stamped into Dan's passport.

Sick on the way

Our family, all seven Lunows, plus luggage, filled the MAF Cessna airplane when we flew out of Anggi to Manokwari. The airplane to Biak Island was a commercial Twin Otter, which is a larger prop plane. There was a small jet on the runway when we landed in Biak and Marie was thrilled, "Is that our plane to go to America?"

Uncle Mike and Aunt Mae welcomed us again and put us up at the Bible School, like they did four years before. Dan and Mike checked in with the authorities. Exit permits and passports were all re-checked when we boarded the plane to Jakarta the next morning. We were given exactly twelve months to leave and return, or have our visa expire.

During the night, Marie got sick. She complained of stomach cramps and ran a fever. Then she vomited. My copiously packed purse yielded some medicine, and I gave her a dose of Benadryl, which helped relieve the nausea. She told me she was better in the morning and I thought she was getting over it. But once we got to the airport and were on the plane, she started with diarrhea and I barely made it to the bathroom with her. After that first episode, Marie was so thirsty she gulped down soda pop, only to vomit it up, followed by the urgency to go to the bathroom again.

The cycle continued with her gulping down soda, throwing it up, then diarrhea until it was only water. By that time, I was afraid of dehydration, so I let her drink all she wanted, and hoped that her system would absorb some of the liquid. Meanwhile, I used a plastic bag to catch what she threw up. The stewardess supplied me with soda, but there was no one else on the plane who could help us. I resorted to using the disposable diapers that I had hoarded for Matthew, and put them on Marie. They were small, but they worked, and I didn't have to worry about getting her to the bathroom quick enough. It was also convenient to throw them away in a used plastic bag, which I had in my purse. The day dragged on, as I held Marie on my lap, praying all the way to Jakarta.

All this time I basically ignored Matthew, but he was doing great as long as someone held him all the time. We couldn't put him down anyway because there was no bassinet for him. Dan and Lorraine gladly took over watching Matthew, passing him back and forth between them.

It was a dawn departure from Biak, and a late afternoon arrival in

Jakarta. What a relief to see the driver of the Guest House van holding a sign at the airport. Even the traffic cooperated and we made it into the city in record time. I immediately asked for someone in charge to help us, "Can you please take us to a doctor. My little girl is very sick."

The woman receiving us at the Guest House was sincerely concerned, and directed the driver to take Marie and me to a local doctor's house where he was having evening hours. Other people were already waiting, but the doctor saw us in a few minutes. I tried to tell him about Marie, but I couldn't understand his rapid responses in Indonesian. Dan stayed at the Guest House with the big kids and Matthew, and so I was on my own. After examining Marie, the doctor gave her a shot. He could tell I didn't understand him, so he didn't try to explain much either. He wrote out a prescription for oral meds and told me, in English, "You must buy this at a pharmacy in the morning. All are closed now."

I stumblingly remembered my manners, "*Terima kasih,* thank you, for helping us. *Selamat malam,* good evening to you."

The driver took us back to the guest house, where Marie finally slept; maybe from the shot? By morning she was still vomiting, but her fever was down and the diarrhea was less. The Guest House driver took Dan to a pharmacy before breakfast. Marie actually took her medicine without much fuss, and she made a turn around and started to improve over the next few days.

We had decided to stay longer in Jakarta, in case Marie needed more medical attention. After such a traumatic flight from Irian, I was thankful to stay put for a few more days. The local doctor knew what he was doing because Marie gradually gained strength and didn't need further treatment. I had planned on going to the US Embassy and asking them for advice, if we needed more medical care for her. I'm glad that wasn't necessary.

Dan called Klaus and Josy, a German-Papuan couple. He was a former missionary in Irian and married a national girl who was educated as a nurse under the Dutch. Klaus worked for a drug company in Jakarta. When they heard about Marie, they invited us to come and stay with them, until she was better. They even sent their chauffeur driven van to pick us up. The place was huge, with many rooms, and servants to care for all of it. Both of them led busy lives with work and social activities, so we didn't have much talk time together. We felt more like we were guests in a hotel, with our rooms in another part of the house and the servants fixing our meals separately. It was an elegant place to stay for an extra week.

While Marie was recovering, David and I came down with the flu. We were both in bed for a couple of days. My first concern was that baby Matthew would get sick from my nursing him, but he was fine and the rest of the family stayed well too.

Shopping in Jakarta

Jakarta was the place to buy small gifts for our supporters and family, since Irian Barat didn't have anything like that. None of us had the energy to go shopping until Josy offered her chauffeur to drive us to a big complex with a multitude of small shops where we could look for souvenirs. By the end of the week, I felt well enough, and the chauffeur not only drove us to the shops, but he waited to transport us back home.

We located an Indonesian craft store and I bought a few small gifts, including several batik tablecloths, with uniquely designed Indonesian patterns. At a fabric place, Lorraine chose a batik piece to make a pants outfit. She was tall and thin and ready-made children's clothing didn't fit her. I bought yards of fabric to sew matching shirts and dresses for us to wear when visiting churches in the states.

We took Lorraine's fabric to a tailor's stall, "*Selamat siang, bapak*, good afternoon sir. Can you sew an outfit for my daughter? I will need it quickly because we are leaving soon."

Right then and there, he took his measuring tape from around his neck and measured Lorraine. She was a little embarrassed to have a man measure her, but didn't say anything. Men are most often the ones who sew in Indonesia.

When I handed him the material, he also assured me, "B*esok sore,* tomorrow afternoon. You come then."

The whole exchange was in Indonesian and I felt good that I understood all of it. By then, I was tired and didn't feel like any more looking around, so our driver took us home. That was the only time that shopping in Jakarta was less than two hours altogether. Maybe not feeling well had something to do with it.

The next day, the tailor kept his promise and had it ready when Josy's driver took me to his shop. Lorraine tried the pants suit on when I got home, and it was a good fit. I was impressed because the tailor didn't use a pattern. He drew a pencil sketch from my description and sewed from that picture.

THE LUNOW FAMILY

Before (1968) and After (1972) the Mission

David, Jonathan, Lorraine, Barbara and Wolfgang Lunow

Wolfgang and Barbara Lunow

LORRAINE, DAVID, JONATHAN, MARIE AND MATTHEW

Afterwards: "The Ending after the Beginning"

India again

Who was to guess that the change of one day for a plane ticket could be so important to us later? After the delay in Jakarta, our airline tickets needed to be changed and re-issued. The kids put their request in, "Dad, see if you can get tickets on Japan Airlines. The kids at school say they are really nice, and they have cool planes."

Dan went in person to the airline office to explain, but when he returned, "Hey, I'm sorry, but I couldn't get JAL tickets. They fly the day before we want to leave. I got tickets for Al-Italia because they fly on our day, and they had enough open seats left for our family. We're all set to go. We still have the same route, going to India, Germany, then the US, but everything is moved back two weeks."

The flight out of Jakarta routed through Singapore, arriving in Delhi, India, at two in the morning. There was a hotel near the airport, and we slept for what was left of the night. In the morning, we got smart and asked the hotel to charter a taxi for us. The taxi offered a comfortable ride, but we all agreed it was definitely less thrilling than riding in the economy bus with the general public. With our windows rolled up and air-conditioning turned on, we lost the distinct smells of humanity, animals and dust. The scenes along the roadside were the same though, working elephants, proud peacocks, water-buffalo wading in the rice paddies, roaming holy cows, and people, people everywhere. The plains were dry and hot, without any sign of rain, as we began the climb up into the mountains.

Our taxi driver took his cue from other drivers and routinely leaned his elbow on the horn. We zig-zagged our way going up the narrow road, barely avoiding head-on crashes with the assorted vehicles coming down. It was all too familiar, the taxi driver hunched over the wheel, driving on a collision course, horns blaring, swerving to the side at the last second, and both cars moving off in opposite directions.

Travel by taxi took us only six hours from the hot plains to the lofty mountains. We drove past the final bus stop, slowly twisted up a little higher, and the driver deposited us on the doorstep of the Olson's cottage. The trip up wasn't as scary the second time, but I was relieved to get there and see Ruth and her two boys again. Alton was gone to pick up their Land-Rover from the garage, and wouldn't be coming back until the next day.

It felt good to be in our friend's comforting cottage for a few days. For whatever reason, I had about as much energy going back as I did going forward to Papua. Of course, I was still nursing Matthew and I was also concerned about Marie. I wanted Alton to examine her and reassure me that I had gotten the right treatment for her.

The next morning, Ruth handed me the Delhi newspaper with news from two days before. The headlines were bold and blaring, and the pictures said it all. What a shock to read that a Japan Airlines plane had crashed on landing at the Delhi airport the morning before we arrived. Only two people survived, the rest were dead. That was our plane! Not really, but it was JAL that our kids wanted us to fly on, but their schedule to India was *the day before* we wanted to leave Jakarta. The travel agent recommended that we fly Italian Airlines instead. IF we had been on that plane… "Thank you again, Lord."

Alton got back with their Land-Rover that day and talked with Dan and me, "I am prepared to do Barbara's surgery in the hospital here. The government subsidizes for birth control and will pay for most of it. It's up to you, but I think now is a good time." We agreed and I checked into the hospital for three days.

It felt a little strange being in a ward with the Indian women. I was tempted to speak to them in Indonesian, but fortunately they welcomed me in very polite British English, "Good day. What is your name? "

"Where did you come from? "

"Are you sick?"

"What will you do here?"

The nurses were very professional and knew their stuff, which gave me confidence in them. My surgery went well. Dan brought Matthew back and forth for me to nurse him. He didn't suffer much without me because his sisters and brothers were very protective and carried him around most of the day. He was happy as long as someone was hauling him around. Ruth also gave him a bottle in between feeds from me. On the fourth day, I went home and Ruth took care of me. I was soon feeling much better, if not quite back to full energy.

Meanwhile, the boys and Lorraine always had something going with Brad and Nathan Olson. Marie made a fuss and thought she was big enough to tag along, but they didn't let her go with them all the time. One day, when I was still in the hospital, we heard loud screaming through the open window. It sounded just like Marie's voice, but I had no one to ask.

The screams continued, and suddenly Lorraine appeared in the ward, "Mom, Marie got her finger smashed in the hinge of the Land-Rover's back door. She's down in the emergency room with dad. What can we do with her? She won't stop screaming."

"Go tell Daddy to just hold Marie, and give her a chance to settle down before they try to fix her finger. If she's quiet, the doctor can see it better."

Well, the screams eventually stopped, but shortly resumed with great, loud bellows. Dan told me later they started again when Marie saw the Indian doctor come in to attend her. She had expected Dr. Alton to see her because she knew him. After scaring the other doctor off, Dan held her tightly, while a nurse bandaged her finger up, minus stitches, and she was free to go. The finger did heal, though a scar remained.

Alton and Ruth also had a young man from our home church staying with them for a couple of months. He was there to see missionary life and help Alton by doing odd jobs. In reality, it was an adventure of a lifetime for John. Our three older kids immediately latched on to him. John and all five of the older kids often went out to explore along the street, and in the bazaar. It was a steep walk, with the houses, roads, food stalls and even the little *kiosks* all clinging to the rocks they were perched on.

The Buggy

One day John and his loyal followers spied a buggy that a peddler used to carry his wares around. How or why they did it, I don't know, but John commandeered the buggy and they took turns sitting in it, careening down the steep roadway until they ran into a blunt, immovable object that stopped them. They apparently made this run several times, so that all the kids got a chance at it. On the second round, someone plowed into an object that not only didn't budge, but the impact was so great the wheels of the buggy came off and the steering handle-bar bent.

A group of sheepish kids came trudging home to show us what their folly had wrought. "We're really sorry. We know we shouldn't have taken it. How can we get it fixed? The man needs it."

They realized they had taken the man's only means of livelihood and broken it, with their fooling around. Dr. Alton checked it out, and tried to bend and mend the wheels. He paid a repairman to fix what he couldn't. The kids had to return the buggy themselves. Some contrite kids learned a valuable lesson about honoring the poor, not taking something that didn't belong to them, and other common courtesies about respecting our fellow man.

Lorraine celebrated her eleventh birthday while we were in India. Ruth baked a cake for her and she was highly honored by the boys singing, or trying to sing "Happy Birthday." They giggled and laughed through most of it, again. Gifts were small. Ruth gave her a couple of little handcrafted etched brass pitchers that are made in India. I gave her a long, batik, maxi dress that I had tailor-made in Jakarta.

While I was recuperating from the surgery, Alton drove us around to look at the sights. We went to a Tibetan temple and saw one of their libraries of sacred books and scrolls. The monks smuggled them out of Lhasa, Tibet when the Chinese communists were invading. Landour, India was their headquarters in exile. We visited a former Maharaja's house and saw all the exotic animal heads and skins hanging on the walls or spread across the floors. He was known as a great wild animal hunter. His house had beautiful oriental furniture and many carved pieces of ivory on display, too. We drove up high enough to an outpost where we looked across the Himalayas into Kashmir and in the far distance was Tibet. The vastness and greatness of that view was totally breath-taking. We were trying to see Mount Everest, but it was cloudy, and we were never sure which peak it was. We just said that we did because we saw all the peaks through the clouds.

On the way home from the trip, a huge boulder came rolling down the mountainside right in front of the car and across to the other side of the road. Alton slammed on the brakes just in time. After the dust had settled, we realized once again that God had His angels working overtime looking out for us. We could have been seriously injured, if the boulder had hit our Land-Rover.

We made one last trip down to the plains and stayed a couple of days in a big rock house of a doctor friend of Alton's. It was near a clinic that he was supervising. On the Fourth of July the kids wanted to have firecrackers. I don't know where Alton found them, but that evening we went up on the flat rooftop and set off flares, firecrackers and sparklers. The sky was lit up with brilliant splashes of color from the fireworks. The next day we went back up to the Olsons' house. It was time to re-pack suitcases for the rest of our journey to the US.

Homeward bound

Four years previously, five Lunows left the ways of the West behind and flew into the unknown jungles of Irian Barat, Indonesia, where we were swallowed up, molded, educated and changed. Then the rain forest spewed seven Lunows out, to return to the West and tell our stories of God's provision, guidance and presence with us on the journey. Sometimes the pathway was crooked, other times steep and treacherous, and yet again the road brought sorrow and loss, amidst blessings and great joys.

Could we, could I, even think about coming back to Papua? I didn't know the answer to that as we left the field the first time. What I could say, positively, was that I wanted to do what God directed me to do, to always obey Him, whatever the cost. (In the years to come, I believe I lived in obedience to the will of God, and God kept His promises to go with me and watch over my little family to the ends of the earth and back.)

"O LORD, you are my God, I will exalt you and praise your name,
for in perfect faithfulness you have done marvelous things..." Isaiah 25:1
(NIV)

The Lunow Family today
David, Lorraine, Marie, Barbara, Matthew, Dan, Jonathan

CPSIA information can be obtained at www.ICGtesting.com
Printed in the USA
LVOW05s2033090514

385121LV00003B/7/P